CHAPTERS

1
one

Robert Smith and Laurence Tolhurst first met on a school bus in September 1964, but they didn't say hello to each other until May 1972.

Robert:

"I got my first electric guitar in December 1972 when I was attending the Notre Dame Middle School, an experimental school whose methods of teaching 11-13 year olds was thought to be revolutionary; very free-thinking, and I liked it. If you were crafty enough, you could convince the teachers you were special: I did virtually nothing for three years. But it was at heart a Catholic school, so there was still a certain amount of religious education. This forced me to skip lessons and, with Lol, Michael (Dempsey) and a few others, go to the music room where, using the school's odd mixture of kettle drums, Spanish guitars, vibes and the like, we learned to play weird versions of various contemporary songs, and by throwing some strange semi-religious words on top, we created a uniquely awful new form of music.

"At the end of the last year, we played a piece to the class: I played the piano, Lol played drums, Michael and a Marc Ceccagno both played guitars, and a kid called Alan Hill played bass. We called ourselves The Obelisk and the whole thing was horrible! But still much better than studying!

"At the age of 13, we all moved to St Wilfrid's Comprehensive and, by then, I had very long hair and was wearing a great big woman's fur coat which stretched right down to the ground – not really to be different but just because no–one else dared. I was suspended from school with Marc Ceccagno for being an 'undesirable influence' but they did eventually take me back."

Lol:

"St Wilfrid's was a strict school, which was a shock after the freedom of Notre Dame. I think that's where the idea of doing something together came from, as a challenge to all that discipline. My friendship with Robert developed – I began to rebel too."

Robert:

"The first real band rehearsal was on 23 January 1976 in the hall of St Edward's Church, Crawley, and, after that, we rehearsed every Thursday evening. I think it all came about because Marc Ceccagno wanted to be a guitar hero. Michael had a bass, I had got hold of a guitar and our first drummer, Graham, had a drum kit. His brother had an amp and a mike so he sang. One evening we decided he couldn't stay – he just couldn't sing – and the same night, around the end of April, Lol arrived and convinced us he could be the drummer. The problem was, he didn't have a drum kit! But we took him on anyway."

Michael:

"We had to teach Lol the drums. We had no aims, it was just something to do, something to talk about."

Lol:

"We called ourselves Malice!"

Robert:

"We started practising three nights a week in October, without Marc because he wanted to play jazz. Lol was going out with this girl whose brother, Porl Thompson was known around Crawley as a good guitarist, so he started coming along. He was working at Gatwick Airport, I remember, and he used to turn up in his waiter's uniform."

Porl:

"I first met Robert in a record shop where I was working. He came in to buy 'Songs Of The Humpback Whale' and we found we liked the same stuff. I joined, and we did covers of Bowie songs, Alex Harvey stuff, Hendrix . . . "

Robert:

"We soon started writing our own songs and, on 18 December 1976, we played our first gig at a place in Sussex called Worth Abbey. It was an acoustic set, we sat on the floor and played bongos. We weren't called Malice for this one actually because, in order to get the booking, we had to pretend we were a folk band! Two days later, though, we played St Wilfrid's with Marc's new band, Amulet. I told the headmaster Malice were a pop group without telling him I was a member because he hated me! We got in this singer, Martin, a journalist with The Crawley Observer with whom we hadn't had a single rehearsal, and he turned up in a three piece suit, a Manchester United scarf and a motorbike helmet which he refused to part with because he was scared someone would steal it! He turned out to be a cabaret singer . . . did good impersonations of David Cassidy. We started playing; 'Jailbreak', 'Suffragette City', 'Foxy Lady' . . . but no-one could distinguish anything! It was just a screaming wall of feedback!

"Three hundred people came, 200 left, and the rest got up on stage! Lol started singing 'Wild Thing', Porl felt so humiliated he hit him and Martin fled with the words 'This is shit!' No-one's seen him since . . . We immediately broke up the group!"

Lol:

"Logically, we should have gone to University, our brothers had gone. But, just then, punk arrived and we turned down University. I went to work in a pharmaceutical lab and we started rehearsing again at Robert's house."

Michael:

"Robert's parents had an annexe on their house and we practised there three or four times a week. Robert would come in with some guitar chords, I'd find a bassline, Lol would sort out the drums and the two of them would write the words."

Robert:

"The group was a way of doing something. I didn't hope for anything, but I found a lot of our songs better than those I was listening to. My biggest influence at that time was John Peel. From 15 on, I used to listen to his show every night, that was the best part of the day. I heard White Riot and cut off all my hair! The Buzzcocks, The Stranglers . . . I used to dream of making a record that John Peel would play.

"We decided we needed another name if we were going to start playing again, so one night in the middle of January 1977, we sat around in my kitchen discussing it. One of our songs was called 'Easy Cure', a song written by Lol, and, eventually, in desperation we settled on that."

During March, the band hired and fired vocalist Gary X and co-opted Peter O'Toole, a demon footballer and Bowie fan who'd never sung before. His debut gig was on 22 April, Robert's belated birthday party at St Edward's Hall.

Robert:

"I remember nothing at all so it must have been good . . ."

During April, Hansa, Germany's largest independent record label, run by Peter and Trudy Meisel and distributed by Ariola, placed an ad for new talent in the British music press.

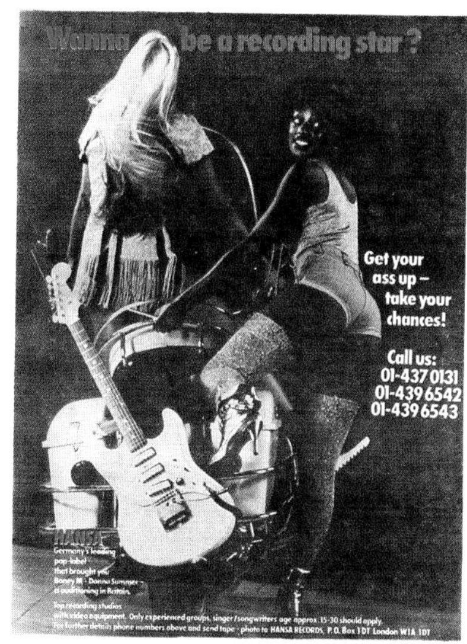

Easy Cure made a tape in the dining room of Robert's parents' house, sent it in with a photo and, within a few days, received a telegram.

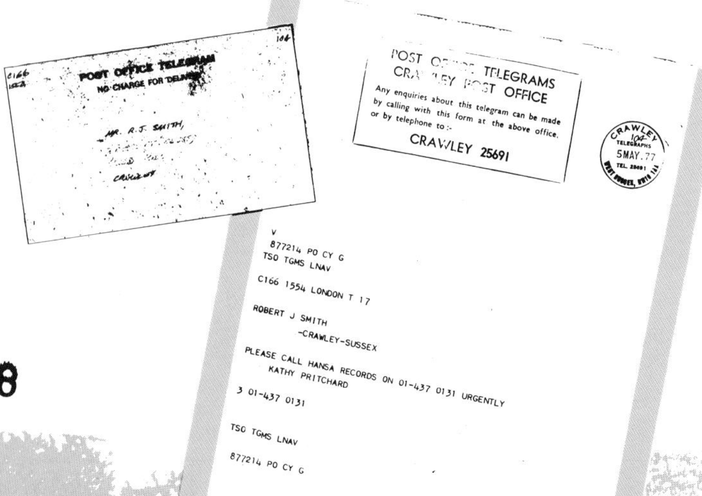

POST OFFICE TELEGRAM
NO CHARGE FOR DELIVERY

MR. R. J. SMITH,

TELEGRAMS
OFFICE

Any enquiries about this telegram can be made by calling with this form at the above office or by telephone to:-

CRAWLEY 25691

CRAWLEY TELEGRAPHS 5 MAY.77

V
877214 PO CY G
TSO TGMS LNAV

C166 1554 LONDON T 17

ROBERT J SMITH
-CRAWLEY-SUSSEX

PLEASE CALL HANSA RECORDS ON 01-437 0131 URGENTLY
KATHY PRITCHARD

3 01-437 0131

TSO TGMS LNAV

877214 PO CY G

An audition was organised at Morgan Studios in London on 13 May.

Robert:

"They had a video camera set up and said 'Just go through a couple of your songs': we did, and they signed us. In retrospect, their only interest was in the way we looked. They thought they could turn us into a teen group like Child. I don't think they even listened to our tape — they just liked the photo!"

Five days later they were sent a Hansa contract. After much debate, they signed. On 6 May, Easy Cure played their first proper gig at The Rocket, a local Crawley pub.

Robert:

"It was Sunday lunchtime and we realised Amulet were supposed to be playing that night and that they couldn't make it for some reason so we just phoned the pub and asked if we could play instead. We realised we needed to play in front of a real audience at some point so we rehearsed all afternoon and went and played. We went down quite well and they asked us back and, within two or three months, we were pulling about 300 people because there was no-one in Crawley who'd ever done anything like what we were doing. We had a really drunken following, and we were really just a focal point, an excuse for people to go out, get really drunk and smash the place up!

"Whenever we played, we all thought it was awful — there was loads of feedback and you could never hear anything except Porl's guitar. That's the only reason we kept getting rebooked, because he became the local guitar hero!"

On 3rd June, Easy Cure played a Peace Concert in Queen's Square, Crawley organised by James and Consuelo Duggan who'd arranged over 100 free concerts in Ireland. They told the local press: "We just wanted people to come along, listen to the music and think about peace. Not just for Northern Ireland but everywhere." Three hundred people turned up and Robert's dad filmed the performance.

'ROCKING' TO THE TOP

A YOUNG Crawley based rock band, 'Easy Cure,' celebrated in Queens Square on Sunday, after signing a £1,000 contract the previous day.

The band, all aged between 18-19, was one of 1,400 bands to answer an advertisement in The Melody Maker music paper.

Only 60 bands were selected for an audition in London from which eight groups were offered a contract by Hansa, a leading German recording firm.

The group's first single will come out on the Antlantic record label.

"There were so many other bands that we didn't pin all our hopes on it," they said.

The group has only been together for eight months, and they have now signed a five-year contract, renewable every year.

One member, Robert Smith, said: "It all happened so fast, but now we are really looking forward to making our first record."

The group consists of Laurence Tolhurst, Mick Dempsey, Paul Thompson, Peter O'Toole and Robert Smith.

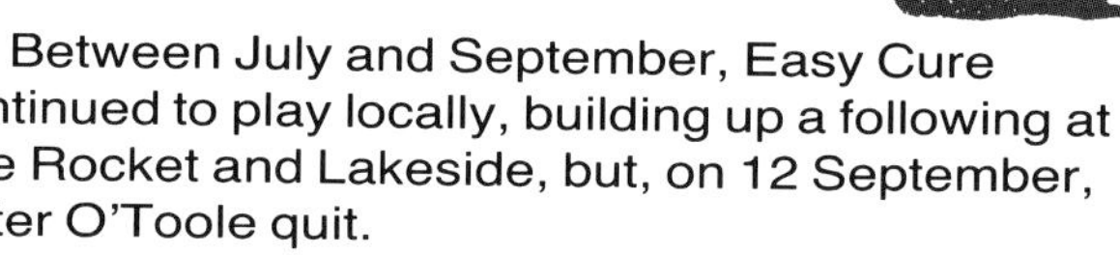

Between July and September, Easy Cure continued to play locally, building up a following at The Rocket and Lakeside, but, on 12 September, Peter O'Toole quit.

Robert:

"He went off to a Kibbutz in Israel and, as I'd sung 'Foxy Lady' at the Peace concert, and we'd already had about four useless *frontmen*, I thought I couldn't be any worse so I decided to be the singer."

Michael:

"I think that's probably the most admirable thing I've ever seen Robert do, take the vocals on himself. I can't remember how he broke the news to us but I'm sure his decision was born out of frustration. We'd had such a hard time with singers."

Easy Cure had made £1,000 from the Hansa signing with which they bought equipment and on 11 October and 15 November, they recorded demos in SAV studios, London. The songs from the first session were 'See The Children' (a sort of punk molester's anthem), 'I Just Need Myself', 'I Want To Be Old', 'Pillbox Tales' and 'Meathook'. And from the second: 'Rebel Rebel', 'I Saw Here Standing There', 'I'm Cold', 'Little Girl' and 'Killing An Arab'. Hansa were dissatisfied with the original material and began sending tapes of songs such as 'I Fought The Law' and 'The Big Airplane Strike' as suggested cover versions. The band refused to comply.

On 16 October, they played Felbridge Village Hall and the police intervened.

Robert:

"I think it was because we were doing benefits for this teacher called Tony Weaver who was sacked for committing an act of gross indecency with a man in a public place. We didn't think someone's sexual preferences should have any bearing on whether or not they were considered to be a good teacher and, inevitably, this incurred the wrath of the local National Front. From then on whenever we played local concerts, there was usually a lot of trouble, so we started gathering together our own Easy Cure Wrecking Crew."

Michael:

"Dr Weaver was a language teacher at our secondary school, probably the first outrageous homosexual we ever met, and a marvellous character. When he left the school, he was persecuted continuously and we admired him because he became a kind of anti-establishment figure."

On 31 December, Easy Cure played at Orpington General Hospital.

Robert:

"It was hilarious — something Michael's brother-in-law set up. He decided he was going to be our manager, had all these cards printed up saying 'Easy Cure For All Occasions' and got us this gig paying £20. Well, we thought, 'we'll play anywhere for £20' but when we arrived, we realised it was full of 40 and 50 year olds and trainee managers who, by 11 o'clock, were getting pretty belligerent because we were playing songs like 'Killing An Arab'."

Michael:

"They wanted a dance band and we really had no grasp on anyone's tunes but our own. We were also expected to play two sets but we knew right from the outset it was dangerous because we played our first set to a lot of booing and hissing. Luckily they weren't sufficiently drunk at that stage to be anything more than vocal."

Robert:

"Porl had a history of playing in cabaret bands and so, during the break, we were wondering what we could do and Porl said he sort of knew how to play 'Tie A Yellow Ribbon'. So we went back and started playing it and this roar of approval went up but, after bashing away at the chorus for six or seven minutes, this bloke threw a bottle and we ended up in the car park getting beaten up by several punters who wanted their money back!

"Michael's brother-in-law immediately destroyed all 500 of his Easy Cure calling cards and we realised then that we couldn't just go and play any old place. We didn't want to learn loads of other people's songs just so we could because, that way, we would have become yet another pub band."

Michael:

"I think we got paid. I'd remember if we hadn't!"

In January, Easy Cure went into PSL studios with producer Trevor Vallis to do more demos for Hansa.

Robert:

"They were giving us all these old songs to cover. We couldn't believe it. This was 1978 and we thought we'd be able to do all these new songs we'd written and all they wanted from us were versions of really banal old rock 'n' roll songs . . .

"Anyway, they said 'This is a very well-known producer and this is your last chance boys', so we went in and did 'Plastic Passion', 'I Just Need Myself', 'Rebel Rebel' and 'Smashed Up' — the worst song we ever recorded. The only really remarkable thing about the whole day was that Lol got knocked over by a bus! We had to spend a couple of hours holding him up in the pub, pouring brandy down his throat. "He spent the rest of the day playing drums and bleeding. It was cack.

On top of all this I had suddenly realised that I actually hated the songs we were doing and that, even if Hansa liked them, we wouldn't follow through.

On 19 February, Easy Cure again played The Rocket, this time supported by Lockjaw, a local punk band featuring bassist Simon Gallup.

Robert:

"They were really hardcore, really like The Clash whereas we had more melody, like The Buzzcocks. All their songs were really fast and it was the only time they ever played The Rocket because the place was torn apart. They only got to play there in the first place because they had a record out and we said they were a big group!"

Simon:

"Putting that record out was a big mistake. We sent a tape to a record company called Raw Records and they thought we were this really good suburban punk band but we were actually shit. They signed us and put out this record — 'Radio Call Sign' backed with 'The Young Ones'. If I see any around today, I break them.

"I actually knew about Lol from school because he was going out with a girl I knew and she used to go around saying he was really hard — I used to cross the street whenever I saw him coming!"

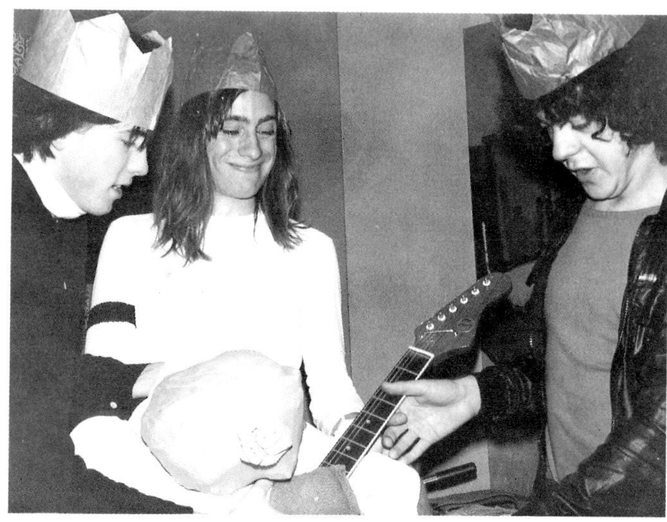

On 29 March, Easy Cure dissolved their unsatisfactory relationship with Hansa when the company refused their request to release 'Killing An Arab'. Robert wisely ensured that the rights to all the original songs reverted to the band. During April, they met up with Lockjaw again in Redhill.

Robert:

"Up until then, I'd only known Simon just to say hello to but we spent a really good evening together drinking from about five o'clock till two in the morning and we became good friends."

Simon:

"When Lockjaw and Easy Cure used to play gigs together, me and Robert used to go off together and ask the deejay to put on things like 'Night Fever' so we could disco dance while all the punks pogoed about."

On 17 April, Robert also invested in some new equipment.

Robert:

"I bought a Bon Tempi organ, a Top 20 guitar and a cacky little WEM amp — my ideal set up. The sounds on Elvis Costello's 'My Aim Is True' album were really cheap and they were the sounds I wanted."

On 3 May, Porl left.

Robert:

"The songs were getting starker, more minimal and I was beginning to loathe Porl's lead guitar. I tried to get him to play chords but he didn't like that and it got even more complicated when he started going out with my sister because we'd be rehearsing in the house when my mum and dad were out and he'd be somewhere else with my sister. I remember we decided we needed to talk about it so Lol, Michael and I went out into the greenhouse for some reason and sweated in 98 degrees of heat discussing the future of the group. We decided not to have any more rehearsals for a couple of weeks and, when we started again, we just didn't tell him."

Porl:

"The music was in the process of changing and, as I was known as the fast guitar player, when punk came along I became obsolete, so I decided to do something else. I did a course at art college and played in two sorts of Roxy Musicish bands; The Exotic Pandas and A Lifetime Of Trials."

The band also decided to change their name.

Robert:

"I had always thought Easy Cure was a bit hippyish, a bit American-sounding, a bit West Coast, and I hated it, which put Lol's back up as he'd thought of it. Every other group we liked had 'The' in front of their name but The Easy Cure sounded stupid so we just changed it to The Cure instead. It upset a few old fans but . . . well, there you are . . . I thought The Cure sounded much more *it*."

On 27 May, the new three piece Cure went into Chestnut, a small studio in Sussex to record an eight track demo financed by Simon's brother Ric who was sick of seeing them kicking their heels. For less than £50, including beer money, they recorded 'Boys Don't Cry', 'It's Not You', '10.15' and 'Fire In Cairo' and sent the tapes, with accompanying letter and photo, to all the major record companies.

Robert:

"Lol was working as a chemist, sitting in a lab doing nothing. Michael was working as a porter in a mental hospital wheeling all the dead bodies out in the morning, and I was fed up with being on the dole. So, we made the tape and sent it out."

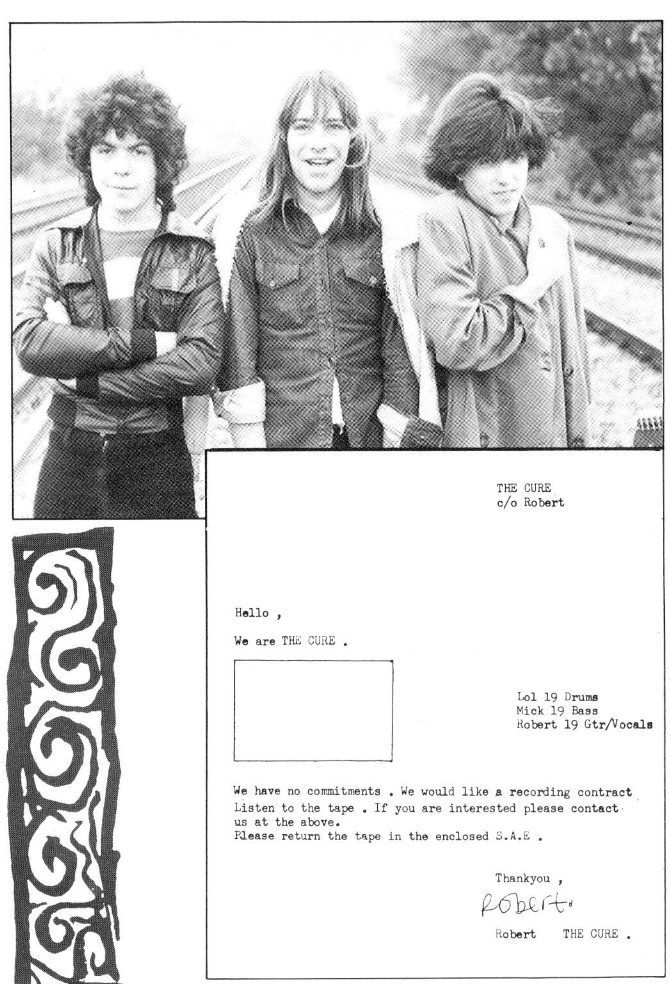

THE CURE
c/o Robert

Hello ,

We are THE CURE .

Lol 19 Drums
Mick 19 Bass
Robert 19 Gtr/Vocals

We have no commitments . We would like a recording contract
Listen to the tape . If you are interested please contact
us at the above.
Please return the tape in the enclosed S.A.E .

Thankyou ,

Robert

Robert THE CURE .

While they awaited replies, The Cure played a special gig on 9 July at The Rocket called 'Mourning The Departed'.

Robert:

"A lot of people said 'Oh, you've got to get Porl back, there's no guitar solos or anything' so we put on this concert where we used this backing tape I had made at home with an organ and a drum machine and church music and we held a 40 minute mock religious ceremony. We had a seance in the pub — brilliant! I nailed a piece of wood to the Top 20 to make it into a crucifix and wore a priest's outfit and we had this kind of Cabaret Voltaire backdrop.

"The best thing that happened was Porl arrived in a hat and an old mac, in disguise, and we didn't know he was in the audience until, just as we finished playing, he walked up and poured a pint of beer over Lol's head! Suddenly we were friends again!"

On 14 July, The Cure played in Brighton with Lockjaw, and five days later, Robert threw a week-long party for all the local punks in his parents' house while they were on holiday. Every day they checked the mail.

Robert:

"Every single company rejected us except Polydor."

phonogram

129 Park Street London W1Y 3FA

28th June, 1978

Dear Robert,

Many thanks for sending in your tape.

Unfortunately, after careful consideratio[n] … A & R Committee it was decided that the … not viable for us and therefore I am so[rry] … that we pass.

Once again, many thanks for sending i[n] … giving us the opportunity of hearing …

Yours sincerely,

David Bates
A & R Manager.

23rd August, 1978

EMI RECORDS 20 Manchester Square London W1A 1ES

Dear Robert,

Thank you for submitting your demonstration recording which we have studied very carefully.

It is with sincere regret that we have to advise you that we do not feel able to help you at this stage. Please do not consider this a criticism, but merely our view related to the current record market.

We are returning your recording herewith and take this opportunity … thanking you for your interest and wish you every … the future.

Virgin Records Limited 2-4 Vernon Yard Portobello Road London W11

23rd …

Dear

Many thanks for your tape, which you will f… this is not the type of material we are lo[oking for] … Anyway, thanks for your interest.

Best wishes,

Helen
A & R Virgin Records

ISLAND

27 June 1978

Dear Robert

Thank you for sending in your cassette of the Cure.

Unfortunately, however, it is not really the type of material we are looking for at the present time and I am therefore returning it to you.

Yours sincerely

BBC

BRITISH BROADCASTING CORPORATION
NEW BROADCASTING HOUSE PO BOX 27 OXFORD ROAD MANCHESTER M60 1SJ
TELEPHONE AND TELEGRAMS 061 236 8444

29th June, 1978

Re: The Cure,

Dear All,

THE KID JENSEN SHOW: BAND OF HOPE AND GLORY

Thanks for sending the tape and information about your band. We have had an enormous response, with hundreds of bands sending material; and obviously we can only use a very small proportion of these bands.

Unfortunately, we cannot use your group: but that isn't to say that your tape is without interest or that the particular group is not good enough. It's just that the combination of qualities we are looking for isn't quite there.

I hope this reply isn't too much of a bring down: always remember that music is a subjective area, so that when you sell your first million albums, you will know we were wrong!

I am returning your tape, photos, etc. with thanks for your interest, and with my very best wishes for the future.

Sincerely,

Tony Hale
Producer,
RADIO ONE

Chris Parry, who had been a successful drummer in New Zealand, moved to London in 1969, took exams in marketing, and joined Phonogram Records in the International Department for five months. In a rut, a friend of his persuaded Wayne Bickerton, Head of A&R at Polydor, that Chris would make a good A&R man so he moved in late '74 and signed The Chanter Sisters who had a hit in '75. Then punk came along.

Parry:

"It struck me as very, very obvious that something big was happening. I hooked up with Caroline Coon and floated around, saw all the most abysmal shows and everything, but I was the first from the record companies there. In my Canadian lumberjack jacket and beard, I stuck out like a sore thumb!

"I saw The Pistols, The Clash, Siouxsie . . . but Polydor somehow didn't think they were worth signing and someone else got the first two. But then Shane, who's now in The Pogues, told me about The Jam and I saw them at the Marquee and I was determined I wasn't going to miss out again."

Chris Parry signed and produced The Jam for Polydor as well as signing Otway And Barrett and finally coaxed the company into signing Siouxsie And The Banshees. But, as they all got bigger and the avenues for promotion closed, he became disillusioned and started thinking about starting his own label.

Parry:

"Demo tapes came in by the sack load to Polydor and I just grabbed a bunch every Friday night. So there I was, Sunday afternoon, browsing through the sports pages and I just heard 'Drip drip drip' and I thought 'That's rather nice' so I played the tape again and '10, 15' and 'Boys Don't Cry' were really very good. The idea of a three-piece excited me too, the fact that they were a little bit spacey and that this little cassette had come from the backwoods and no-one else had touched it.

"My reaction was it had mood, it was atmospheric and I liked it, so I wrote them a letter asking them to get in touch."

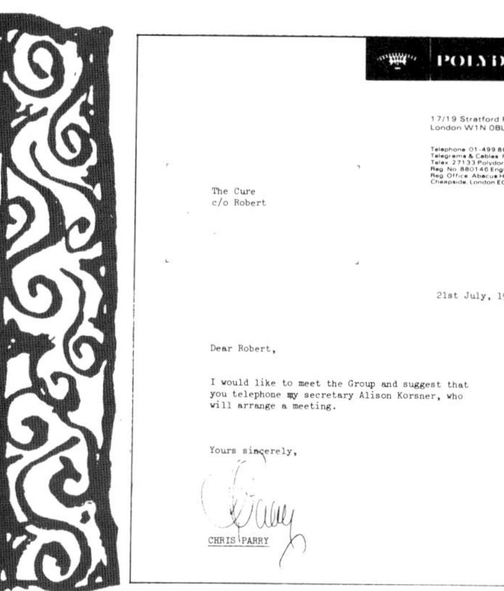

POLYDOR LTD

17/19 Stratford Place
London W1N 0BL

Telephone 01-499 8686
Telegrams & Cables Polydor London W.1
Telex 27133 Polydor (Ldn)
Reg No 880146 England
Reg Office Abacus House, Gutter Lane, Cheapside, London EC2V 8AH

The Cure
c/o Robert

21st July, 1978

Dear Robert,

I would like to meet the Group and suggest that you telephone my secretary Alison Korsner, who will arrange a meeting.

Yours sincerely,

CHRIS PARRY

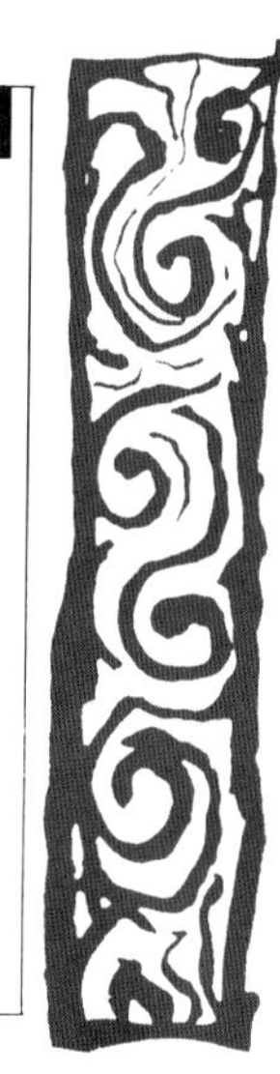

On 10 August, The Cure met Chris Parry.

Robert:

"The Polydor letter was the only good one we received so obviously I phoned up. Parry asked if we would play in London and I said no, we should meet first and just talk. It would have been stupid if we'd played our first concert in London and it had been awful — not our audience — so we arranged to meet him first at Polydor."

Michael:

"We arrived absolutely on time and a doorman of military bearing told us he wasn't in so we waited, frustrated, in the foyer. Eventually we asked if he was coming back and, just at that moment, this figure went past the door. The man said 'There he is' and Parry looked as though he'd committed some criminal act,

which he may well have done for all I know. He looked very much like he was related to Colonel Gaddafi — same sort of army bouffant hairstyle and craggy jowl."
Lol:

"He looked Italian, very suave, a bit like a bank manager. We went to the pub and, as he talked to us, he was absent-mindedly spilling his beer on his shoes. That's when we decided he was the one for us — someone totally capable of embarrassing himself."
Parry:

"We actually met in my office. They walked in and I liked the look of them from the beginning. I was struck by Smith in his high-waisted trousers, and I was pleased to find out he was the singer. We got to know each other over a drink. I had a couple of pints and fell over a bit, and they appreciated that."
Michael:

"We weren't really used to drinking at lunch time so our heads were reeling."
Robert:

"It was quite a pleasant afternoon really. We just got very drunk on Directors bitter. He had bird shit on his shoulder — the first person we'd met involved in the business who didn't take himself seriously. He seemed to be doing it because he enjoyed it.

"I remember this gypsy woman was pushing an enormous plant along Stratford Place in a wheelbarrow and he just turned around and said 'I've always wanted a plant like that. Excuse me lady, how much d'you want for your plant?' She said '£15' and he said 'I'll give you £12' and handed over the money. We thought it was a set-up. He just stood there with this huge plant with a pink flower in the middle, smiling like an idiot. When he got it home though, he discovered the pink flower was false — just stuck on."
Parry:

"The flower *was* attached, and remained so for years. *They* pulled it off actually, at a party. Now there's symbolism for you!"
Robert:

"He said I can't offer you the world and we appreciated that, but when he told us that he actually wanted to sign us to his own label we were obviously a bit disappointed – we thought he was going to sign us to Polydor. After he had explained his ideas more clearly, however, we decided that we liked the sound of it after all."
Parry:

"They were all quite happy people, quite sharp. I liked Dempsey's understated English sense of humour. Lol was flapping around here and there, but it was obvious that Robert was the leader and had views on things, checking me out more than the others."

Parry decided to take Robert's advice and check out the band playing in their familiar surroundings so he drove to their gig at Lakers, Redhill on 27 August with a mate called Dave Alcock, a hospital porter, who Lol immediately mistook for Robert Stigwood . . .
Michael:

"Lakers was a hotel which held gigs on Sunday nights featuring this jazz/funk/reggae fusion band called The Hotpoints. They headlined and we had the non-stage."

Parry:

"They were playing on the floor, not on the stage. Dave and I joined the few people down the front and I remember I turned round to him and said 'This band are gonna make me an awful lot of money'. It's not that I'm very money-orientated, it just came out that way. I instantly thought they were going to be very successful. I thought they had a very universal appeal which is why I must have translated my excitement into money terms — because bands with a universal appeal can't help making a lot of money. I thought 'This is really sharp and incisive and young'."
Robert:

"He saw us play and then we went to this other pub called The Home Cottage where everyone used to go after our gigs because it sold such horribly strong bitter. He talked more about his ideas for the new label, about how it would go through Polydor and how he'd been looking for a group to start it off and he wanted to know if we'd be prepared to take the risk, otherwise he said he'd sign us direct to Polydor. Well, we'd given it a lot of thought by then and decided that we'd be better off on an independent anyway, more comfortable. We thought Polydor would try to hype us and, after our experiences with Hansa, we decided to sign with Fiction.

"Actually, he was going to call the label Night Nurse but we said we wouldn't sign if he called it that so he changed it to 18 Age which was also useless. We said 'What happens when we get to 20?' So Fiction it was."

Michael:

"He never explained what he saw in us. We were a three-piece, The Jam were a three-piece and I got the feeling that maybe he thought 'I'll go for another one' — not consciously but like when you need a pair of shoes and there's a tendency to go and buy a similar pair to the ones you're used to."

TWO

By 13 September, The Cure had signed a six month contract with Parry's new label and on the 17th he drove Adrian Thrills of the New Musical Express to Lakers to see the band.

Parry:

"He got quite into it but he didn't really go for them as I thought he would. I mean, I really thought they were quite exceptional. I remember playing him Billy Mackenzie's *Mental Torture* tape on the way back and he said it *was* mental torture, so obviously Thrills was not the right guy because I thought Billy was brilliant too, my other new protege to be signed to the label."

On 20 September, Parry, who'd acquired the obscure nickname "Bill", put the band back into Studio 4 at Morgan and by five-thirty the next morning they'd recorded five tracks: 'Killing An Arab', '10.15', 'Fire In Cairo', 'Plastic Passion' and 'Three Imaginary Boys'.

Lol:

"I was still working at the time so I had to pretend I was ill. I said I had boils on my bottom! After that, for my sins, I got them!"

Parry decided the band should gain experience playing and booked them two dates with Wire, at Kent University on 5 October and London Polytechnic on the 6th.

Robert:

"They were so much better than us, I was horrified. They used white lights, dressed in black and white and their music was rigid, dramatic and very powerful, I immediately wanted to change in that direction, to get harder because we were small and lightweight in comparison.

"I remember we were very nervous because this was the first proper concert we'd ever played and, on the way home, we crashed our van into a wall and nearly decapitated ourselves.

"The next night we didn't make it to the venue. We got a lift from this bloke Phil who lived in Horley and had a van. But the van broke down and we had to wait for someone to come and fix it so we arrived at the gig at about eight-thirty, much too late, and Wire had just gone onstage. We asked if we could play after them but they thought it was a ploy and said no.

"I remember Bill was really furious. He said 'You just can't do this or people won't book you'."

Parry:

"I wasn't very happy. We went across the road to this pub and they started going on about wanting to turn professional, wanting to get paid for it. So I agreed to put them on £25 a week or something. I thought 'Fuck it, why not?' Again a major decision made under the influence of alcohol!"

Michael:

"Lol and I were working — I was still a porter in a mental asylum and Lol had left college and was looking to be a research chemist — so it wasn't a lot of money but it gave us a sense of purpose that all our waking hours could be channelled into the group."

On 12 October, they went back into Morgan with a view to recording enough tracks for a debut album.

Robert:

"We recorded solidly for two days and nights and got home at 8am on the 14th. Some of the songs were atypical of what we wanted to be like but we didn't have any control over the production side of it. Bill wanted to produce in a certain way which horrified me and he got in Mike Hedges, a tape-op, to engineer because he wanted someone young with few preconceptions.

"We had so many arguments — I liked the production we'd done on our demo which was, after all, the reason he signed us, but he was quite adamant about it and, as he was paying for the sessions, he had us over a barrel.

"I liked 'Killing An Arab', '10, 15' and 'Boys Don't Cry' but I hated 'Object' and I was unhappy because, up till that point, everything we'd done, we'd done ourselves and he was still a sort of outsider who'd taken over. Hedges was on our side though, he'd mediate and moderate in his own inimitable fashion!"

Parry:

"I had a production concept — here was a three piece but, rather than make them sound like a five piece like I did The Jam, I wanted to make it totally different, elusive, translucent, stripped right down to the bones. I liked the lyrics and I liked Robert's voice and I was convinced, after the punk thrash, that people would want something more mysterious.

"I wanted to give The Cure, and the label, the option of anonymity rather than being another label marketing another three chord thrash. I had an advantage over Robert. I had a clear idea of what I wanted to do whereas Robert had a clear idea of what he didn't want. We had many arguments — he'd get sulky and my temper was worse then than it is now so I would take umbrage. I'd think 'Fucking hell, I've got enough problems trying to sort out the label without this. Why can't they see I've got their best interests at heart?'."

Hedges:

"The band didn't really know what was going on. Everything was new for everyone except Chris. Robert knew what he wanted but he didn't know how to express it. We used very little technology. He just wanted to use his old Top 20 guitar which cost 20 quid in Woolworths and a cheap HH amp which was the worst in the world for distortion."

Parry:

"He wouldn't change his amplifier and we had an argument late one night. He liked the sound and that was okay but it didn't work for some songs and anyway, after the guitar solo on 'Three Imaginary Boys', it fell to bits. He was also unwilling to change his £20 guitar and I thought 'Jesus, here I am investing money in an album for some git who refuses to listen to reason'.

"We could have had a rough Kinksy-Stonesy sort of sound but it wouldn't have worked internationally, I knew the punk thrash was never gonna get beyond Britain so I said 'Fine, if you wanna be a punk band, all dirgey and turgid, which you will be if you continue to use the equipment you've got, you can. But you'll be thrown off the label'.

"If Robert felt I had him over a barrel, he was perfectly right. I had other problems too. Getting a performance out of them was hard because Lol was a very temperamental drummer and could only play well if he felt well. Dempsey wasn't playing well either and, listening to it now, I think the album's highly flawed."

On 25 October, The Cure were booked to support The Young Bucks at The Windsor Castle in Harrow Road before returning to the studio for an all night session.

Robert:

"That was the concert where Bill decided we should also change our image. Before we played he said we all had to shape up and we thought 'He's going too far now, asking us to *look* different.' Back in the studio, Dempsey was really upset, really drunk, and he *never* got drunk. He couldn't play but he insisted he was okay. I was horrified — he kept telling me and Lol that we were playing out of time!

"That sowed some seeds of doubt — I mean, Bill could have waited until after the show to have his say. The only good that came out of it was that he gave us some money to buy some clothes."

Parry:

"Dempsey looked a dork so I told him so. I mean, here I was with a lot of faith and belief in the band and they'd just amble on stage looking horrible, fucking disgusting. I liked their view that style wasn't going to be thrust upon them but Dempsey wore corduroys, Hush Puppies and a grandpa jumper, Robert had a coat that he wore a lot which looked very nondescript, and Lol used to turn up wearing any sort of trousers and shoes, a white shirt, and a bit of a beard and I thought 'These guys are the dog's breakfast! The music is great but they look shit'."

Michael:

"Robert would have none of it. Maybe he bought himself a pair of brothel-creepers or something but I bought myself some awful clothes. The only image we had was this leather jacket that belonged to a hoodlum we knew. Lol somehow got hold of it and started wearing it. So did Robert."

Throughout the next two months, they played gig after gig under Parry's toughening-up scheme. One particular favourite among all the dross was supporting The UK Subs at the Moonlight Club in West Hampstead on 20 November. Charlie Harper, the Subs' singer/leader with the immaculate perm, had previously asked Lol to join his band when they'd met at the Croydon Greyhound.

Robert:

"What a fucking glorious night! They were everything I loathed about that particular part of punk culture — old rock 'n' rollers. Horrible. I remember they said 'Hey, we gotta use your gear man' and I said 'You can't call me *man*. This is 1978!' We were really good that night, really aggressive."

On 24th November, The Cure embarked on an educational string of dates supporting Generation X, driving back after every gig to sleep on the floor at Parry's house near Watford.

Robert:

"I remember we arrived at High Wycombe and this bloke said to me 'Are you using the lights?' and I thought 'Well, obviously we want to use lights otherwise no-one will be able to see us' so I said yes. Then he said 'D'you wanna use the PA?' and I said yes again so he said 'Okay, £25' and I said 'Is that all?' I thought he was saying, if we used the lights and PA, that he could only pay us £25. He looked at me peculiarly and I suddenly realised that he was charging us! So I said we hadn't got the money — we only had about £15 for petrol and stuff to get back from High Wycombe — and he said 'No £25, no lights or PA'. So I said 'Right, we won't use them then'.

"We'd brought along these two Yamaha A40 bins which we used in pubs as our PA system and we were going to use them as monitors and I had this HH mixing console as I always mixed from the stage with someone in the audience giving me signals for bass up or vocals down, so we wheeled it out and we had two standard lamps either side of us and we played like that.

"The blokes who were doing the lights and sound for Generation X were called Mac and Nigel and they thought it was great that we reacted like that. So the next night, at Northampton Cricket Club, they came up to us and said we could use the lights and PA for nothing."

Mac:

"I thought they were really nice people. It took me some time to get used to their music though — I didn't think it was that brilliant at first."

Robert:

"Mac was my older brother's age and we thought he was kinda funny. Nigel and he were amazed to be able to talk about Hendrix and Nick Drake with 18 year olds."

On 30 November, the Generation X tour played Hales Owen Tiffany's. The Cure were attacked by skinheads, and then stayed in a hotel for the first time, as the Polydor executive had travelled to see them.

Lol:

"All the Polydor people were going 'Great show lads' and buying us free drinks. I remember drinking loads of Southern Comfort and thinking it was really good and, about two hours later, lying with my head down a toilet thinking it wasn't that good at all."

Robert:

"We all had to share a room, two beds between the three of us, so Lol went on the floor because he was so drunk. He threw up in the sink and all over the carpet and it was really humiliating because, when we woke up, he'd completely ruined the room, sprayed vomit all over the walls and everything and it was our first stay in an hotel!"

Michael:

"I must say I don't think I enjoyed that time on the road. It wasn't exactly tiring because it was still quite fun but we were always really hung over on cheap and nasty beer, playing in front of people who neither knew us nor wanted to know us.

"When we asked Parry why we were playing these places, he had a good way of dealing with it. He was always very jokey, very avuncular, and there was no way you could pin him down. As soon as we complained, he'd say 'Oh c'mon, have a beer'. I think he wanted to build up what he called a grass roots following. He had two expressions he was constantly bringing out at that time to do with his grand scheme – one was *grass roots following* and the other was *ground swell*. I think he got them from a book of economics or something. He had another expression – *atomise* – but that was mainly used in connection with The Associates."

On the 3rd December, The Cure played Bristol Locarno.

Lol:

"After the gig, I wandered back through Gen X's dressing room to go to the toilet but someone at the door said I couldn't go in there. Well, I was desperate so I pushed past and went in, and there was Billy Idol up against the urinal in a rather compromising position with a young lady. He gave me his famous sneer but I thought 'Sod it, I'm not going away, so I walked right up next to him and pulled out my willy. He was going 'Don't be nervous, don't be nervous' and I turned to him and went 'Alright Billy' and pissed all over him!"

Michael:

"Lol had this unfortunate ability to stumble across people in some sort of carnal act."

Robert:

"We did one more date on that tour before they kicked us off and that was Dunstable California Ballroom because I don't think they could get anyone else to do it. The toilet incident obviously didn't go down too well but, as well as that, we were beginning to get too good a reaction, and that made them nervous."

On 4 December, the Cure recorded the first of many sessions for John Peel's late night show on Radio One, performing 'Killing An Arab', '10:15 Saturday Night', 'Boys Don't Cry' and 'Fire In Cairo'. Four nights later, they found themselves at The Corn Dolly in Oxford, a famed heavy metal watering hole.

Robert:

"That was *the* worst gig we ever did. It was snowing, we broke down, we ran out of petrol, we loaded all the stuff in and it was about 10 feet square. I started singing without any drums because Lol had gone for a piss outside and there were only about 20 people there anyway, all blokes, really drunk, and one just shouting out all night 'Play that drip drip drip one again!' We played '10:15' about eight times because it was the only song he wanted to hear and every time we got halfway through something else, he'd throw a beer glass at us and shout 'Play that drip drip drip one again!' Horrible."

On 16 December, The Cure received their first coverage in the national pop press courtesy of the New Musical Express. The article, written by Adrian Thrills and entitled "Ain't No Blues For The Summertime Cure" made a fuss about the band's deliberately primitive instrumentation:

" . . . Hands up those of you who still reckon you need expensive instruments to play rock 'n' roll? I suggest you catch The Cure immediately."

Thrills referred to the band as "an abrasive light metal trio", "a breath of fresh suburban air in the capital's smog-ridden pub and club circuit" and "a triumph of impulse and spontaneity". Robert told him: "We see so many of the people we went to school with doing absolutely nothing. A lot of them are talented enough but they just don't bother themselves. There are so many people playing music that is absolute rubbish and getting somewhere doing it. You just think 'If they're doing it, why don't *you* when you know you're so much better." On 19 December, The Cure played The Hope & Anchor in Islington and the NME feature had the effect Parry'd hoped. The place was packed with curious punters and, as was now customary, the band played a curious set.

Robert:

"I had flu and was doped up on Night Nurse and disprins. Halfway through the set I collapsed with a temperature of 102. We were really worried that the gig was gonna be reviewed and that people would think we were always like that."

The Cure

Hope and Anchor

This was a cruel date on The Cure's calendar.

Guitarist Robert Smith had flu and Lol Tolhurst's drumkit kept falling over. The Hope's basement displayed the charm of a cross-Channel lorry deck, and the PA vied with the gas heater in the inadequate stakes.

Ostensibly, The Cure had little going for them; yet they salvaged this unluxurious event from oblivion, largely through their own embryonic musical talent and their ability to inject a dose of enjoy-serum into the Mivvied corpuscles of punters present.

Despite their charity-rack instruments, the band played a crisp set. Their sound was compact and effervescent. Each song was a two-minute cameo of ferrous punkrock. Their *coup-de-gig* was the Camus inspired ditty "Killing An Arab": a zany crossbreed of 4/4 thrash and Moorish bazoukie fever.

The Cure's novel approach to rock is emphasised by bassman Michael Dempsey's skilfully versatile handling of lead and melody lines played over a rhythmic drum / guitar backdrop. Intriguing, but it tended to make things top-heavy. Such is the nature of three-piecedom: streamlined impact is often gained at the expense of amplitude. The Cure are competent enough to add a fourth hand to the crew without sacrificing the excitement and originality of their live performance.

A youthful nervousness, dotted with moments of controlled deadpan enhanced their stage presence; they played with sufficient enthusiasm to overcome the Spartan test-tube conditions of this chilly niterie.

Hollering for two encores, the crowd risked frostbite to clap for The Cure.

Rick Joseph

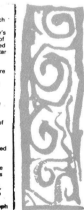

On 22 December, the band played twice in one day – in the afternoon they were booked to provide the knees-up for the Upjohn Christmas Party.

Robert:

"My dad worked there and pulled strings to get us booked as the cabaret. It was really funny – we got no reaction at all! We played for 25 minutes, got very drunk, then drove like madmen to the Music Machine where we sat outside for two hours because the bouncers wouldn't believe we were the support group to The Pirates."

Around this time, The Cure's first single, 'Killing An Arab'/'10:15' was released on Small Wonder, an indie label chosen by Parry when it was evident that Polydor would be too inflexible to market any Cure product before Christmas. The deal was that the band were sub-let for 15,000 copies with the knowledge that, should these sell, Fiction would have made enough money to press another 15,000 themselves.

Parry:

"It was so completely different that I knew the punters would like it. It was something you could pogo to, so it was a winner for punks and, among those punks, were the people I really wanted to get at – the people who read music papers, the active ones. So I made sure we got a really good poster campaign. I used Bill Smith to do the designs – quirky but right for the time, a little bit different.

"The design certainly wasn't to Robert's taste, I knew that, but I wasn't terribly concerned. I just wanted him to concentrate on the music. He had a lot of good songs and I was worried we weren't gonna get them down or that someone would come along and do them better.

"I thought, 'This band are just enjoying themselves too much; they lack weight, lack concept, lack awareness of what they've got in their hands'. So, I picked this old man's face, reversed it to make it look more ugly, then put it out on posters throughout London."

Robert:

"The reaction was astonishing. One minute we were nothing and the next we were the New Existentialists!"

SINGLE OF THE WEEK
THE CURE: Killing An Arab (Small Wonder).
Apparently based on Albert's *The Outsider* and, if so, quite possibly the straw that broke Camus' back. Cymbals crash · once, twice, three times. A guitar, full of eerie promises, slithering like the sprog of some belly-dancer and a poisonous reptile. Pause. Compact bass guitar motif, descending alone. Then those vocals — taut, terse, tense intonation, very much wired and emotional, the scream that a nervous system might make on the verge of metabolic breakdown. A voice like that feeling you get watching the faces on the workaday tube ride after stepping out at dawn for the third time without sleep. Clipped, concise urgency, occasionally cracking when it arrives at a word or phrase it considers particularly emotive — ain't nothing but another beach party on an alien sandy shore! Kick off your Scholl sandals and listen. Monotonic chant:

"Standing on the beach/With a gun in my hand/Staring at the sea/Staring at the sand/Staring down the barrel at the Arab on the ground/Can see his open mouth/But I hear no sound./I'm alive/I'm dead/I'm the stranger/Killing an Arab."

And racism has got nothing to do with it."

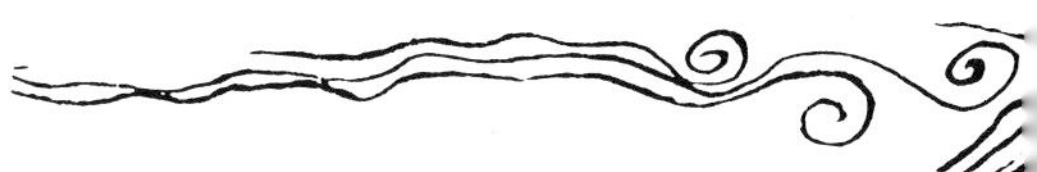

THE CURE
Railway Hotel, London

KILLER CURE

AS the country slips into a non-operative stasis, here comes some good news. The subject of the bulletin is the Cure, a brand new three-piece from Crawley.

Last Wednesday, Robert Smith (guitar/vocals), Mike Dempsey (bass) and Lol Tolhurst (drums) played what I'm going to describe as modern pop. Don't groan — this is one of those occasions (happily growing more numerous) when the handle fits. All three members are in their late teens, and evince the kind of apprehensive excitement of discovery that make for interesting and invigorating sensations.

Of course, I'm not saying that they are ready-made saviours. There are rough patches (a new PA backline caused some nervy moments), and they need to work on projecting their act, but despite these teething troubles they showed a glorious potential.

Tolhurst is sturdy, while Dempsey and Smith manage to be both rhythmically sound and melodically inventive. Smith's voice is a lot stronger than it appears to be on their current single on Small Wonder, "Killing An Arab" (a sort of distillation of Camus' novel, The Stranger) coupled with "10.15 Saturday Night" (which should have been the top-side).

At the moment, though, their real strength lies in the material, which is generally co-written by the trio. The songs mesh a stylishly understated plundering of classic Sixties poprock with post-punk economy and drive. The effect is tight and open-ended, considered but on the right side of rough.

Take a song like "Boys Don't Cry," for example: reminiscent in structure of a Beatles' flipside around '64/'65, its appealing choppiness and ebullient angularity meet contemporary needs pretty well dead on. Mix in some imaginative lyrics (often tersely evocative narratives) and the experience should be far from unpleasant.

Don't let them pass you by. — IAN BIRCH.

Ian Birch wrote in Melody Maker: "As 'Hong Kong Garden' used a simple oriental-styled riff to striking effect, so 'Arab' conjures up edginess through a Moorish-flavoured guitar pattern."

The flip-side, '10:15', was eulogised too. Sounds' Dave McCulloch wrote: "It hits upon the value of sparseness in rock 'n' roll like no other record has in, oh, as far as I can think back. There's scarcely any playing on the song at all. Everything is left to your imagination . . . ". He also remarked upon the "bored, effortlessly tired vocals . . . " while NME's Nick Kent called it " . . . Something of an isolated vignette, hopefully portraying a whole mood of rejection."

From 8-10 January 1979, The Cure were ensconced once again in Morgan Studios working on the album.

Michael:

"Parry sat in the chair next to Hedges so I suppose that's tantamount to producing. Trouble is, he'd been a drummer in his former life and, like most people who play, he had an affection for his particular instrument so the first day of recording always consisted of poor Lol hitting the snare to get what Parry considered the all-important element of the song. After that things went very quickly – there were no overdubs apart from a little lead guitar and Robert's vocal and, because we'd played the songs so many times, it only took us three or four takes. We whipped through very quickly.

"Parry even managed to persuade Robert to invest in a Fender Jazzmaster guitar and a Roland JC160 amp to enhance the sound."

Following the unprecendented publicity surrounding 'Killing An Arab', Sounds featured The Cure on the cover of their 27 January edition. The interview, conducted by Dave McCullough and called "Stars In Embryo", took place at the Natural History Museum at the band's request and featured a foetus sucking its thumb in the background of the photographs.

"God, they look so young it's not true," wrote McCullough. " . . . Robert resplendent in baggy, singularly silly and unhip pants. He's skinny and alarmingly handsome . . . They look younger in the way that most grammar school kids from fairly safe family backgrounds look younger. Unexposed and clean."

Attending a gig at the Moonlight, he continued: " . . . Like the early and late lamented Buzzcocks, nothing is spared, the whole set is minimal glory . . . Robert's lead is killing but it's that bass sound that steals the evening's honours, Mick using it like a lead instrument and pushing the whole sound along quite superbly."

He concluded that the band had "direction through indirection . . . Very musical. Almost rootless, which makes them very contemporary . . . The Cure brought back the spark of rock 'n' roll to me. Youth. Energy. Endless potential and hope."

Of the same Moonlight gig, Ian Birch wrote in Melody Maker: "The songs mesh a stylishly understated plundering of classic Sixties pop-rock with post-punk economy and drive. The effect is tight and open-ended, considered but on the right side of rough."

From 31 January to 9 February, The Cure continued to record and mix in Morgan, playing intermittently in and around London.

Robert:

"The thing was, not living in London, I didn't know about these places. The only time I'd ever been to see a group was in Brighton or Croydon, we never used to bother going to London – it cost too much money to get there and back. I'd read about The Marquee, Hope & Anchor and The Nashville but I couldn't believe what they were actually like; they were horrible.

"We played The Nashville on 9 February and the National Front turned up because they thought 'Killing An Arab' was really about killing an Arab. There was continuous fighting. The NF were distributing leaflets which mentioned 'Killing An Arab' so we had to publish denials and ended up playing the single down."

THE CURE

Marquee, London

10.15 on a Friday night, and it's obvious that all is not well. At one end of a dismal refectory hall in Hounslow Poly, still under the glare of houselights, The Cure are concluding an introverted and undistinguished set. The audience is sullen and unresponsive, and the atmosphere uneasy as the evening's contingent of shaven-headed intellectuals clamber onto the stake. The band struggles through and returns, unnecessarily, for an encore.

The Cure seem to have benefited little from the praise heaped on their debut single, "Killing An Arab." Its self-conscious literary references and contrived jingle-like tune suggest a calculated cleverness of approach which, in actuality, the band do not possess. Either way, their set did little to diminish the preconceptions of this audience.

And so to the Marquee for the second of the band's four Sunday-night spots. First up were Fashion, a band so original that they even have a synthesizer to assist in their turgid sub-Doctors dirges, thereby at least ensuring the results are spectacularly boring. The most exciting moment came when the synthesizer broke down, but from then on the set became simply boring and interminably drawn out.

The Cure take the stage, opening with the single's superior B-side, and they impress. There follows a breathless stream of 15 other songs, compressed into just over 40 minutes, each one compact, perfectly conceived and performed with control and vigour. Although basically the same set as at the earlier gig the results are incomparably different.

The songs have in common a taut, tightly-drawn structure, within which are contained more hooklines and melodies than many bands can muster in a lifetime.

Lead singer and guitarist Robert Smith is the archetypal high definition performer, at times resembling a younger, fresh-faced Tom Verlaine, spitting out lyrics and rolling off lightning guitar phrases in a jumble of sustained discord and harmonics. Mick Dempsey, on bass, takes as many solos, weaving around the song structures, and leaving much of the rhythmic impact to Lawrence Tolhurst's echoed, imaginative drumming.

Comparisons could range from Pere Ubu to Buzzcocks and Wire, and at times the band played with a detachment that belied the inherent warmth of their songs, informing but not engaging the audience. Lyrically, they work best when dealing with specifics ("Boys Don't Cry", "Subway Song" and others) and not with suspect literary concepts as in "Killing An Arab" and "Fire In Cairo", the latter possibly the next single.

In the final count, The Cure are doing what few of the other new bands have done: writing traditionally melodic songs, embracing experiment to a point short of self-indulgence, and at the same time being intelligent about it. They are very young. They will also be successful. — **JAMES TRUMAN.**

On 3 February, Sounds ran a snippet of gossip claiming The Cure had been gobbed on by skins for "Their blow-waves and baggies" and, later in the month, 'Killing An Arab' was featured on '20 Of A Different Kind', a post punk compilation released by Polydor featuring, among others, 999, The Jam, The Skids, Sham 69 and Generation X.

NME's Paul Morley called the album "An insulting, corny joke . . . hopefully an intentional parody of the established K-Tel, Arcade and Ronco con guides."

From 4 March inclusive, The Cure played a residency of four Sunday nights at The Marquee in Wardour Street. One of their support bands was Joy Division.

Robert:

"They were all full and the stage was regularly invaded. On the first night they let in 900 people, even though the capacity was supposed to be 800."

Lol:

"I remember Ian Curtis had a very sad aura about him. I wasn't all that shocked to hear about his suicide later."

Robert:

"I can't remember Joy Division at all. Backstage at The Marquee is about as big as a toilet and there were always about 20 people in there. We couldn't go out to see them play because we were too nervous anyway, so how the fuck Lol noticed Ian Curtis was sad, I'll never know."

On 7 March at Bournemouth Town Hall, some girl pulled her boyfriend's ear off and the next morning the local paper ran a story entitled "Man Loses Ear At Pop Concert". The next day, at Hounslow Borough College, security – who were all off-duty firemen – clashed with skinheads who took exception to the reggae support band. The Cure played on only to discover later that their jackets and money had all been stolen.

On 30 March, in West Runton where the band were playing the Pavilion, Robert saw the cover artwork for the album for the first time: a fridge, a hoover and a lampshade. He was horrified.

Parry:

"He thought it was absolute cack and he was very disappointed that he wasn't in control. It was my decision to make it pretty obscure and, when I showed it to them and he started to bitch, I just said 'Well, we've done it anyway' so he had to go along with it.

"My problem with The Cure was, here was a band without an image but with strong music so I thought, 'Let's make it *completely* without an image' rather than go for the sort of blood, gore and angst display that was popular for album covers at the time.

"I thought, 'Let's make it completely dispassionate, let's pick the three most mundane things we can possibly find'. And, rather than giving song titles, we gave clues – the whole thing was a headache for programmers but it was an interesting angle. People might be upset and think it pretentious but that was a risk I was prepared to take."

Michael:

"I didn't dislike it. In retrospect, I'm rather pleased that it was done because it created a mystique which couldn't be construed as pretentious because it wasn't ably enough done. I think Robert was disappointed that it was done by someone who obviously had nothing to do with the group – the in-house artist or someone – and that it was presented as a fait accompli."

Lol:

"We didn't want to be judged on what sort of look we had; so I'm the hoover, Robert's the lampstand and Michael's the fridge."

The band's only say in the cover was to be the list of names on the inner sleeve – a kind of who's who of characters who'd cropped up in their history, a kind of thank you in case they never got the chance again.

On 24 March, an interview conducted by Ian Birch appeared in Melody Maker in which Robert claimed that being a three piece "broadens rather than limits us. You can do much more with less instruments. That's why the single sounds different. If someone else had done it, they would probably have thought it needed a keyboard or a rhythm guitar playing along with the bass. Because it hasn't got that, it makes people think 'Ah, there's something a bit wrong because it sounds slightly unbalanced'."

Robert goes on to explain The Cure's perplexing instrumentation: "It's not that I dislike playing lead, but it's very hard to do things that aren't cliched. Playing lead on the bass is, as yet, relatively unexplored."

Dempsey, meanwhile, had his say on image: "Pretence is presenting yourself in a way that you don't like or that you find over-the-top. Presentation, on the other hand, is just the way you are. I'd like to think that we have a little more integrity, a little more honesty to present ourselves the way we are rather than present an image. We're our only yardstick."

The tour continued and on 5 April, after a gig at Chesterfield Fusion Hall, claimed to be the first pop concert there since Pink Floyd had played in 1968, The Cure tour was busted.

Lol:

"Some of our roadies used to smoke dope and someone shopped them. I was sharing a room with Robert when, at about five or six in the morning, someone knocked on the door and announced themselves like the BBC. It was the police. They searched the whole room – we didn't really know what was going on. They didn't find anything in our room but one of the roadies was arrested and had to go to court."

On 6 April, The Cure played Watford College and, again, there was trouble, local skinheads doing battle with police dogs. On the 7th, Chris Westwood, suspicious of Parry's marketing methods, wrote a piece in Record Mirror: "The Cure, may be a hype," he claimed, "but it may also be three young people geared in the same (positive) direction, creating not a new form or attitude for and towards rock and roll, but refocussing some of its more vital elements, forcing the observer to adjust his stance, to think and enjoy . . . A spinal, basic sound, stripping down and refocussing the instruments . . . the drums, particularly, are dominant, hard, driving and surprising, characterised by a glorious cheap-cymbal tish. For once the drum kit becomes far more than a mere rhythm box . . . The Cure are about precision, tempered and channelled energy, ideas and provocation of thoughts. They are not an essential life-force. They are merely very good."

In the same article, Lol explained his stance: "I suppose we're anti-rock 'n' roll but only in the sense that we dislike all the overplayed glamour that goes with it."

On 29 April, the band played Northgate Community Centre in Crawley with Amulet in another benefit for Dr Weaver.

Robert:

"He was thrown out of Crawley College for exactly the same reason he was thrown out of school – gross indecency – so he obviously hadn't learned his lesson. We had more status now, we'd become minor celebrities in Crawley so we thought we'd draw attention to his plight by doing a concert with Amulet, the band we played the first one with.

"The NF turned up again and went berserk. They ringed the community centre and tried to burn it down while we were playing. The whole night was a disaster really, pure violence from beginning to end, as all the Anti Nazi League people turned up as well. It was a shambles, but it made the papers . . . "

In the 5 May edition of Popstar Weekly, Robert described some of the grief the band had been subjected to, especially during their Marquee residency: "The gobbing was bad, I held my hand out and it was like it was covered with elastic bands. A lot of people came to check us out and a lot of people didn't like us, because of what we looked like I suppose."

That same week, The Cure released their debut album, 'Three Imaginary Boys' featuring the set the band had been building live since its inception. Robert's favourites were 'Accuracy' – "the most perfect of songs, few words, little music" and 'Grinding Halt' written by Lol and shortened by Robert so it only comprised the start of each sentence about apathy and decay. 'Another Day' was "purely about boredom and repetition", ostensibly about Robert at home and 'Object' was a fake horror, a black joke, Robert's attempt to appear "unwholesome. A pastiche of a sexist song". 'Subway Song' was a story, a typical Smith fantasy: "I had this habit of telling people I knew someone who'd been murdered in a subway. It wasn't true at all."

'Meathook' was one of the first songs The Cure ever wrote "and probably the worst too. It's an in-joke of sorts, arising from an incident during the Hansa days when an old producer kept complaining that one song had no hooklines". 'Fire In Cairo' was a vivid word painting, and 'Foxy Lady' was a typically irreverent and minimal assault on the Hendrix classic of which Adam Sweeting in Sound International wrote: "Imagine Hendrix without the guitar flash, phasing and stereo trickery and you're left with a sparce, twitching skeleton . . . You lose the dream and get, instead, an uncomfortable necessity". The title track was the first of many songs based on Robert's dreams.

But, amid all this eclecticism, 'So What' stood out for its sheer deliberate mundanity. Robert, drunk, couldn't come up with any lyrics so he read the special offer for a decorative cake-icing set off the back of a sugar packet. "I like the music but not the lyrics. Funny – it seemed a good idea at the time."

Adam Sweeting also wrote: "I can't remember a band which has displayed such a basic format so richly since The Who . . . it's like an introspective reverie on a wet afternoon."

Parry:

"The reviews were generally very strong except Morley's. Funnily enough, if anything was ever like what he's done with ZTT, it was the first offering from Fiction Records."

THE CURE
Three Imaginary Boys
(Fiction)

Aaah! More alert and anguished young men chalking up more sanctioned and sactimonious marks. Do not applaud them. This glistening long player contains twelve self-conscious variations upon the smoothly quirky theme, somewhere between hypnotic and indifferent, that brought the world, somewhere between hype and anonymity, the pleasureable 'Killing An Arab'. For one whole album that pretty bending and doodling does a lot less than please, and a lot more than irritate. The Cure's formula is not that marvellous.

But The Cure are not just making pop music. They make things m[illegible] worse than they could be by packaging this insubstantial froth as if it had some social validity. As if it were going to alter our conceptions of what is real and what is unreal. They garnish their twelve little ditties with unreliable trickery, not content to let ordinary songs die ordinary deaths.

The lads go rampant on insignificant symbolism and compound this with rude, soulless obliqueness. They are trying to tell us something. They are trying to tell us they do not exist. They are trying to say that everthing is empty. They are making fools of themselves. They are represented on the ice cream colour cover by three bulky, ageing household gadgets. Lol Tolhurst (drums) is a fridge. Michael Dempsey (bass, voice) is an upright Hoover. Robert Smith (guitar, voice) is a standard lamp. Each song is represented on the back sleeve by a picture and on the label by a symbol.

Thus a typically dehydrated interpretation of Hendrix's 'Foxy Lady' is matched with a polaroid snapshot of a slinky lady in pencil skirt and stillettos striding along a metropolis pavement. "So What' is represented by a picture of two bags of granulated sugar spilling over the floor. All clever stuff. All this charming, childish fiddling about aims for the anti-image but naturally creates the perfect malleable image: the tantalising enigma of The Cure.

They try to take everything away from the purpose and idea of the rock performer but try so hard they put more in than they take out. They add to the falseness. Good luck to them.

The Cure, really, are trying to sell us something. Their product is more artificial than most. This is perhaps part of their masterplan, but it seems more like their naivety. The way it is, The Cure set themselves up as though they float a long way outside the realms of anything we can understand. They are scandalous, fulfilled aliens, and they look down on us. What do they see?

Not much that'll shoot your being through with vigour or sudden understanding, but they never stop nagging. Willowy songs wallow in the murk and marsh of tawdry images, inane realisations, dull epigrams. Sometimes they sound like an avant-garde John Otway, or an ugly Spirit. Sometimes a song is as pretty as 'Killing An Arab': 'Accuracy' (a target over a man's eye) or 'Fire In Cairo' (palm tree in the desert). Most of the time it's a voice catching its breath, a cautiously primitive guitar riff, toy drumming and a sprightly bass. Nowhere is there anything alarming, nowhere is there anything truly adventurous. Not that I demand adventure at all costs, but The Cure do suggest that they're on a worthwhile expedition.

Neither do I constantly demand anything that's going to make my life a little bit better but, again, The Cure hint that they're doing this and more. What they've done here is the equivalent of an album of Enid Blyton readings packaged as reading from Angela Carter. No, it's maybe not that awful-good.

It's just that in 1979 people shouldn't be allowed to get away with things like this (The Cure are absolute conformists to vaguely defined non-convention). There are just too many who do (Doll By Doll, Punishment Of Luxury, Fischer Z). Fatigue music. So transparent. Light and — oh, how it nags.

Paul Morley

★The Cure: 'Three Imaginary Boys' (Fiction).
Although 'Three Imaginary Boys' is hardly an unqualified success, there is something highly appealing about the Crawley trio's quirky, melodic brand of modern rock. The Cure burst on to the scene little over six months ago with the delightfully ambiguous 'Killing An Arab', and seemed prime candidates for the 'too much exposure too soon' syndrome that has been the downfall of many a group over the past couple of years. But they've clearly landed butter side up, the sloppy lapses being far outweighed by the group's muted and original playing. This is primarily down to guitarist/singer Robert Smith's penchant for unusual timings, often creating a singular Eastern effect, and sense of melody. At their best ('10.15 Saturday Night,' 'Accuracy', particularly 'Another Way'), the

Cure are reminiscent of the early Only Ones, if without their vision. But comparisons are unfair. The Cure, for the most part, are out on their own; it's just from this first effort it's impossible to decide whether they are a major force in the making or merely another fascinating diversion. But then, the complete cure always takes time. (Mick Houghton).

THE CURE
'Three Imaginary Boys'
(Fiction Fix I)*****

THE RECIPE: take three intelligent, sheepishly good-looking, nice middle-class boys who have a flair for original, stylish music and who don't mind leaving their souls in the hands of a fourth, streamlined highly successful party. Take this latter party's financial genius, add a pinch of wry, good-natured self-studying humour and here in one lavish package you have . . . The Cure.

On 'Three Imaginary Boys' the recipe belongs to that essential fourth Cure, producer, mentor, minder, keeper, Chris Parry. Parry's the undoubted epicentre of The Cure, the Onassis, Merlin and only sometimes the Banquo's ghost of this boy's band, the figure that walks and provides the ostensibly decadent, Dark Side Of The Moonish packaging gimmicks (dumb postcard and all) that furnish and inevitably and intriguingly both denigrate the album and perversely enhance its cheaper charms. The cover portrays a lamp, fridge and hoover, which if really serving as personality symbols of the Cure trio provides a witty metaphor.

However, packaging is packaging: if it affects or despoils the music or the band's expressionistic, aesthetic approach it's the tik tat of disaster. As it happens, on 'Three Imaginary Boys' the treatment and approach of the songs are so strong and of such unity that they aren't put down by the decadence. 'Three Imaginary Boys', fridge and all, is a powerful album.

The Cure (Lol Tolhurst: drums, Michael Dempsey: bass, Robert Smith: guitar and vocals) are unique in that they are ploughing a path of 'different', off-centre music, but retaining within their innovation, which is slight but is total at the same time, no little energy, drive, emotion and tasteful integrity. Their pretension is given enough gloss, enough tatty superficiality, enough awareness of its existence to keep it restrained and light. This album is full of tongue-in-cheek and expert satire (new musik laughed off as instant, gross and hollow). The Cure take these norms and throw them away with one great hollow thud of a bass drum.

The album reflects The Cure's excitement of ideas, their quite stunning sense of the reserved, the sparse, the low-key: they achieve what others employ battalions on with the simple unit of bass, drums, guitar and voice. Satire? The gross becomes the intense. The chic becomes the workable.

Opening with the colossal 'IO.15 Saturday Night' the lp ticks mightly along, taking you totally by surprise if crashing, meatheaded chord swopping was expected. 'Grinding Halt', the new single, for instance, uses an old 60's soul bass-line to structure a tight, fast, just over the two minute mark pop song that reminds you of The Isley Brothers (string-bare) or The Buzzcocks (middle period when they were still good), while 'Object' sounds at once funky, punky and Q.H.M. like (quite heavy metal-like). 'Another Day', like 'IO.15' relies more on achingly dramatic, sparse splashes of musical light and shade. Side one's closer 'Subway Song' barely exists at all: mumbles, muted bass and flickering harp convey an astonishing array of ideas.

Side Two opens with a stupendous 1.53 version of Hendrix's 'Foxy Lady' and continues in similarly punchy, explosively condensed fashion with the jazzy 'Meat Hook', the elegant and shapely 'Fire In Cairo' which like the rest of the songs on the album has been transmuted brilliantly from the rough stage prototype to a polished monster of an album track, ending with the sultry, phasy nursery-rhyme title track, again an explosively understated, brilliantly dynamic reflection of a song.

So the weetabix is can't beatabix is cheatabix trappings don't matter when the music stops. 'Three Imaginary Boys' is powerful stuff, an album that's assured growing, getting better, sounding richer material. The Cure are going somewhere different on each track, the ideas are startling and disarming, but the unfussed lightness of expression is superbly maintained. I'd say: catchy and catching. I'd say; the missing link between the new Damned single and Leslie Crowther. I'd say: the cure.

DAVE McCULLOUGH

The Eighties start here

THE CURE: "The Cure" (Fiction Deluxe FIX I)

THEY have an almost embarrassingly appropriate name. At a time when many new bands are agonising over all sorts of dilemmas — do you provoke rather than entertain? do you borrow from or reject past traditions? do you subvert from within the biz or set up an alternative alongside it? — the Cure have slipped in with a masterful debut that goes a long way to resolving all the contradictions.

The key to this success lies in the discreet strength of their songs, which (bar Hendrix's "Foxy Lady") are all group-penned, and in the comprehensive originality of their approach. Everything about this album is just so practical, purposeful and democratic.

The chemistry was clearly right from the start. Producer Chris Parry shows an intuitive understanding of the Cure psyche by giving each member an equally dynamic share of the action. The band might be a three-piece, but Parry knows that they have completely cast aside the old, lumpen notion of a trio being basically a frontperson and two salaried extras.

Consequently, all the conventional areas of tedium are chucked out of the window. Instead of spotlight-hugging guitar breaks (aaargh!) or loads of vocal histrionics, the mix darts buoyantly, evenly and with superb economy between the three component parts. Of course, the band wouldn't have had it any other way, but such a situation only works when the empathy is exactly right.

Parry is also not averse to an occasional flash of studio trickery. When he adds something, however, there's always a good reason behind it. A couple of times, for example, he splices echo or mild distortion onto Robert Smith's surprisingly agile vocals. It isn't bogus window-dressing but a smart underlining of a specific sentiment. Even the nuclear howl that concludes "Subway Song" escapes cliché by being short, contained and entirely fitting for the song's sense of impending attack.

But then his job was made that much easier by such distinctive material. There are ten cuts which both create a unified framework and display how flexible that framework can be.

This is the result of careful selection and assessment, knitting together all the parts and filtering them through a strong corporate personality. They evince a healthily distanced respect for quality Sixties pop-rock, but never fail to sound contemporary. The tradition isn't abused; simply updated.

Their songs run through a whole gamut of moods which grow out of everyday situations: anger, mischief, disillusion, scorn, wistfulness and humour. Their appeal is immediate but still has the kind of depth that allow them to resonate in your head a long time afterwards. They're tightly structured, but also open-ended enough to be accessible to everyone. They are astute without being condescending, provocative without losing sight of that basic aim of entertainment.

I could go on and on. This is great pop that you should waste no time discovering. The missing link between the Kinks 1966-style and the Banshees 1978-style? The lean and friskily alert music of the Eighties? Find out for yourself. — **IAN BIRCH.**

THE CURE

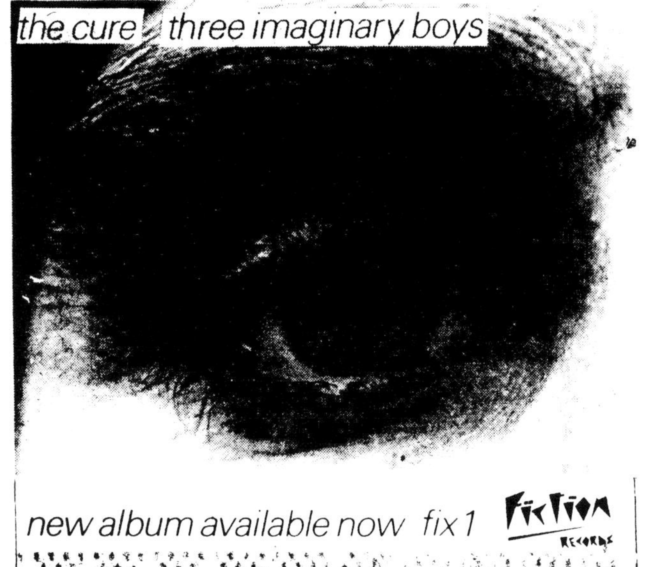

Robert:

"The reaction to 'Killing An Arab' had been universally good – even Tony Parsons didn't slag it – and it surprised us immensely. It went into the alternative chart, Peel played it virtually every night and I really didn't think it would have such an impact because I didn't think it was so radically different. Then again, I was listening to Captain Beefheart at the time so I probably thought what we were doing was tame . . .

"When we did 'Killing An Arab', no-one knew who we were – it was a single with no preconceptions but, when we brought out the album, we'd had a certain amount of press coverage, people knew what we sounded like and what we looked like and it got slagged horribly. Because of the way it was packaged, people thought it was arty."

Robert and Parry both wrote to Morley at the NME and, in their next Peel session, Robert changed the lyrics of 'Grinding Halt', parodying Morley's elaborate prose style and ridiculing his claims.

Robert:

"What irritated me was that I agreed with some of what he said but the bit about the packaging making claims for social validity was nonsense. He was saying that we were trying to do something and then not achieving it, which was obviously not true.

"I didn't actually like the record. I didn't think it sounded like The Cure at all. A lot of people said they liked it for its diversity but that's the exact thing I didn't like about it. It sounded like a compilation album or something."

On 19 May, in an NME article entitled "A Demonstration Of Household Appliances", Nick Kent remarked: "In a business full of parasites, fools and all other species of human inadequacy going under the handle of the middle man, Parry is the proverbial good guy – a man worthy of high esteem due to the fact that his sojourn as A&R man for a major record label gained him great credibility and a reputation for maverick manouvres and high stake gambling."

Kent didn't get on so well with the boys: "They are not rude or particularly cliquish but the interviewer senses that the ongoing interview situation is not one that they feel particularly at home with, that they find the process bemusing, almost quaint in its ridiculousness. As personalities, drummer Tolhurst appears the most democratic and business-like while guitarist Smith, definitely older than his age, is the creative, shoulder-shrugging one . . . Between this pair, bassist Dempsey blends in without adding any particular dimension."

Still, he persevered and, following a phone call to Robert later, concluded: "What will follow may well be some of the finest pop of the Eighties. The Cure, and Smith in particular, are to be watched closely. Middle class boys keep swinging, stopping only to check their bearings out in suburbia, changing tacks, making observations that are not hollow or bogus."

With a view to releasing a second single, Parry sent out white labels of 'Grinding Halt' but the reaction of radio programmers was less than enthusiastic so the idea was dropped although not before it was erroneously reviewed in Record Mirror.

The band's next notable gig was on 1 June at Carshalton Park on a mod revival bill with Secret Affair and the Merton Parkas. Record Mirror's Philip Hall noted "Lots of ideas but little identity" while The Crawley Advertiser praised "The delicate blend of bass and lead guitar which makes a pleasant change from the 90 miles per hour music offered up all too often as a substitute for talent".

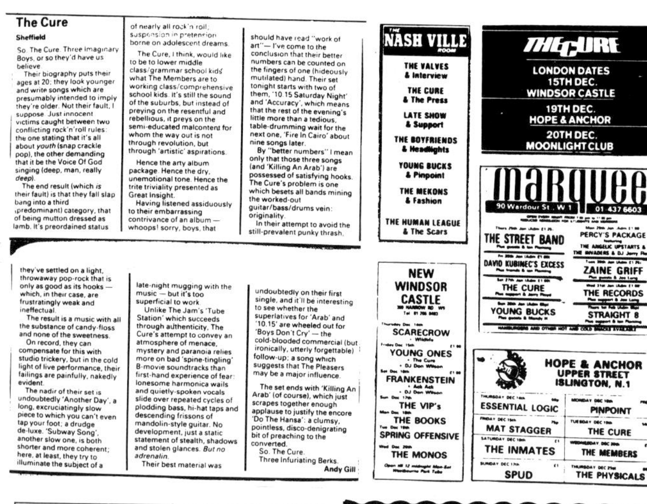

The Cure

Sheffield

So. The Cure. Three Imaginary Boys, or so they'd have us believe.

Their biography puts their ages at 20; they look younger and write songs which are presumably intended to imply they're older. Not their fault, I suppose. Just innocent victims caught between two conflicting rock'n'roll rules: the one stating that it's all about *youth* (snap crackle pop), the other demanding that it be the Voice Of God singing (deep, man, really *deep*).

The end result (which *is* their fault) is that they fall slap bang into a third (predominant) category, that of being mutton dressed as lamb. It's preordained status of nearly all rock'n'roll; suspension in pretension borne on adolescent dreams.

The Cure, I think, would like to be to lower middle class/grammar school kids what The Members are to working class/comprehensive school kids. It's still the sound of the suburbs, but instead of preying on the resentful and rebellious, it preys on the semi-educated malcontent for whom the way out is not through revolution, but through 'artistic' aspirations.

Hence the arty album package. Hence the dry, unemotional tone. Hence the trite triviality presented as Great Insight.

Having listened assiduously to their embarrassing contrivance of an album — whoops! sorry, boys, that should have read "work of art" — I've come to the conclusion that their better numbers can be counted on the fingers of one (hideously mutilated) hand. Their set tonight starts with two of them, '10.15 Saturday Night' and 'Accuracy', which means that the rest of the evening's little more than a tedious, table-drumming wait for the next one, 'Fire In Cairo' about nine songs later.

By "better numbers" I mean only that those three songs (and 'Killing An Arab') are possessed of satisfying hooks. The Cure's problem is one which besets all bands mining the worked-out guitar/bass/drums vein: originality.

In their attempt to avoid the still-prevalent punky thrash, they've settled on a light, throwaway pop-rock that is only as good as its hooks — which, in their case, are frustratingly weak and ineffectual.

The result is a music with all the substance of candy-floss and none of the sweetness.

On record, they can compensate for this with studio trickery, but in the cold light of live performance, their failings are painfully, nakedly evident.

The nadir of their set is undoubtedly 'Another Day', a long, excruciatingly slow piece to which you can't even tap your foot; a drudge de-luxe. 'Subway Song', another slow one, is both shorter and more coherent; here, at least, they try to illuminate the subject of a late-night mugging with the music — but it's too superficial to work.

Unlike The Jam's 'Tube Station' which succeeds through authenticity, The Cure's attempt to convey an atmosphere of menace, mystery and paranoia relies more on bad 'spine-tingling' B-movie soundtracks than first-hand experience of fear: lonesome harmonica wails and quietly-spoken vocals slide over repeated cycles of plodding bass, hi-hat taps and descending frissons of mandolin-style guitar. No development, just a static statement of stealth, shadows and stolen glances. *But no adrenalin.*

Their best material was undoubtedly on their first single, and it'll be interesting to see whether the superlatives for 'Arab' and '10.15' are wheeled out for 'Boys Don't Cry' — the cold-blooded commercial (but ironically, utterly forgettable) follow-up: a song which suggests that The Pleasers may be a major influence.

The set ends with 'Killing An Arab' (of course), which just scrapes together enough applause to justify the encore 'Do The Hansa': a clumsy, pointless, disco-denigrating bit of preaching to the converted.

So. The Cure.

Three Infuriating Berks.

Andy Gill

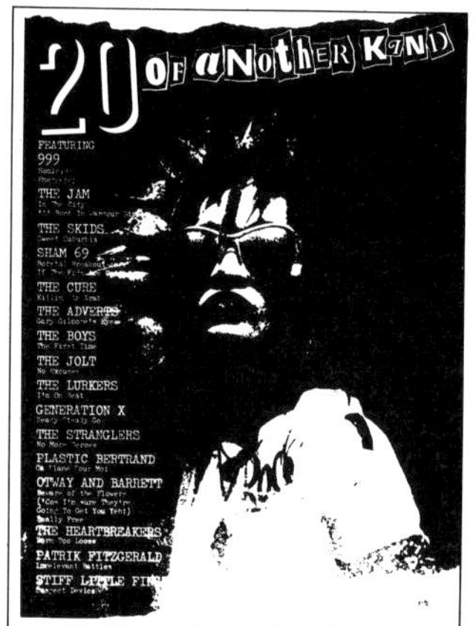

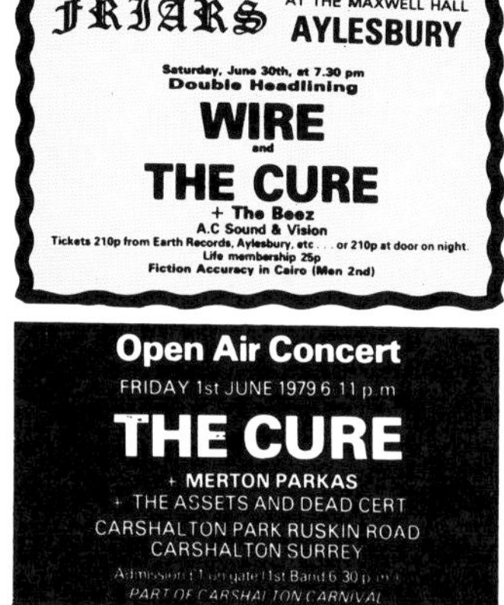

In late June, The Cure released 'Boys Don't Cry'/ 'Plastic Passion' as the second single. Ian Birch of Melody Maker had already noted the song live: "Reminiscent in structure of a Beatles flipside around '64/'65, its appealing clappiness and ebullient angularity meet contemporary needs pretty well dead on". Record Mirror's Giovanni Dadomo had reckoned it "brought to mind the image of John Lennon at 12 or 13".

Parry:

"On 28 June, in Port Talbot, Robert sat me down and said 'Look Bill, I don't want to be like The Boomtown Rats'. That made me laugh and gave me an insight into Robert's character, the first indicator of what was to come. I thought 'What *does* he mean? There's no way in the world he could be like The Boomtown Rats'. It got me thinking and it was only later that I supposed what he meant by that was that he wouldn't be manipulated. I took it as a sign of inherent weakness in terms of how much he'd be prepared to take to see through what he was doing and I started thinking about just how far this band could be pushed. It's very frustrating when someone says something like that to you – you just want to say 'Fuck off, get like The Boomtown Rats and *then* change it. Don't back off before you've found out what the water's like'. And the seriousness on his face, the worry of it all, struck me as very odd."

Reviewed by PAUL MORLEY

NEW POP OF THE WEEK

1). THE CURE: Boys Don't Cry (Fiction). I still find the 'Three Imaginary Boys' LP as empty as a yawn and the frowning self-elevation that surrounded the dust just as tedious. This is magnificent. Just (just!?!) as a single, a sound, a sprint, something I can quite easily see at number one. The clarity, the skimming speed and the overall make-up confirm the notion that there is a distinct Sound Of The New Pop forming — not yet a formula, though. A light rush, an alert melody and an elusive genius. Buzzcocks started it, The Undertones, Smirks, The Distractions and others have followed it through and now The Cure prove that they know the way. 'Boys Don't Cry' is a light trippy riff, with an eloquent one-string motif, chatty, ambiguous, yearning vocals and a series of understated, unexpected twists. It is classic new pop. That means absolutely addictive. The Cure can be a great singles group, and realising that there is nothing wrong with that should cut away all the defensive enigma trimmings and get on the swing. At least they've stopped sobbing.

Parry:

"I knew that 'Killing An Arab' would be fun but 'Boys Don't Cry' was my pick for the Top 10. It didn't get there because Polydor stitched us up. 'Boys Don't Cry' was a hit song and it *should* have been a hit. Robert was disappointed and he had a right to be. It was a farce."

On 1 July, The Cure played The Lyceum with The Ruts.

Lol:

"We topped the bill; the promoters mixed bands without giving a fuck about compatability, all they wanted was to fill the place."

Robert:

"I remember Malcolm Owen, The Ruts' singer, came to see us in our dressing room and was well pissed off that we'd managed to convince his fans we were good."

Still, some remained unconvinced. Mike Nicholls of Record Mirror wrote: "Halfway through '79 and The Cure can consider themselves prime contenders for The Most Frustrating Band Of The Year Award . . . No hoover, fridge or lamp onstage, just a nice fat ventilator to keep 'em cool and casual. And further fine hardware in the form of attractive lights beaming blue and yellow on the band and white on the audience . . . Did you know they were the Pink Floyd of the new wave? Well, Robert Smith carries off an admirable Syd Barrett drone and their general art school and smoke bombs approach has definite hippy appeal."

During July, Robert set about some ancillary projects to The Cure. One was recording The Obtainers' 'Yeah Yeah Yeah' for his and Ric Gallups Dance Fools Dance label.

Robert:

"They were like an accapella group, just the two of them, 10 or 11 years old, singing and playing on pots and pans. They just dropped a cassette through my front door and the songs were brilliant. I played it to a lot of people and everyone said they wanted a copy so I thought, rather than copy tapes, it would only cost £50 to get 100 records pressed and we could sell them for 50p each. So, that's what we did. We put Simon's band, The Magspies, on the other side, and all the copies sold. Peel played it quite a lot and I thought it was fun. I'd never realised it was so easy to make, package and sell records."

The other project was Cult Hero, a bit of fun that unwittingly served to illustrate tensions within the band.

Robert:

"I wanted to record with Simon. I never really knew Michael, we never had that much in common. I would chat to him but I would never really *talk* to him. There were lots of little differences in our characters and, if it weren't for the group, I wouldn't have socialised with him at all because I don't think we particularly enjoyed each other's company. There were other people I had more in common with and it got difficult on all those journeys to all those places just the three of us, sharing a room. Lol and I grew closer because we would laugh at the same things and get angry at the same things but Dempsey wouldn't.

"Sometimes it would go quiet for two or three hours, no-one would say anything, and Lol was always trying to break the ice, patch things up, make everything right and I just wouldn't indulge in small talk because I knew, at some point soon, that I was going to have to stop playing with Michael.

I wasn't enjoying going on stage or anything. It was fine when we were just rehearsing once a week and playing at The Rocket but, when we were on tour, doing three or four concerts a week, I began to find it very difficult."

Lol:

"Michael always used to take as many vitamin pills as possible and yet he was always ill."

Robert:

"We just began to diverge and then it began to spill over into the music. I was then going out drinking on a Saturday with Simon and his lot in Horley and I thought it would be great if Simon was in the group, it would be much more fun and really take off."

Michael:

"Simon and Robert both had a liking for Indian food and it was my undoing. I hated it."

Robert:

"I was in the pub one night with Simon's crowd and someone said that Frank Bell, this local Horley postman, had always felt he had the makings of stardom. I knew him – he was one of the wrecking crew and he used to wear a tee-shirt saying 'I'm a cult hero'. So I thought 'Get him in the studio and write him a disco song'. I wanted Simon there and I got in Porl, and Janet, my sister, as well so it wouldn't look like I was just replacing Michael with another bass player."

Lol:

"The atmosphere in the studio was very different to how it had been over the previous couple of months. Everyone was falling about – it was really good fun. Then we invited another 10 or 15 people from Horley and they all arrived about seven o'clock clutching their bags of goodies and we stayed overnight."

Michael:

"I'd been on holiday and, when I came back, Simon had already learned the bassline. It didn't bother me actually so I went down to the studio and played some synth with a wine bottle. I think that's the moment when Robert came to see that Simon was more suited to the group. He felt more at ease with him, they had a lot more in common."

Robert:

"We recorded it with Hedges at Morgan. Bill didn't object. There was no 'Is this a good career move?' He thought it peculiar that Frank sang and not me though – he didn't understand that particular part of it."

Parry:

"I like spontaneity but I had the sense to say 'Well, get the backing track done first, *then* we'll have the party'. It made immense sense to me – the only thing is, I think we picked the wrong side. Robert wanted 'Cult Hero' but 'I Dig You' is really the one the Americans went for."

Robert:

"It did very little except in Canada where it sold about 35,000 copies: so there it worked; there Frank *is* a cult hero!"

On 29 July, The Cure played an open air festival in Sterrebos, Holland, their first trip abroad as a band.

Lol:

"It was pissing with rain and we thought we were going to get electrocuted on stage. But we liked the gig so much that we went to a club that evening and

played a second gig at the request of various people. I remember they paid us in drinks. And then we went on to Amsterdam, we had rooms booked in a hotel that looked alright from the outside but, after 10 flights of stairs, we arrived in a room with six camp beds, dirty curtains and an open pipe running across it giving off this stinking smell. We went back out immediately and stayed out drinking 'till five in the morning before we could face going back."

On 3 August, back in Britain, Robert met Steve Severin of The Banshees at a Throbbing Gristle gig at the YMCA off Tottenham Court Road.

Robert:

"I was watching Throbbing Gristle and it seemed they were pumping car fumes into the audience from a truck outside so I went to the bar and Severin was there. Bill was there too and he introduced us and we just chatted over a few drinks which set the scene for the next five or six years really. I remember the occasion distinctly – I was wearing sunglasses and my green check Charlie Cairoli suit and it made Severin laugh."

Severin:

"We'd signed to Polydor thanks to two people, one of whom was Chris Parry. When he left the company to start Fiction, he gave me a copy of 'Killing An Arab' which I really liked so, at the YMCA, he introduced me to Robert who was wearing a strange green suit. The first thing I asked him was why he lived in Crawley as I couldn't understand how he could be in a band and not live in London. He replied that it was more peaceful there."

Robert:

"I was pleased to meet him because I liked The Banshees a lot, they were really good, and so when he asked me if we'd be interested in going on their tour, I said yes."

On 24 August, The Cure played Reading Festival on a bill with The Tourists, The Police, Wilko Johnson, Doll By Doll and Motorhead. They shared a caravan with Lemmy, dedicated 'Boys Don't Cry' to "the Motorhead men" and went down remarkably well.

On 5 September, they played Belfast as support to Siouxsie & The Banshees.

Lol:

"We drove into Belfast and stopped at a police post to ask directions to the Europa Hotel. I was wearing all black at the time and I leapt out of the car and ran towards this policemen and the next thing I knew I had a gun in my side.

"That was just the start! When we arrived at the Europa, there was nothing on the first four floors except a bar and there was this 15 foot high fence all around it. It was horrific, you had to go through all these searches to get in. When we got to the Ulster Hall, we found the crew had all fallen asleep in Liverpool so there was no gear whatsoever, nothing. So Terry Hooley, who ran Good Vibrations, scouted around all the bands that he knew and we played after The Banshees with all The Outcasts' gear. One of their guitars disappeared as I remember and they weren't very happy about that."

The next date of the tour was in Aberdeen and everyone arrived off the ferry to discover massive policing because Maggie Thatcher was in town. The traumas continued that night when, after a frosty public appearance at a record store, Kenny Morris and John McKay, The Banshees' drummer and guitarist, pinned their tour passes on their pillows, took a train to London and quit the band. This didn't exactly come as a shock to The Cure.

Robert:

"I remember after a warm up date in Bournemouth, we'd finished our set and we were sitting backstage and Severin and Sioux came in and chatted to us, just getting to know us, but Morris and McKay wouldn't say anything. If we bumped into them and said hello, they'd just turn their heads away like superstars!

"The first we really knew about them leaving was the pandemonium backstage at the concert. Dave Woods, The Banshees' manager, was in a panic as we came off from playing our set and asked us if we could go back on and play some more. I said okay and Sioux and Severin went on and made the announcement. The crowd started chanting and we went back on and played some unfinished new songs like '17 Seconds', ones that we'd written the music to but not the words. I think we did 'M' and then they joined us for 'The Lord's Prayer'. Severin was shouting to me 'E! Just play E!' and, as it turned out, that wasn't to be the last time he shouted it at me either!

"I thought it was a good night. We went back to The Banshees' hotel afterwards and I ended up staying there with Sioux and Severin getting drunk together for the first time. They were discussing what they were going to do and I wanted the tour to go on. It was important to us so I just suggested that I'd play with them if they needed me. Severin told me they'd audition some guitarists and it was left at that."

On 8 September, Sounds published an article by David Hepworth in which he vividly described the agonies of attempting to interview The Cure: "Had there been a handy exit, I'm sure I would have used it. Smith, who was inhabiting some lurid green suit that looked like a cross between a bull-fighter's costume and a Charlie Cairoli cast-off, floated across the bar like a man who is just too damned effete to live, offered a hand like a portion of under-cooked haddock, asked if there was anything non-alcoholic to drink, simpered that the rest of the band couldn't make it and then leaned wanly against the wall and made only token efforts to return my pathetic attempts at conversation."

Later, though, over a glass of wine or two, Hepworth warmed to Robert as he elucidated the concept behind 'Three Imaginary Boys': "The reason for the non-image was that, as a group, we weren't particularly affiliated with anything. There was no left wing, no right wing, no nothing. People think that, if you're in a group and you enjoy playing the same sort of music, you have to have the same beliefs or like the same things or stand for the same things. I don't think it really follows. If it was a co-operative like The Mekons, I could understand it, but with us it's just a musical thing. I don't really socialise with Mick and Lol. I never socialise with anyone really."

Robert goes on to deny that poverty is a prerequisite of having something to say, admits to going out with the same girl for five years and says he has nothing to do with any all-lads-together-on-the-road business. On the lack of success of 'Boys Don't Cry', he said: "It's like commentators in cricket. They always say 'Oh, he's doing really well' and then he gets bowled out." He also claimed he was glad it wasn't a hit because it freed him from having to duplicate for the sake of success.

Finally, Robert voiced his opinion on the idiocy of interviews: "It's ridiculous. You put out an album that's greeted with some measure of critical acclaim and you're immediately in a position where people should listen to you . . . It might be flattering to know that people want to know what you think but I don't really see myself as one of the top three original thinkers in the world today so I'm not in any position to expound my philosophy of life."

SIOUXSIE: She is getting help from Crawley's The Cure.

Siouxsie's remedy – Crawley's Cure

DESPITE the break-up of Siouxsie and the Banshees, the concert at Brighton with Crawley's successful pop group *The Cure* still looks like going ahead.

One of the three Crawley boys who go to make-up The Cure, drummer Michael Dempsey, told the *Courier* this week: "As far as we know it's still on.

"Our guitarist, Rob Smith is standing-in for the one who walked out, Siouxsie has got someone to replace the drummer and the tour we were doing with her starts up again on Tuesday."

Siouxsie who was left in the lurch by two of her Banshees at a concert in Aberdeen last week is on tour with The Cure — Michael Dempsey, Lol Tolhurst and Rob Smith, three 20-year-olds from Crawley — and last week there was worries that the tour would have to be cancelled because of the split.

"But it all seems to have worked out alright now," says Michael, "I only hope Rob has enough energy to play with both bands."

The Cure are currently having their third single mixed, called "Jumping on someone's (or somebody's we haven't quite got the grammar worked out yet) train", it should be out in six weeks to two months' time just at the start of The Cure's own headlining tour when they expect to play ten universities and ten Continent gigs.

The Brighton concert is at the Centre on October 10 and tickets are available from the box office.

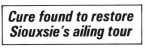

Cure found to restore Siouxsie's ailing tour

SIOUXSIE RECRUITS

SIOUXSIE AND the Banshees this week resume their truncated British tour, with Siouxsie and Steve Severin joined by two recently recruited musicians.

These are Budgie, former drummer of the Slits, who takes over on drums, and Robert Smith, guitarist of the Cure. Smith will not be leaving the Cure to play the gigs — just playing two sets a night with the Cure and with the Banshees.

At the end of the tour Siouxsie and Severin intend to find permanent replacements.

•Most of the tour dates remain unaltered but Bradford St George's Hall is now September 24. Oxford New Theatre is now September 26 and a gig has been added at Liverpool Empire on September 30. Taunton Odeon has been cancelled. Tickets bought for the original dates will be valid for the re-scheduled dates and refunds can be obtained from box offices.

SIOUXSIE and her new-look Banshees, plus The Cure

Siouxsie starts again

SIOUXSIE AND THE BANSHEES were back in action again this week — resuming their British tour with replacements for guitarist John McKay and drummer Kenny Morris who quit the band just before a gig in Aberdeen.

The temporary replacements in the band are guitarist Robert Smith from The Cure and drummer Budgie from The Slits. Permanent replacements will be made at the end of the tour. Smith will now be playing two sets a night on the tour as The Cure are special guests on all dates.

The band picked up the threads of their tour at Leicester De Montfort Hall on Tuesday. The tour has been slightly reorganised, but most dates remain as originally scheduled.

Bradford St Georges Hall has been moved to September 24, Oxford New Theatre will now be on the 26th. Taunton Odeon has been cancelled and replaced by Liverpool Empire on the 30th. Tickets bought for the original dates will be valid. Rema Rema will not now be playing any of the dates as a second support act.

· Siouxsie's new single, 'Mittageisen', will be released by Polydor this weekend.

On 10 September, The Cure played the Rotterdam New Pop festival, playing in front of 10,000 people and televised nationally. On returning to Britain, the band went back into Morgan and worked on their next single, 'Jumping Someone Else's Train'/ 'I'm Cold'.

Robert:

"It was a reaction to the mod movement that was going on at the time – that explains the sub-Pete Townshend opening chord. I remember writing the words in the bar at Morgan. The tune was a left over –I was writing songs like '17 Seconds' by then. I thought it would make a good single but it was about the last thing we did like that and I realised it would be the last thing we did with Michael. We'd had a couple of rehearsals and he didn't like the new stuff. I wanted the basslines to become really simple and he wanted to get even more flowery."

Michael:

"It was really the last Cure song in that style. It had a little bit of everybody in it, all the groups we'd been following around. There was a syn drum, a poppy bassline and a little bit of The Jam in there. Robert just gave me a tape with a chord structure and no lyrics, Lol only had one beat so we knew what that was going to be and that was it really. We didn't work on it together so I don't know if Robert hated the song or if he liked it."

Robert:

"Sioux and Severin came to visit us while we were doing 'Jumping Someone Else's Train' and Sioux sang on 'I'm Cold', the B-side, wailing backing vocals. It was an old song from when Porl was in the group, so we recorded it normally and then slowed it down to half speed, just so I could put psychedelic guitar on it!

"The Banshees had had two days auditioning guitarists and then they'd invited me down as they hadn't found anyone else who could play what they wanted. I'd rehearsed a couple of their songs so I could be really impressive! I think we probably actually covered six or seven songs because I knew them, and it was then they decided I'd be right. So they finalised everything – they'd found Budgie from The Slits – and they told me the news at the Morgan session. Everyone was quite happy about it, although they initially wanted another support group. But I said I'd only do it if it was The Cure."

The Banshees tour reconvened at Leicester de Montfort Hall on 18 September, Robert playing two sets.

Robert:

"I don't remember it being difficult. After what we'd been doing for the past two or three years, it was a piece of piss really. We were driven around, there was food in the dressing room and the only difficult thing was the mental strain of the first few nights because I knew people were looking at me, thinking 'Is he going to be able to do this?'.

"I got through it okay, though it was the first time I'd ever tried to copy a guitarist. I found that peculiar, but more rewarding than exhausting."

NME journalist Deanne Pearson, who'd joined The Cure on tour, came to different conclusions. In an astute article entitled "No Image, No Style, No Bullshit", she described Robert thus: "He looks ill, thin and pale, isn't eating properly, isn't sleeping properly, his mind a constant whir of activity. He doesn't want to let anyone down, least of all The Banshees."

Robert, for his part, described the band's predicament: "I think people are disappointed because we have no image. There's nothing for them to identify with and imitate like there is with The Clash or The Ramones or The Banshees . . . I even wear the same clothes onstage for The Cure and The Banshees sets as I do offstage – and that's nobody's idea of a pop star! . . . It would have been so easy for us to cultivate an image. We could have dyed our hair pink or dressed up in leather or something but then we'd have to live up to that image all the time and I just couldn't be bothered."

Lol revealed that he, too, had offered himself as a temporary Banshee should the need have arisen and Michael seemed resigned to The Cure being lacklustre as a sacrifice for the tour continuing. He also took the opportunity to denigrate the album cover: "It was someone else's idea and it proved only detrimental to us. We had kids coming up asking us to explain our album and we couldn't. How do you explain someone else's artwork . . . it's impossible, and that's when our prefabricated image began to crumble."

Michael also disapproved of Robert's sudden celebrity overshadowing the group as a whole: "I don't want people to think of The Fatman (as he'd taken to calling Lol) and I as the Bruce Foxton and Rick Buckler of the band, y'know, the two jokers. We're not really silly all the time."

But, Robert admitted, they were all over-awed: "I think The Banshees and the roadies and everyone think we're rather silly and naive at times because we all get so excited about things . . . Sometimes I smile, like when Budgie and I make mistakes, we look at each other and grin. We can't help it but that's not The Banshees' image is it? They're supposed to be all deep and dark and brooding." Of the relationships within The Cure, he revealed: "We only talk to each other on a very superficial level now, cliquey jokes and witty comments at breakfast and so on, because you run out of things to talk about when you're constantly together . . . But I don't get bored because I've got so many other things to think about."

Pearson surmised he was putting on a brave face, especially as his parting shot was: "I dreamt I packed it all in last night and it was such a relief", a hint of what he confessed, later in the year, to Blank Space: "It wasn't until about the fifth or sixth date that I realised I was holding back during The Cure's set, as if that was the starters and the real thing was still to come . . . Before I'd go on for each set, I'd have to prepare myself in the tune-up room. It was like a schizoid thing, a different me with each band . . . the hardest thing to get over, a really odd sensation."

Things got a lot odder still in Newcastle on 3 October.

Robert:

"It was a very peculiar night. I got into a fight in the lift with these three businessmen which carried on down the corridor. I put this bloke's head through a glass door and his two mates really did me over.

"There wasn't much I could do about it. I did manage to get out at my floor with them still after me, and I pounded on Lol and Michael's door, shouting 'Help me! Help me!' but, of course, they thought I was pissing about. By the time they eventually rescued me, I was really scarred. I had cuts all down the side of my head and my hand from the glass door and I felt terrible.

"I wrote virtually three-quarters of the '17 Seconds' album that night. I just stayed up for seven or eight hours and wrote because I was so unhappy. It was one of those nights when I felt filled with all the horror of the world.

"The other great night on that tour was in Hull on the 8th. Me, Lol and Severin were drinking seriously in the bar when Lol decided suddenly to go for a walk. When, about two hours later, he still hadn't returned, we thought we should go and find him.

Lol:

"All I can remember about that is going out to the Humber and never making it back."

Robert:

"It was really foggy and Severin and I were walking along with a lighter each so we wouldn't get lost. Every now and then, we'd stumble over an empty bottle on the footpath so we knew we were on the right track. We eventually found him asleep on the banks of the river, but as he wouldn't move, we just left him there covered in mud to sleep it off!"

Lol:

"I remember there were all these bullrushes by the side of the river and there was a point where I thought I had to grab hold of something and I just went down, bathing in the rushes. Good one that."

Robert:

"Severin really liked Lol after that and the three of us became a sort of group within the groups because he could have a type of fun with us which he couldn't with The Banshees."

Out of choice and necessity, Robert was spending more and more time with The Banshees.

Robert:

"I don't think Lol minded so much because he was really enjoying the fact that we were touring with them but Michael didn't particularly like them and I think he resented the fact that I had even started to travel around with them.

"They had a luxury bus while Lol and Michael were travelling around in my green Maxi. The Banshees didn't want me travelling in that because they thought it might break down – which it frequently did – and they thought 'Why jeopardise the entire show?'

"There was also one other particular incident, I think it was in Birmingham, when we'd been swimming, but Michael wasn't there, and we were sitting around the breakfast table with Siouxand Severin and a few other people and Michael came down and there wasn't room for him. He had to go and sit at another table and I thought 'Oh no, this is going to be the last straw!'

"I realised that, after The Banshees tour, I couldn't just go back to The Cure as it was but I was really looking forward to The Cure as it was going to be. The Banshees tour had given me time away from

Lol and Michael to think about what I wanted The Cure to be."

Michael:

"I think Robert was going through a lot then. Lol and I were, well, not blind functionaries, but we were just on the tour, whereas he was looking forward to the next thing. I remember him saying he wanted to make the next album really boring and I couldn't quite grasp that concept. Still, at that point, he was still decent enough to realise that Lol and I would be worried that he might join The Banshees – I'm sure they tried to persuade him – so he tried to divide his time between everyone."

Parry:

"I thought 'Fuck it, if the guy wants to play with The Banshees, something will come of it though Lord knows what!' Robert's in love with life – he'll do just what he wants. During that period, I had lots of other things going anyway – The Passions, The Purple Hearts, The Associates. I was a label boss so I was really unaware that Robert was spending a lot of time in the company of The Banshees."

On 3 November, the British music press reviewed 'Jumping Someone Else's Train'.

THE CURE: Jumping Someone Else's Train (Fiction).
CULT HERO: I'm A Cult Hero (Fiction). Two new Cure singles on the same label in one week, showing just how much the band have come on in the past year. I mean, it's a long way from the Laker's Hotel, Redhill, to Hammersmith Odeon with the Banshees.

The sardonic attack on fads, 'Jumping Someone Else's Train', lacks the compassion that distinguished 'Boys Don't Cry' and there are hints that the formula is wearing a little thin, but it's the best of their new songs. 'Cult Hero' is a bit of discofied studio nonsense concocted by the group and a drinking buddy that should never have seen the light of day.

However, I await the impending addition of an organist with interest — it should give them the fuller sound they need. And surely sooner or later, whether it be with The Cure, Passions or Purple Hearts, Fiction are going to have a hit.

reviewed by CHRIS BOHN

THE CURE: "Jumping Someone Else's Train" (Fiction Records). The Cure's biggest problem is trying to replace the innocent charm which helped flesh out the bare bones of their early singles. Obviously after a year's hefty touring that innocence is gone, but the bones are still showing, though Robert Smith's done a lot to cover them up with sparingly-used guitar over a hustling rhythm. The song's a twist on bandwagon jumping, which Robert sings from a catarrhal distance, if you know what I mean.

REVIEWED BY ALAN LEWIS

THE CURE: Jumping Someone Else's Train (Fiction). Someone should get a medal for the sound quality, which slices out of the speakers with icy precision, perfectly matching the harsh but detached tone of the song, a sneering rebuke to trendies and bandwagon-jumpers. Anyone who found the Cure's first efforts interesting but musically a little limp and empty will be shocked by the concentrated vigour of this one.

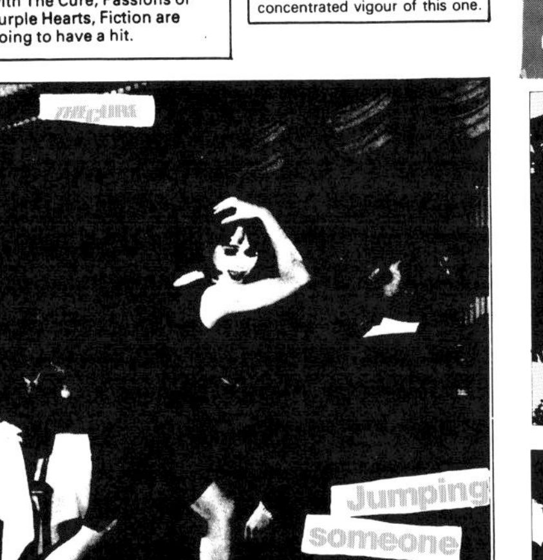

Parry:

"It was probably the best-sounding of all the early singles, a fine moment for Dempsey, a swan song."

The Cult Hero single was also released during November.

Reviewed by CHRIS WESTWOOD

THE CURE: 'Jumping Someone Else's Train' (Fiction). The Cure are gradually edging towards something of a pop paradox where the absolute state of the art hardly makes an impression of those ugly charts.

They lack the insight of U2 but possess a rich sparkle and imagination of their own. 'Jumping Someone Else's Train' is better though less instant than the throwaway 'Boys Don't Cry' — it's more growing, more paced, more structured. It builds into an incessant and fetching commercial song. Typically Cure ... which means it doesn't communicate a great deal but points at what you can do with rock structures given a modicum of inspiration.

CULT HERO: I'm A Cult Hero (Fiction). Apart from backing from The Cure; the person responsible for this is Frankie Vell, a 26 year-old postman who's fat, drinks a lot and likes mushy peas. That's all we need, another singing postman!

Parry:

"After the tour, I looked at The Cure long and hard and decided that they had to become an international band. I was bored with going up to Birmingham and Manchester and, fair enough, you use bands as your passport to travel, don't you? You push them out and share experiences.

"So, I called them in and said 'There's a whole world waiting out there and I want to take you round it' and, typically, Dempsey said 'Why Bill? Things not going very well in Britain then?' but Robert said very little and I kept looking at him, wondering what was wrong.

"Anyway, after a few platitudes, they piled into Robert's green Maxi and shot back home and, later, Robert phoned me and said that he was going to change the line-up of the group. I remember he said 'Don't worry Bill. It'll be okay'."

Talking to the NME some eight months later, Robert reviewed the band's situation: "It just became like a job . . . The more it went on, the more unbearable it became . . . Michael wasn't criticising or joining in on any level and we were getting really banal . . . sticking to the same set night after night . . . the whole thing was getting like a joke. None of us were enjoying it . . . There wasn't much point in carrying on."

Playing with Severin had strengthened Robert's resolve to pursue a purer, more skeletal style.

Robert:

"After the tour I spent time making tapes on my own at home. I used my sister's Hammond organ which had bass pedals and a little drum machine and I wrote almost all of '17 Seconds' with a bossa nova or swing beat. I had the words from Newcastle, I strummed out the chords on the Top 20 and I'd built up six or seven songs within a week.

"I remember I had Michael and Lol round to listen and Lol was really excited but Michael was . . . well . . . cool, he just continued reading his paper so I thought 'Right that's it!' and I went straight round to Simon's house and played the demos to him. He was really enthusiastic, especially as the band he was in at the time were playing fairly icky pop songs and I knew he was frustrated so I asked him then and there if he wanted to play in The Cure. I remember he said 'Why, have you got rid of Michael?' and I said 'No, not yet. But if *you* come and play bass, *he* won't be able to will he?'"

Simon:

"I always felt I ought to be their bass player but I never dreamed Robert would ask me. I was resigned to spending my life working in the factory from 7.30 to 5.30, coming home, playing bass for a couple of hours, spending the rest of the evening with Carol, my girlfriend, and then, at the end of the week, going down the pub with my 18 quid."

Parry:

"Robert wanted to tighten it down to strict disciplines, he wanted to strip it down to the real basics and, if an open E string was plucked endlessly for five minutes, that would do him. But it didn't interest Dempsey. He was, and still is, a very eloquent bass player.

"I wasn't that happy with the decision because I thought they were the perfect pop trio, better than The Police, better than The Jam. But Robert wasn't interested and he closed the doors.

"Well, I thought, 'I'm not gonna knock my head against the wall. The boy wants a change, he's either gonna be successful or he's not and, if not, I'll find another band'.

"It was hard to say goodbye to Dempsey though because I rather liked him and still do. He's a very funny, dry, witty man, very underestimated in his abilities. I can spend more time with him, sitting down chatting in a hotel foyer than with almost anyone else I know. But I thought 'Well, life's like this . . . bitch . . . bitch . . . we change course'."

Robert:

"I don't know how I actually told Michael. I probably didn't. I probably left it to Lol."

Lol:

"I actually phoned him and it seemed as if he didn't really care about it at all."

Michael:

"I knew something was in the air. I had a long conversation with Robert – quite a friendly one under the circumstances – and he said he didn't care about the band, that he couldn't go on the way it was and that he was prepared to change the name if necessary. I said there was no need. Simon was very suited to them anyway. He was very much the New Wave bass player who could play his bass at pelvic level. I could never do that, I had to have it under my chin like some sort of funkster. Maybe that was my undoing!"

In November Matthieu Hartley, keyboard player with The Magspies and hairdresser by day, also joined The Cure.

Lol:

"I used to see him wandering round Horley with different coloured hair every week."

Robert:

"I thought it was a bit much asking Simon to step in, I thought he might be resented by his mates in Horley so I asked Matthieu to join as well. I didn't know him very well at the time and I wasn't even sure we'd need any synth lines but I knew we'd need another instrument at some point and, also, it would mean Simon wasn't the new boy, wasn't the odd one out.

"Matthieu had a Korg Duophonic synth which was perfect because you couldn't play more than two notes at a time and we just started rehearsing straight away. I was really excited at the time – we started setting up concerts before we even had the songs ready. We set ourselves a deadline and rehearsed for seven or eight days solid."

Matthieu:

"When Robert asked me to join The Cure, I said yes immediately because the prospect was so exciting. My role was reasonably detached though, I wasn't an integral part of the band but I wasn't on probation either. I just did what Robert told me to do."

Parry:

"Given hindsight, I think it was a rather hedonistic choice – bang two in instead of one. But I quite liked the idea of four – it shattered previous illusions and I felt 'We're going somewhere!'

"Robert rang me and said 'I think you'd better come down and listen to what we're doing' so I went down to his mum and dad's house in Crawley and, I must admit, my gut reaction was less than enthusiastic. I instinctively took a liking to Simon and a disliking to Hartley – I found him a bit overbearing. Simon was nervous, Lol was trying hard, Robert was trying to please but Hartley was just boorish."

Matthieu:

"There was something between Chris and me from the start – a personality conflict. I didn't hate him, I just didn't get on with him, that's all."

Parry:

"They played and I felt better – I automatically noticed the downbeat quality of it which, musically, was a bit of a shock, and I wasn't quite sure where this thing was going to go. But, I'll give Robert his due, *he* knew where *he* wanted to go."

On 10 November, the story of Dempsey's departure broke in the British music press. He told NME: "I suppose you could call it a clash of personalities but I was definitely booted out and I'm looking for another gig." He told The Crawley News: "I didn't want to leave The Cure at that moment. I didn't have any money to finance any future projects", The Crawley Advertiser claimed he was getting a band together with Porl but he finally teamed up with Parry's other proteges, The Associates.

Michael:

"Certainly the period after I left was awful but Chris pretty quickly picked me up and I soon found that The Associates were, musically, more mature than what I'd been doing before. The Cure were a sound that you had to be part of but The Associates were more lively so I recovered reasonably quickly."

On 16 November, the new four piece played their first gig at Liverpool Erics as part of the Future Pastimes Tour, a package involving The Associates and The Passions.

Robert:

"Something happened – I think the bus broke down or we ran out of petrol or something but, anyway, we didn't arrive at Erics till about 10 o'clock and The Passions had already played. There were only about 100 people there so we just went to the bar, got a beer, got onstage and played. We were really just playing for ourselves, chatting between songs and that. I remember we'd been drinking on the way up and I couldn't remember which words went with which songs so I just started making them up.

"It was the best concert I'd done by far and I suddenly realised how awful the last six months had been. But now I was onstage with people who were really enthusiastic. It was a new start."

Simon:

"It was great – the first night I'd ever had free beer. I remember thinking 'So this is stardom!'."

The next day, the new Cure played the London School of Economics.

Robert:

"We stopped at a motorway cafe on the way back down from Liverpool and I ate some very dodgy sausages. That night, 10 minutes before we were due on stage, I was suddenly stricken. It was fucking freezing and I was shivering like a dog.

"It was a good show though. A lot of the Horley crowd came up and it got so boisterous I forgot I was ill until just towards the end when I threw up all over this punk in the front row."

It was on this tour that That Cure entourage learned the whole soundtrack to Walt Disney's 'Junglebook' off by heart. Jolly times but . . .

Robert:

"All the bands used to drive around together and it was a pretty volatile mix. There wasn't really that much good feeling on that tour. The only thing that held it together was, if it was cack for one group, it was cack for us all. We were only headlining because I guess Bill pinned more hopes on us, but there wasn't any sense of priority. We all shared the same dressing room. In fact, at one point I think there was even talk of alternating headlines but we thought that was stupid because we'd never be able to decide who should headline in London."

Even the bad times are good

The Cure
Durham

THE CURE are searching. Maybe they don't know exactly what for. The Cure are finding. Maybe they don't know exactly what. But what's clear is that they happen.

Confusingly the new line up played even more hangdog songs than its predecessor (including a new number wryly labelled 'Bleak One') with such vibrant force and thrust that their audience at Durham Students Union was compelled to respond by dancing. A bad-time good-time band doesn't sound possible.

The two opening songs presented their extremes. '17 Seconds'. A death march drum, a wailing vocal and I couldn't understand it at all. What goes on in the '17 Seconds'? 'Accuracy'. Immediately and conversely a portion of perfect clarity and acute insight on the destructive side of close relationships where self respect can be murdered with a cunning word. 'We sit in the same room/Side by side/I give you the wrong lines/Feed you' Precise music matched the idea. The cool blue surge of guitar and drums made you dance around the black story. It felt wrong-right but what can you do? Shake a leg now, ask questions later.

The 'drip, drip, drip' bit in 'Saturday Night' was great with each word like a small bomb blowing up and so was the spelling-out-the-title bit in 'Fire In Cairo' — all-action substituting for solid subject matter quite acceptably. More new ones. 'Play For Today' and 'Bleak One'. The surprise was their power and the regret, in the light of 'Accuracy', was their lack of verbal and musical clarity so you had momentum without shape in their less effective moments (probably not all blameable on acoustics, PA etc.)

They overcame this lapse though. Robert Smith advised two hecklers "If you don't like it why don't you get out!" Then the Cure pulled together into more and gripping new material. 'AM' was compressive, a slow squeeze, the music rolling simply and Smith attacking the vocal with lungfuls of emotion. '44 F' was such a strong section of clipped, punchy rock'n'roll instrumental that might even give them an atypical launch into the singles chart sometime.

They closed with their established faves and much rejoicing from the audience which showed how instantly they can make contact, because they had never played anywhere near Durham before.

The new boys? Simon Gallup fitted in on bass so you couldn't see the join, whereas Matthew Hartley was less sure of what his keyboard might add to the Cure — but all four are convinced they'll grow into it. Watch them grow.

PHIL SUTCLIFFE

On 7 December, the tour wound up at Crawley College, an event heralded by The Crawley News in an extraordinary article entitled "Split No Remedy For Cure's Ills": "I hope they will reconsider for, together, The Cure were something, apart, I believe they will be nothing . . . " wrote the zealous hack. "I only have to look at today's most successful groups to press home my point. Led Zeppelin has never gone down like the lead balloon it takes its name from largely because it has never changed. Deep Purple is dead and gone because it did. Only death has changed the line-ups of The Who and Rolling Stones. I may be jumping the gun but I think The Cure will start to fail tonight . . . "

Robert:

"Some skinheads came and smashed the place up – they always did in Crawley. I remember we came off pretty disgusted because it was our home town concert and there were a lot of people there who liked us and wanted to see us and all I could see was people bottling each other."

Simon:

"There was a lot of jealousy too. I remember going to the local record shop and people'd say 'My mate's much fucking better than you are. I don't know why you got the job'. We never played Crawley again."

In December, the foursome also travelled abroad together for the first time. On the 10th, they played Eindhoven.

Robert:

"We all really went to town. We thought 'This is it – the start of a new era'! We had a day off and got taken to a cafe in the morning where we ended up drinking 13 bottles of red wine between the four of us. Later, Lol went into a coma. We were sitting in someone's room back at the hotel when he suddenly started screaming and flipped out. He went running down the corridor puking up red wine everywhere."

Simon:

"Me and Robert followed the trail – like a sick paper-chase. Really good."

Robert:

"He kept going into different corridors, trying his key in different doors so, eventually, I took pity on him and let him in my room where he commenced to enter the bathroom with, he said, the intention of committing suicide."

Lol:

"They were all banging on the toilet door, going 'Let us in! Let us in!' and I was groaning 'Let me die! Let me die!' I lay with my face in the turned on shower for hours, woke up about five in the morning and crawled to bed."

Robert:

"I pissed in his suitcase as retaliation; he was still alive!"

The Cure played in Amsterdam and then Paris, where they made the gossip columns of the British music papers by getting lost and refusing to eat lobster boiled alive. They then turned to Britain where Robert told Blank Space: "We'll be forgotten very quickly if we don't do something good the next time around. I accept that . . . "

On 3 January 1980, rehearsals commenced for the '17 Seconds' album at Robert's house. From 13th to 20th, they recorded all 11 tracks at Morgan and between 4th and 10th of February, they were all mixed – a fairly swift process enhanced by many of the songs having already been played live.

Parry:

"The last time we'd worked at Morgan, they'd stayed at my house to keep the costs down but not this time. Robert didn't want to, it affronted him, he said it felt like walking back.

"On the first day in the studio, I was fiddling about with the snare drum and Robert came on the microphone and said 'Don't bother Bill, it's not what we want'. Well, I thought, the guy's obviously got his own ideas' and I left him to it. I remember I said 'I don't think I'll come in tomorrow' and he said 'Well, if you did Bill, you'd be bleeding' which was his way of saying I was best to back off. Fine. I was working across the street so I'd come in for a little while every now and again and then disappear, y'know . . . "

Robert:

"I had to ask Bill not to come into the studio because he was trying to produce the record and I wanted to do it with Hedges. I knew exactly what sound was needed for '17 Seconds' – I wanted it to be inspired by Nick Drake with the clear, finished sound of Bowie's 'Low'. I imagined it sounding rather accoustic. I'd been listening to a lot of cello music and I thought it would be good to have drums, bass and guitar with a huge hole in the middle. I wanted a very

particular sound."

Hedges:

"I really appreciated the musical direction – morose, atmospheric, very different to 'Three Imaginary Boys'. Everyone was thrown back on their own resources.

"At the time, we didn't realise we were doing a lot of experimenting by using odd recording techniques, we weren't thinking about commercialism or potential popularity at all. I followed Robert's instructions – he wanted a certain sound. But, above all, we did what we liked and the album turned out to be crucial to my career because a lot of musicians liked it and, after that, no-one ever took me for a pop producer."

Matthieu:

"Simon and me were excited because it was our first time in a studio. Robert and Lol were excited too because they were doing something new. It was strange – no-one actually felt the way the record sounds; rather sad."

Robert:

"Because the lyrics had all been written beforehand, they were quite down but the actual recording was really spontaneous."

Simon:

"I'd just come off the nine to five slog so everything delighted me . . . staying up until three in the morning . . . drinking . . . "

Hedges:

"When I try to remember it, all I can see is a party."

Lol:

"We knew exactly what we were gonna do, even if Robert *was* rewriting the words in the studio. Most of the time, we slept there. It was a former church with a weird roof. With the lights off, after we'd gone to bed, you could hear a lot of bizarre noises. Scarey . . . someone said there were ghosts . . . "

Simon:

"When I arrived, 'M' and 'Play For Today' had already been written but there were some songs, like 'In Your House' and 'A Forest' which we put together on stage. We had 12 or 13 definite songs and four that we knew the chords of but didn't really have a structure. 'A Forest' was one that just used to go on . . . and on . . . the drums would stop, Robert would carry on playing guitar and I was never sure when he was gonna stop so I'd just carry on after him. Then I got some effects pedals and I found I could experiment and make all sorts of bizarre noises . . . "

Parry:

"I was called over to hear 'A Forest' and it was wonderful – a most pleasant surprise. The whole album had been done very economically which was great. They worked all the hours of the day, went to bed at four in the morning, the bloody hoover came in at 10 or whatever and woke them up a bit grumpy but they were young enough to take it and that created a kind of mystique that that was the way to record."

Robert:

"February 4 was Lol's birthday so me, Simon and Matty went out to buy him some presents. We bought him pigs' trotters, a pink nightie, a copy of Zipper magazine and a feather boa because the tape op at the time was falling for him! We dressed Lol up in all this garb and the boy went mad; he was in love!"

Matthieu, meanwhile, was recording his "Piano Concerto", and Severin, too, made a guest appearance to disrupt proceedings.

On 18 March, The Cure played The Lakeside, Crawley, and Porl joined them onstage to play 'Cult Hero' as an encore. Five days later, supporting The Passions at The Marquee, The Cult Hero band played its one and only real gig. With one day's rehearsal at Robert's house, the band, comprising The Cure, Frank Bell, two schoolgirl backing vocalists and an awful lot of alcohol, played a set based on a Top Ten from 1973 that Robert had taped from one of Jimmy Saville's Sunday radio programmes.

Robert:

"We played Gary Glitter's 'Do Ya Wanna Touch?', Thin Lizzy's 'Whiskey In The Jar', Sweet's 'Blockbuster', something by T Rex, a David Cassidy number, something else by the Detroit Spinners . . .

"It was a great night, The Cure wrecking crew came along, about 400 from Crawley and Horley, and they all sang along . . . "

While The Crawley News was noting at this time that "Bassist Simon Gallup now sports the popular Sid Vicious look with greased-up hair and biker's leather jacket", Robert was doing backing vocals for The Associates LP. On 3 and 4 of April, he also played guitar at the Rainbow Theatre in Finsbury Park as a member of The Stranglers. Their singer, Hugh Cornwell, had been busted and imprisoned and an all-star band was assembled to play in protest.

Robert:

"I was in the studio with Billy Mackenzie and I arrived at the Rainbow late. I did the opening two songs and I think Matthieu did some keyboards but what I distinctly remember was being in a room backstage having a bizarre conversation with JJ Burnel and Steve Hillage about European cabbages. The whole thing was very naive in a way, but very nice."

On 5 April, 'A Forest'/'Another Journey By Train' was reviewed by the British music press. The B-side, Robert claims, was "a pisstake – a way of disassociating ourselves from the previous Cure sound."

THE CURE: 'A Forest' (Fiction). The Cure take a trip to the BBC radiophonic workshop in search of Dr Who and find the ghost of Hawkwind. An over long introduction leads into a song which is so atmospheric. The vocals are well down in the mix with lots of echo and there's the usual economic guitar and drums. Sparse but never boring. There's the added keyboards too. This isn't what you'd call an immediate song but there's something very attractive about it.

The tune has the best production to date and like the Banshees' excellent 'Happy House' it leaps over trivia into the 80s.

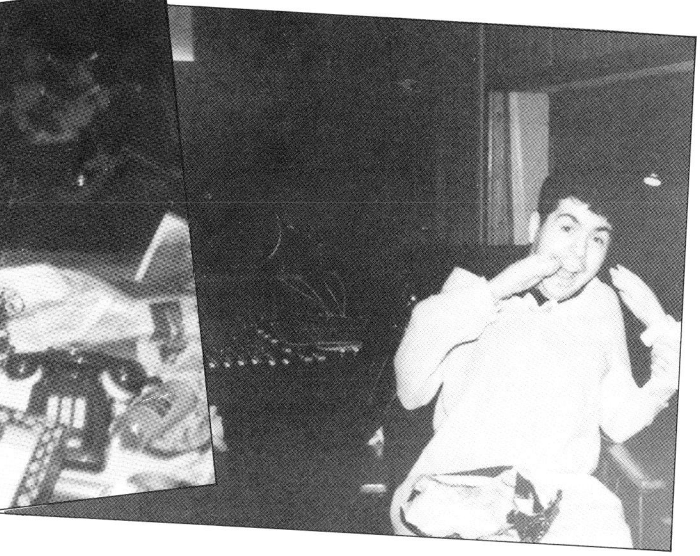

In the NME, Julie Burchill accused them of "trying to stretch a sketchy living out of moaning more meaningfully than man has ever moaned before . . . without a tune too."

Robert had told Sounds that 'A Forest' was based on a childhood experience but, in Stand And Deliver fanzine, he admitted: "I made up the story about childhood experiences because it sounds more interesting for the daily papers. It's just about a forest . . . "

Looking back, he says: "Releasing it as a single was a good move because it had good repercussions. We weren't releasing it to get airplay but, in fact, it did far better than any of the previous Cure singles. I think Bill accepted then that I'd reached a point where I knew exactly what I wanted The Cure to sound like and it had swung full circle and was now back in our hands."

On 10 April, The Cure went to America for the first time.

Robert:

"We'd obtained cult status out there but we only played New York, Philly, Washington and Boston. We played three nights – 15, 16 and 17th – at Hurrah in New York and it was packed."

Simon:

"It was done on a shoe-string budget but it was lots of fun. Instead of having cans of beer backstage, we'd have shots of Southern Comfort!"

Robert:

"It was like a holiday. Even at this point, everything we did, we didn't think we'd be doing again so we used to go to bed at about five in the morning and get up again at eight just to go out and see New York."

On his return, Robert told Record Mirror how America meant "being bombarded by people who all ask the same questions and all want to shake your hand . . . you just find yourself getting sucked into the whole rock 'n' roll trip which we're trying so hard to get away from" while Sounds' Phil Sutcliffe, who'd accompanied the band to New York, told, in an article called "Somebody Get Me A Doctor", how Robert had done his utmost to avoid having his picture taken with Debby Harry.

Robert:

"My 21st birthday happened in Boston and, after the gig, Bill and the four of us got taken to some art media event by this guy who was making a video of us. We had some drugs. I remember a TV and a set of homemade videos and we got bored and insisted this bloke drove us back to our hotel so he took us in his Beetle – the five of us and his girlfriend!

"It was a little cramped so I got out and sat on the bonnet – it was about five in the morning so we thought we'd take the risk. Bill then decided to drive and went the wrong way round a roundabout without thinking. When he realised it, of course, he just kept on going round, laughing insanely and then he got hysterical, got a flat, slewed across the road and I fell off the bonnet.

"I tried to change the wheel – I don't know why I was doing it – but I couldn't understand why the hub-cap wouldn't go back on so I started kicking it, and it was only a few seconds later, when the pain suddenly reached my brain, that I realised the reason the hub cap wouldn't go back on was because my thumb was trapped underneath it. I'd just reduced it to pulp!

"After that we drove to New York overnight but ended up in Cape Cod because Bill had taken a wrong turn! We eventually arrived at the airport just in time to catch the plane to get back to London for Top Of The Pops."

Simon:

"We were all very tired when we got there and we spent all our time in the bar, trying to avoid the other bands."

Robert:

"I hated Top Of The Pops because I was getting to this phase where I was really anti everything like that, anti pop. I didn't want The Cure to be a pop band though I was convinced we should do Top Of The Pops because I realised, even then, that, if we didn't do it, someone else would and it made no difference to the majority of the people watching whether we played or not.

"But Simon and Matthieu had a different attitude, they were much more *up* and were really looking forward to doing it. When we got there, it was just like I imagined it would be, but Simon was really disappointed because he thought it would be like playing in a really good disco.

"We came across looking very morose and disinterested, which we were. I was suffering a great deal – all the blood was collecting in my thumb – and Lol was in his stone-face phase and they sat him right at the front of the stage. It was ridiculous."

Lol:

"All you could see on the telly was Robert's huge bandage moving up and down the neck of his guitar. It was hysterical."

Setting a precedent for future appearances on the programme, the deejay got their name wrong and, aided and abetted by their dismal display, the single immediately plummeted down the charts.

On 26 April, '17 Seconds' was reviewed in the press. Chris Westwood of Record Mirror asked: "Why don't The Cure come out of their shell? Why don't they come out to play? This is a reclusive, disturbed Cure, sitting in cold, dark, empty rooms, watching clocks."

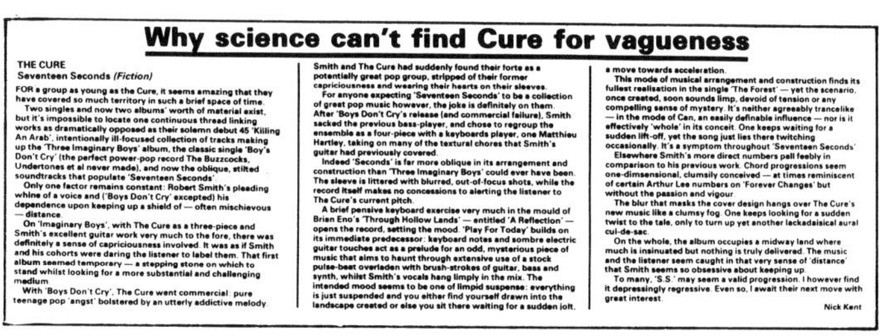

Why science can't find Cure for vagueness

THE CURE
Seventeen Seconds *(Fiction)*

FOR a group as young as the Cure, it seems amazing that they have covered so much territory in such a brief space of time.

Two singles and now two albums' worth of material exist, but it's impossible to locate one continuous thread linking works as dramatically opposed as their solemn debut 45 'Killing An Arab', intentionally ill-focused collection of tracks making up the 'Three Imaginary Boys' album, the classic single 'Boy's Don't Cry' (the perfect power-pop record The Buzzcocks, Undertones et al never made), and now the oblique, stilted soundtracks that populate 'Seventeen Seconds'.

Only one factor remains constant: Robert Smith's pleading whine of a voice and ('Boys Don't Cry' excepted) his dependence upon keeping up a shield of — often mischievous — distance.

On 'Imaginary Boys', with The Cure as a three-piece and Smith's excellent guitar work very much to the fore, there was definitely a sense of capriciousness involved. It was as if Smith and his cohorts were daring the listener to label them. That first album seemed temporary — a stepping stone on which to stand whilst looking for a more substantial and challenging medium.

With 'Boys Don't Cry', The Cure went commercial: pure teenage pop 'angst' bolstered by an utterly addictive melody. Smith and The Cure had suddenly found their forte as a potentially great pop group, stripped of their former capriciousness and wearing their hearts on their sleeves.

For anyone expecting 'Seventeen Seconds' to be a collection of great pop music however, the joke is definitely on them. After 'Boys Don't Cry's release (and commercial failure), Smith sacked the previous bass-player, and chose to regroup the ensemble as a four-piece with a keyboards player, one Matthieu Hartley, taking on many of the textural chores that Smith's guitar had previously covered.

Indeed 'Seconds' is far more oblique in its arrangement and construction than 'Three Imaginary Boys' could ever have been. The sleeve is littered with blurred, out-of-focus shots, while the record itself makes no concessions to alerting the listener to The Cure's current pitch.

A brief pensive keyboard exercise very much in the mould of Brian Eno's 'Through Hollow Lands' — entitled 'A Reflection' — opens the record, setting the mood. 'Play For Today' builds on its immediate predecessor: keyboard notes and sombre electric guitar touches act as a prelude for an odd, mysterious piece of music that aims to haunt through extensive use of a stock pulse-beat overladen with brush-strokes of guitar, bass and synth, whilst Smith's vocals hang limply in the mix. The intended mood seems to be one of limpid suspense: everything is just suspended and you either find yourself drawn into the landscape created or else you sit there waiting for a sudden jolt, a move towards acceleration.

This mode of musical arrangement and construction finds its fullest realisation in the single 'The Forest' — yet the scenario, once created, soon sounds limp, devoid of tension or any compelling sense of mystery. It's neither agreeably trancelike — in the mode of Can, an easily definable influence — nor is it effectively 'whole' in its conceit. One keeps waiting for a sudden lift-off, yet the song just lies there twitching occasionally. It's a symptom throughout 'Seventeen Seconds'.

Elsewhere Smith's more direct numbers pall feebly in comparison to his previous work. Chord progressions seem one-dimsensional, clumsily conceived — at times reminiscent of certain Arthur Lee numbers on 'Forever Changes' but without the passion and vigour.

The blur that masks the cover design hangs over The Cure's new music like a clumsy fog. One keeps looking for a sudden twist to the tale, only to turn up yet another lackadaisical aural cul-de-sac.

On the whole, the album occupies a midway land where much is insinuated but nothing is truly delivered. The music and the listener seem caught in that very sense of 'distance' that Smith seems so obsessive about keeping up.

To many, 'S.S.' may seem a valid progression. I however find it depressingly regressive. Even so, I await their next move with great interest.

Nick Kent

As with 'Three Imaginary Boys', the album cover was deliberately obscure. The four photos of the band members on the back cover are blurred beyond

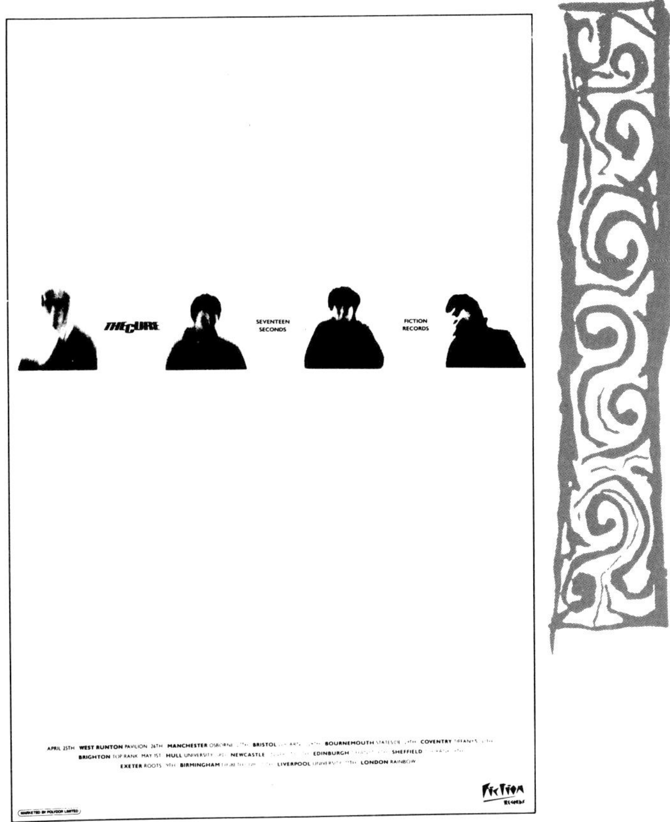

recognition because, according to Robert "showing ourselves clearly would have made things too obvious. With us, the record's always been more important than our appearance so what's the difference if we're elegant or filthy? At the time, we were still unknowns so we didn't have to present ourselves in any particular way and, when we did '17 Seconds', I didn't want us to become famous. At concerts, for instance, we could still join the public and watch the other bands play because no-one knew who we were.

"Because I didn't get a say in the cover of 'Three Imaginary Boys', I demanded to see the cover design this time because it was an album that I'd put so much of myself into and it was far more important than the records that went before. It was a bizarre cover for its time – everyone, including Bill, thought it was going too far . . . It all seemed to suggest a band that was too difficult.

"But, if '17 Seconds' hadn't been like that, everything that happened after it would've been different. It's the most important record we ever made – it decided the way the public thought of us for at least three years.

"The songs can seem sad . . . or angry. I was 20 when I made it and we were all realising that we were no longer young. But I didn't want anybody to think I was going to stay melancholy all my life. I realised that we didn't have much time to do that kind of music because people would get tired of it quite quickly – me quickest of all."

Although Paul Morley actually liked '17 Seconds' and asked to interview the band, the press, on the whole, weren't too keen on The Cure and the feeling was mutual.

Robert:

"Because of the change from 'Three Imaginary Boys', they could never quite believe it was the same band. I agreed with many criticisms of that first album but I couldn't bear anyone to say anything against '17 Seconds' because it was such a good record."

Simon informed Sound International that "our aim on the album was to create a mood. Not a series of moods but just different aspects of one mood" and Robert described to the NME in detail, the state of mind that went into creating the album: "It was a really condensed incident, a rush of feelings that I'd found in myself had been watered down, mainly by playing in a group. It's a really strange situation but I find touring and things like that shut me down. I harden and get very reculsive, sort of shun people. I'm not naturally an extrovert person but sometimes I get really withdrawn and it irritates people. They think I'm doing it on purpose. Sometimes I don't like talking to people, which isn't important, but I don't like people saying 'Oh no, here we go again, he's not being sociable!' and it's just something that happened, all the things that I'd been shutting down just came out in a big rush and, for the following two weeks, every day I'd be thinking about that one particular incident. One day I'd wake up wanting to kill somebody, the next day I wouldn't even bother getting up. It was awful.

"I was letting myself slip in order to write songs. I wasn't fighting it whereas, in everyday life, you'd have to control those feelings. But, it's good that it happened. At the time I was shutting down and didn't feel like writing any more songs, I just couldn't be bothered; and it was through actually being in a group! Through actually playing songs! *That* was causing me to stop writing songs!"

And he told Record Mirror: "There's no point in trying to intellectualise about it because it's a genuine emotion on the album. There was no policy, just that it turned out like that and I was aware beforehand that a lot of reviews would bypass the emotion and just concentrate on the *reasons* for it turning out like that. The whole point about The Cure is that we've been completely unpredictable so far and we *haven't* been going in the same direction all along, that the next set of songs will probably turn out completely different."

He went on to say: "Despite what the press think, there's no hierarchy in The Cure. If there's one drink on the table, we all fight for it", while Matthieu told Sounds' Phil Sutcliffe: "Robert could appear to be selfish, he does have the most say in things but that's fine because, to my mind, he's the most capable." Simon agreed: "Sometimes I wonder why he isn't a nervous wreck . . . I don't think there's a better band or better friends. Our girlfriends get jealous because, if we're split up for four days, we miss each other. The other three are like brothers to me."

Matthieu:

"Dear old Lol, he's the master. We beat him up, wind him up, frame him up, but he understands. He knows we have to release our tensions in some way and he's the target."

He also compiled for Sutcliffe a perfect place for each band member to live: "Mine would be a vegetable garden I could eat my way through forever. Simon's town had everything made of leather, even the houses, and inflatable wimps you could chain to your leg and kick as you went along. Tolhurstville was a long street with a sweet shop then a pub then a toilet then the same again and again into infinity. Robert's place would be full of people in separate rooms sitting and staring at walls."

Robert revealed: "If I wasn't in love, being in a group would be an ideal existence but, for me, it's getting more and more difficult, really schizophrenic. To function at all, I have to keep the being in love completely separate from The Cure otherwise I would lose perspective and get sucked into the rock 'n' roll syndrome. On the road, I close down my emotions. That's why I don't enjoy company. I'm walking around in a daze. But there's a responsibility on me because I know if I stop, The Cure stops. So why bother to play in a group? Why bother to do anything? Because you have to work away from negatives like that."

On 25 April, The Cure embarked on a British tour which included a headline show at the Rainbow on May 11 with The Passions, Au Pairs and The Fall.

Robert:

"We had this mental Ted roadie, an old rocker called Elvis who used to wear drainpipes and creepers and a quiff. He used to spend a lot of time just doing his hair and I remember he thought we were 'a right bunch of scruffy cunts'. I never understood why he was our roadie but he was brilliant. He was rucking all the time. We were completely alien to his culture yet he stayed on with us for about 2 years.

"A bunch of his Ted mates came to one of our concerts once and gave him a really hard time because they thought he was working with a rockabilly band!"

The tour moved on to Europe.

Robert:

"All through the history of The Cure we've had people *supposedly* working for us but *actually* working against us and they've all been employed by Bill . . . I never know where they come from. Lawrie Mazzeo was this Welsh wizard character, the sort of bloke who thought time was something you kept in a spice rack. He was our tour manager and, the first hotel we stayed in with him, we got this knock on our doors 'Be downstairs in reception in 15 minutes'. So we went down and the next thing we knew Lawrie was whispering to us, 'Take your bags to the van then boys. Go on, sit in the van and I'll settle the bill'. So out we went and Elvis was sitting in the van, chatting to us when suddenly Lawrie came hurtling through the hotel door and rushed down the street chased by several people. He was shouting 'Start the engine up! Drive! Drive!' and he threw himself into the sliding door as we roared off.

"He hadn't paid the bill and he said 'Well lads, that saved us a few bob, eh?' And we said 'But Lawrie, we had to hand our passports in at reception!'. When we checked into the hotel in the next town, of course, the police arrived within 15 minutes.

"Everything with him was bizarre. We'd get to a venue and say 'Lawrie, none of the gear is here' and he'd say 'I've booked a lovely little French restaurant for after the show'. 'But Lawrie,' we'd say, 'there's no equipment here. No PA or anything.' and he'd say 'Don't worry about that, it'll all turn up and sort itself out and then we'll get the show over with and go for a lovely meal'. The whole tour revolved around a series of restaurants. It was only because of the good humour within the group that we managed to survive."

On 25 May, the band got arrested.

Robert:

"We used to go to Holland a fair bit so we got to know a few people there and we would usually go to this club in Rotterdam called The Heavy Club – actually it was just an after-hours drinking place. One night Lol disappeared into the phone booth and couldn't find the light switch. He claims he thought it was a particularly small toilet and this woman found him in the booth with his trousers round his ankles so we got thrown out. We then went off in the van, the four of us and Mac, the lighting man, to the beach for some swimming – this was about 6.30 in the morning. The other three fell asleep but me and Mac went in. There was actually a No Swimming sign but we threw that in the sea. Unfortunately, some old lady looked out of her window and was affronted by what she saw and called the police.

"It was quite surreal. I was really dazed; we were walking out of the sea when over these sand dunes, came a police van, two police cars, and four armed policemen with their guns out, all shouting at us. Well, we thought 'This *can't* be happening!'. We picked up our clothes and they immediately threw us in the back of the van and said we were under arrest for public indecency.

"None of us had any real money – we just emptied out our pockets of change and said 'Take anything you want. Divide it between you. Just let us go and we'll get back to the hotel and go to bed. It will be much easier'.

"Mac had a fit, I was actually holding him down. He was shouting 'Call the British Embassy'!' and I said 'Mac, we're not calling anyone and they're going to shoot us if you shout anymore'. They took a couple of cassettes, rifled through what we had and let us go. It could have been worse!"

31 May in Herford, Germany, was Simon's birthday.

Robert:

"It was one of those places with a British army base and the British groups always end up entertaining the lads. They were the worst concerts we had to do. They used to take Union Jacks along and I always used to feel embarrassed about that – being on stage, you could see people were being wound up by the football songs and stuff between numbers. The four of us and Elvis were confronted by all these squaddies and, sometimes, it was like living on a real knife edge. We knew, at some point, we'd suffer real damage because we never had a minder but, then again, we didn't want anyone with us who was a thug – it would have spoiled our fun. Most of the time it was enough for them to be confronted by this crazed Ted in full regalia taking his jacket off!"

Simon:

"We did a song called 'Three' which we'd improvise around every night, and Robert decided to sing 'Happy Birthday' to me over it – it went really well. But Matthieu went absolutely mental that night. He was getting a lot of beer spat at him and he didn't have a great deal of patience at the best of times so he picked up his synth and threw it into the audience.

"Later, Robert and I ended up on the bathroom floor of my hotel room with a bottle of Scotch. We woke up in the bathroom too – good night that!"

On 5 June, The Cure were supposed to play Lyon University.

Lol:

"We got lost and found ourselves somewhere in the mountains in the snow. We kept having to stop to fill up the radiator. When we eventually got to Lyon, it was midnight so we left the van with everything in it and took a taxi to the University. The organisers had sent the crowd home – 800 people – and at first they didn't want to let us sleep on the campus as arranged. So Matthieu got mad."

Robert:

"I was sharing a room with him and he went outside, uprooted a tree and tried to knock down Lol and Simon's door because he wanted a light for his cigarette. Lol and Simon were terrified – they thought he'd killed me. Matthieu eventually came back and went to bed. He woke up covered in blood and bits of wood . . ."

Lol:

"The next day, we left discreetly but it was impossible to find the van. The police had impounded it and the pound was shut so we had to take the train to play in Belgium. We wore the same clothes for the next 10 days and borrowed all our instruments. At one gig the synth that someone'd lent Matthieu started playing its memory sequences in mid concert so he threw it into the drums. No one came near us because we smelled so bad."

On 14 June, The Cure returned to France to play a festival with UFO, The Clash and Kevin Coyne. There was a riot, the police tear-gassed the crowd and headliners Roxy Music refused to play.

On the 18th, 19th and 20th, they played in Scotland and, in early July, played a string of outdoor festivals in Holland where the band were becoming increasingly popular. NME's Paul Morley met the band around this time and said of Robert: "He's always on a fine line between agitation and boredom, and such a balance turns out faintly, deviously charming. He's no pretentious mock-recluse, perpetually feigning intensity of vision. He's never quite sure what to say. He's never quite sure about those around him. Does he take himself seriously? 'I do take myself seriously but there's a point beyond which you become a comic figure.'"

Deeper into the article, "Days Of Wine And Poses", Robert reveals: "I sometimes think I might be in someone else's idea of heaven" and claims "I've always written things down, ever since I could remember. Mainly because sometimes I get really angry. I've got a really violent temper but it's not physical because I don't think I should vent my frustrations and depressions onto anyone else. I don't throw tantrums or anything like that so I go off somewhere rather than smash the room. I write things down. It's a release. But I haven't got over the idea of separating communicating from preaching, a failing in a sense. I worry that my words aren't going to interest people because they're mainly about me, and how I feel, they're not about world situations, and alternatives.

"I've got faith in what I'm doing from a personal point of view but as to whether I go down in history, I'm very doubtful about that so I don't let it worry me. If I let that worry me along with everything else, I'd crack up before I'm going to anyway."

On 24 July, The Cure embarked on their first Antipodean tour. First port of call: New Zealand, where, on the 29th and 30th, they played the Mainstreet Cabaret in Auckland.

Robert:

"The tour was very successful but ultimately unsatisfying onstage. The concerts were not as good as the European ones that Summer – we'd played too much and were becoming very jaded and I was getting sick of doing the songs because I had to remember why each song had been written, go back and feel unhappy. But, after the shows, we were the drunkest, funniest band you could hope to meet. It always surprised people."

The next stop was Australia.

Simon:

"We played in little clubs with tiny stages. If Robert moved, his guitar hit me on the shoulder. If I moved, my bass hit him. The rooms were so full that there were people vomiting at our feet . . . people fainting . . . it was so hot we'd leave the stage soaked even though we were only wearing tee-shirts. It was like coming out of the shower.

"We did tons of concerts like that because the promoters hadn't thought we'd sell very well whereas, in fact, we packed the clubs. It was great, they just kept adding gigs and, in the morning, we'd just go to the beach, swim, bury Lol in the sand, run about . . ."

Robert:

"To start with we were only supposed to do seven or eight dates but, in the end, we did 24. It was pretty horrific – hardly any days off, maybe two or three."

Parry:

"It was brilliant. It's hard to out-pub or out-club the Australians but we broke house records everywhere. The Bondi Livesaver's about as big as the Marquee plus a bit of an open area and we had 2,200 in there. They were dying. We took Australia apart!"

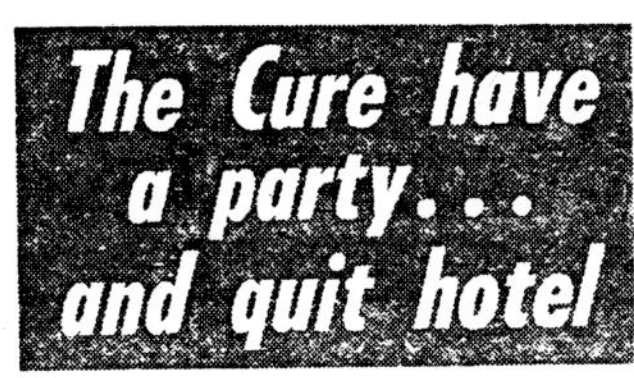

The Cure have a party... and quit hotel

By DAVID DAWSON

Members of English new wave band The Cure mysteriously left their hotel on the eve of their first Australian tour.

The four-piece band left after a late night party.

A door and several items of furniture were reportedly smashed during the party in Auckland.

A hotel employee said: "The band's tour manager paid a bill for the damage and they checked out."

The Cure moved to a nearby hotel and continued its New Zealand tour.

Band leader Robert Smith denied the group wrecked its hotel room.

He said: "We're not the type of band who smash furniture . . . we're not The Who.

"We left the hotel on principle. We arrived late, stayed up and just had a good time.

"It was just part of our working day. It was obvious they preferred us to leave so we went to another hotel."

The hotel manager, who declined to be named, said: "They left yesterday morning because of something which happened. I'm not going to comment any further."

The Cure arrives in Australia next Friday for a club and pub tour.

They are promoting their first two Australian album releases, Boys Don't Cry and Seventeen Seconds.

Robert:

"We couldn't get booked into any hotels after that. Matty was becoming more and more unreasonable by this time and I'd woken him up by playing music or something and he just snapped and chased me through the hotel. So, I locked myself in this room and he kicked the door down and started to beat me over the head. Then he went back to bed. He may have been jet-lagged but, well, I thought 'I'm not having this' so I went back to his room and just jumped at the door and the whole thing went in. By this time, the hotel people had been aroused . . .

"It just all started to go wrong with Matty. He was getting very grumpy, very tired and moaning that he couldn't get any vegetarian food – lots of little things upset him. It wasn't really us, it was the lifestyle.

"I remember going out to this hippy studio in the country and having an argument with Matty. He said I was being patronising to these people who were, in fact, tedious old musos. They were saying things like 'It's great to be in rock 'n' roll isn't it man?' and I was saying 'Yeah, it's unreal, outta this world man' and Matty was saying 'Don't patronise them!' I could see that things were going badly wrong.

"He used to take it out on Lol – he used to beat him up and get at him all the time because he didn't feel he could do it to me."

Simon:

"In the end it got to the point where we weren't talking to him and he wasn't talking to us. He'd go off on his own and drink a bottle of vodka, things like that, and, instead of getting lifted up by drinking, he'd get more withdrawn and we just grew further and further apart."

Robert:

"Simon, Lol and I would play football on the beach but he'd stay in his room. He used to go off before we went on stage, he wouldn't be in the dressing room and, when we came off, he'd go off again on his own. The first free day we got, we were invited on a yacht trip and it was the first chance we had to talk seriously. On that boat, in the space of a few hours, it became clear that Matthieu was no longer a part of us.

"At the beginning, we were supposed to be a democracy but it was often me who took the decisions. Democracy existed in that everyone got the same amount of money and everyone was credited for the songs but that's all. I wanted it to be like that to avoid the possibility of someone in the band coming up with a bad song and me having to accept it. So it was democratic, but generally accepted that I decided the sound. Matthieu was disappointed by that – he would have liked to have had more say.

"On stage, he'd try to play things I hated, useless things, like trying to play a chord at the beginning of 'A Forest' instead of a simple note. When I asked him why he was doing that, he said he thought it was good so what was the point in arguing? By the time we'd reached the end of the tour, in Perth, the three of us had decided that Matty shouldn't be in the group anymore. We'd thought about it long and hard and realised we weren't enjoying it. It wasn't like with Michael where he couldn't see anything coming. Matthieu knew. We'd been talking about what we were going to do next and I wanted to concentrate more on the songs like 'At Night' whereas he wanted to play ones like 'Play For Today', more pop. So he could see a point where he wasn't going to be musically very happy. He was so grumpy anyway, I thought 'Fine. Just don't take it out on the group'."

Matthieu:

"I was starting to get pissed off with the direction the band was taking, not my style of music at all. Also I was treated strangely, childishly. Robert stopped talking to me. So did Lol. I'd had enough . . . it showed when we played and, after the gigs, people would come up and ask me questions about the songs and I couldn't answer them. They used to ask me if I liked Joy Division and, I mean, they were exactly the kind of group I can't stand and I realised that the group was heading towards suicidal, sombre music . . . the sort of thing that didn't interest me at all.

"The music and Robert's attitude ate away at me, and Simon was ill at ease; he felt guilty without knowing why."

Simon:

"When you travel every day, the slightest thing can irritate you – especially when you're at that age. We were all about 20 and we weren't used to being together 24 hours out of 24. When one of us was in a bad mood, someone else would be affected by it, especially me. I always thought it was my fault."

Lol:

"Matthieu snored. At the time, we couldn't afford single rooms and that was fatal. I was the only one who could share with Matthieu because I sleep very deeply. He drove the others crazy."

Parry:

"I'd flown back earlier to do various things and I met them at Heathrow. We'd hired them a pick-up job and when Robert, Simon and Lol squeezed in the front and Matty got in the back with the gear I thought 'Here we go again. Another one out'.

Matthieu:

"When I got home, I rang Robert to tell him I was leaving. I knew he would never have rung me, partly because he was scared and partly because he was tired."

Robert:

"I thought it would be difficult but Matty was really good about it. He didn't hold any grudges and nor did I so it was easy. He phoned me up and that was it. And it was such a relief."

4
Four

On 9 September, The Cure, a trio again, began to rehearse for their next album.

Parry:

"From here on, it just got more and more intense, it was bad – you, me, no-one was gonna get inside that triangle and that was Robert probably playing at being as incestuous and tight and mean-spirited as I've ever seen him. Nobody, but *nobody* could fit inside that thing.

"I started to lose interest: I wasn't bothered anymore. I went one way and they went the other."

Between 27th and 29th September, the band attempted, and aborted, demos at Morgan.

Robert:

"We tried 'Primary' and 'All Cats Are Grey' but they were slow, plodding and sounded very dead. We wanted to get something that sounded funereal but they just sounded dull."

During October, they toured Europe again and, in November, Britain, this time with a different support band every night, having asked for, and received, hundreds of tapes from hopefuls. The band were working on new songs in performance and encoring with Gary Glitter's 'Do Ya Wanna Touch?'. Their jackets were nicked again at Bradford University, 'Grinding Halt' was included on the movie soundtrack to 'Times Square' and Simon told Sounds: "If we didn't mess around, we'd just crack up and, if any one of us three left, The Cure would be no more."

On 18 December, The Cure held their first Christmas party at the Notre Dame Hall off Leicester Square. A private affair, The Associates, Scars, Tarzan 5 and Cure assisted by The Banshees all played, the music never stopped from seven in the evening till one the next morning and everyone who attended was given a badge!

Simon:

"We were all really loud on stage and there was a lot of screaming and a lot of drinking."

Robert:

"And who do you think was in charge of the hall? Doctor Weaver! He was using it as a centre for some French youth cultural exchange. All very coincidental and all very dodgy!"

Between 2nd and 11th of February 1981, The Cure went into Morgan Studios to record their next album, 'Faith', a tortuous process which eventually consumed the whole of the month as the band went from Red Bus to The Roundhouse to Trident to Abbey Road in a bid to capture what Robert was after.

Robert:

"Lol's mother became very ill at this time and Lol and I used to talk about death a lot, about how easy it is to turn it into something abstract until it turns up on your doorstep.

"I used to go and write songs in church. I'd think about death and I'd look at the people in the church and I knew that they were all there above all because they wanted 'eternity'. All of a sudden I realised I had no faith at all and I was scared. Before Christmas I'd been thinking about the album as an exploration of ideas. I was thinking about how, when you're young, you are indoctrinated and forced to believe in something.

"I wanted to get at different expressions of faith, to understand why people have it, to see if it was a real thing. I was living a sort of second childhood, I wanted to know what was going on. I asked myself questions about the people around me, why they were doing what they were doing, why some of them devoted their whole lives to something they would only get after death.

"I immersed myself in it and I found it stupid: and 'Faith' became a difficult album to make – we just couldn't get the songs to sound right. We just kept doing songs over and over and then scrapping them.

"The problem was, I was in the right mood when I was on my own with the words and the music but, when I was with the others, it was wrong. It was too happy."

Simon:

"It was really strange recording but really good fun. Lol and I were a bit green about things and, when Robert would be trying to do a vocal, we'd tend to get a bit drunk which would upset him – us pissed, him trying to work; quite understandable. Once Robert explained to us, though, we were fine."

Hedges:

"'Faith' is more intense than '17 Seconds', more atmospheric, darker, grey, misty. Most of the songs are songs to hang yourself to."

Parry:

"I think 'Faith' is a superb album, the most streamlined and stylish of things, ethereal, but it was such a strain to make. I got involved in it midway through, not in the mixing or anything, but just booking the studios, it was going on and on. Y'know, the drugs were coming, the demands were coming, lyrics were being written on the studio floor . . . I could see that they couldn't carry on like that."

Hedges:

"Robert and I were good friends, we knew each other too well and we started reaching the limits of our possibilities together. If that album had been my first piece of work with them, I'd have put more of myself into it to prove what I could do. But I had nothing left to prove and that made for a bad situation. All the same, the album turned out well."

Robert:

"We laid down the tracks in a completely disinterested way, as if someone else was doing it and not us. But whenever I started to sing, the whole atmosphere went black. After a while, we just did nothing at all, I didn't even want to sing anymore. And it was difficult, too difficult . . . "

Parry:

"I didn't want to come to anymore sessions because I didn't want there to *be* anymore sessions. I wanted it wrapped up but I found myself there because I was concerned.

"Y'know, someone would say something funny in the control room while Robert was doing a vocal in the studio and Hedges would just turn him off, have a joke and a laugh, then turn back and Robert would be waiting and we'd *lost* it. He needed someone to say 'Right, that's great Robert, now *c'mon!*' – that's what it's about; an athletic approach and Hedges didn't seem to have it.

"I was happy with the way the album turned out but it cost a lot more than it needed to."

Robert:

"Once we'd finished, there was an empty space. Then we realised we'd have to play these songs for the next six months . . . "

Meanwhile, Simon's brother, Ric, had been working on a minimalist animated film to accompany the band on tour instead of a support band. The film, 'Carnage Visors' – an antonym for rose-coloured spectacles – was shot in Ric's garage but, when he got it back from the processors, he realised the light exposures had all been wrong and that barely anything had come out.

Simon:

"Ric had a lot of good ideas but he was a bit naive and lacked the material and experience. He had to redo about two months work in three days. He wanted to hang himself! Consequently, it wasn't as good as it could have been."

With the British tour fast approaching, Robert decided they'd have to record the soundtrack "blind" so they went into Point Studios on 16 March, using the day shift.

Robert:

"We rehearsed it for three days and then did it in one go. I played bass along with a Dr Rhythm drum machine, Lol counted out the beats on a stopwatch and held the treatment for me to read and Simon had a bottle of wine which he poured into my mouth every other minute. We'd got through three bottles of wine by the time we finished it, then Simon did some bass overdubs, I did some keyboards and that was it. We didn't actually see the film until just before we went on tour."

The Cure's next single, 'Primary'/'Descent', was reviewed by the British music press on 28 March. It was the first Cure record to boast a Porl Thompson sleeve.

Porl:

"I was at art college and I didn't like The Cure's sleeves and I said as much to Robert, adding, of course, that I thought me and my friend Undy could do much better. So he gave us the chance and we went crazy. This was Parched Art. I forgot all about college and threw myself into it. As with all the later sleeves, I waited for the music to be finished before starting work, and I used to go to a lot of their recording sessions and rehearsals to impregnate myself with a piece."

Reviewed by

ADAM SWEETING

Under doctor's orders

THE CURE: "Primary" (Fiction). This is a triumphant return to The Cure's rushing rhythmic roots after the limpid wanderings of the "Seventeen Seconds" album.

Robert Smith has rediscovered the fine tuning control installed in his unusual musical sensibility, and as a result "Primary" is unbearably urgent, matching a new-found sense of space with a brilliantly focused precision. Smith's propulsive guitar drone is punctuated by crashing waves of percussion, and his voice floats yearningly over the top.

It's oddly like a more tightly-reined U2, and is a far better pretext for a national holiday than the forthcoming Royal Wedding. Also available as a 12 inch.

singles

by David Hepworth

THE CURE: Primary (Fiction). My admiration for Robert Smith aside, I do wonder how long The Cure can continue to prop their songs against the same chord progression, with its clambering bass and deadpan drums. At the moment their fast song (this one) sounds just like their slow one speeded up.

Record Mirror's Simon Tebbutt called it "Pleasant but heavily phased and everyone sounds incredibly bored." When the band appeared on Top Of The Pops, it was almost a repeat perforamcne of their first visit. The presenter forgot their name and assumed this was their first appearance, the band did their utmost to avoid all the other acts and dressed up their instruments in clothing to expose the idiocy of miming, and the single, which was at 38, duly careered down the chart with an anvil round its neck.

In mid April 'Faith' was released with the soundtrack to 'Carnage Visors' as the B side of the cassette version. The album cover – misty and grey – was actually a building dear to Robert's heart.

Robert:

"When I was a kid, I used to play beside it on my holidays. It's hundreds of years old and the way it is on the cover, is the exact image I'd retained of it. It's one of my oldest memories."

Porl and Undy actually created the cover from photographs of Bolton Abbey and the record company was far from happy with the result.

THE CURE

THE CURE
Faith *(Fiction Records)*.

A CONFESSED rockist writes Wasn't Hank Williams wearing a great suit in *Heroes of Rock and Roll?* A man who was wearing a suit with musical notes on it way back then has to have had a lot going for him, *n'est ce pas?* Unfortunately, I'm here to talk about the new Cure album instead of the aforementioned garment. Does an album called 'Faith', featuring eight tracks called 'The Holy Hour', 'Primary' (even now charting, as we ace reviewers have it), 'Other Voices', 'All Cats Are Grey' (honest!), 'The Funeral Party' (rib-tickling, isn't it?), 'Doubt', 'The Drowning Man' and 'Faith' sound like a barrel of laughs to you?

In *Sniffin' Glue*'s glory days they used to write happily of hurling records out of the window if they didn't come up to the exciting standards of the time. This one would have gone straight out, no messing about. Young English groups have created a whole new songwriting category known to experts as Grammar School Angst, and this collection represents a major contribution to the genre. It's very well played, beautifully recorded, and says absolutely nothing meaningful in a fairly depressing way. One unrecorded aspect of the present government's economic policies is that thousands of young people

Gloomy? Gothic? Us?

are forming bands when they would really be more suited to chartered accountancy or a career in market gardening, say.

I just can't understand what the driving force is behind albums like this. A burning desire to get in a recording studio and sing lines like *"The innocence of children, dressed in white and slowly dreaming, stops all time"*, in an anaemic English whine, is a force I cannot comprehend. When I was a kid, aspiring rock and rollists wanted to be bigger than Elvis or own two hundred Cadillacs and ingest drugs and drink in unhealthy quantities while fornicating with beautiful women. You know, something worthwhile and life-affirming. Too many bands nowadays just want their bloody personal problems in purple prose.

Records about pain and misery and the hurt of rejection are successful when they transcend the misery and the singer learns from the process and informs the listener of his findings. That's why a lot of John Lennon's solo work was unsuccessful, he was simply describing his misery and producing miserable records. Joy Division were the only angst band that actually said anything. Ian Curtis's obsessions were obviously real and one could learn something real and instructive from listening to him.

Back at the booby-hatch, the singer's just informed a waiting world that he *"lives with desertion and eight million people"*. Well, don't we all, love. Really, this is just the modern face of Pink Floydism. I think it was the aforementioned ex-Beatle who once said "Sporrans will go. They will shrink and fade. We're bigger than Robbie Burns now." Me, I'll take Hank Williams' suit to the cleaners any day.

PS I take it that you're all still in possession of your Hucklebuck footwear?

Roy Lowry

THE CURE
'Faith'
(Fiction FIX6)★★★★½

IF WE didn't know better, we could all throw rocks with the words 'Joy Division' printed all the way through at The Cure. Fact is, 'course, they were doing this sort of thing – and minus the distasteful wordplay with deathcamp imagery – years before. Perhaps someone should 'phone the insanity squad?

Enough! The Cure are above such peurile games of grammar and solipsism. At best (Joy)/Division offered an unhealthy, vicarious snapshot of the darkness (but how soon everyone wore their badge!) and the press, poor leeches living lives by proxy, flocked to their falsie nerve-ends.

The Cure pretend to no such Genetesque aesthetic of degradation. They would never "die for you". 'Faith' has exactly that: beyond the surface of cynicism, this dance of giants glows with positivism and life, from its boot soles upwards.

'Faith' is hardly new. 'Primary' goes fast, its phased binary beat slicing somewhere between Neu and the Doctors of Madness. 'Doubt' also takes it at a fair lick, a classy lyrical dance number. Neither of them are particularly historic, but both are infused with an epic quality by The Cure's sense of strong, haunting melody.

The rest commutes between modern-day Dusseldorf and the Sixties of the Floyd at the Middle Earth and the Doors in Miami. There's a Neu-ish sense of smudged melody, soft tones flowing around a languorous, groaning bass. Pieces like 'Other Voices', a chill offshore dub written for a spaghetti western, and the seductive cathedral voices of 'All Cats Are Grey', with a ritual drum beat I could whirl to all night, have an overwhelming anthemic atmosphere. Like 'The End', they have some strange sense of importance, of personal commitment, that I can't quite fathom. It's almost as though listening to 'Faith' requires a personal act of involvement, the reward being a sense of belonging.

That may sound completely wacko, but 'Faith' wins. It swings like a warm summer night, its warm breezes and rarefied beat transcend everyday dance music. But whatever symbols I pin on its entrancing map, the only steps you'll take here are those of an irresistable dance to music like brilliant light.

And a word to the wise: 'Faith' and its constituent parts trade under a namemark of broadly 'religious' cynicism, dismissing catechism, belief and observance. It may (should?) knock down some icons, but you should read between its lines. Reverse psychology may be passe, but 'Faith' uses these as a front for its own deep-rooted hope and belief. As Smith repeats at the end of the title track, "There's nothing left but faith." Without that they couldn't have made this album. This is life and I want more of it.

JOHN GILL

Robert told Record Mirror: "I've always tried to make records that are of one piece, that explain a certain kind of atmosphere to the fullest. If you're gonna fully explore something, you need more than one song to do it. That's why I always liked Nick Drake's albums or Pink Floyd records like 'Umma Gumma' . . . I like a lot of music that is built around repetitions – Benedictine chants particularly, and Indian mantras. These musics are built around slow changes, they allow you to draw things out."

Record Mirror's Mike Nicholls, though, was far from complimentary: "Whereas PiL, for example, continue to radically rewrite their rule book, The Cure remain stuck in the hackneyed doom-mongering that should have died with Joy Division . . . The Cure are lost in the maze of their spineless meanderings . . . hollow, shallow, pretentious, meaningless, self-important and bereft of any real heart and soul . . ."

Free Voice was slightly more generous: "It is seductive and enjoyable but its equation of despair with profundity is vacuous."

Absolute Zero asked Robert whether he'd read the NME review: "No, I've been told about it though . . . they had a picture with Matthieu in it, so I wouldn't read it on principle. If they couldn't get the picture right then it's unlikely they got the review right."

In an interview with Sound International, Simon expressed the current feeling within the band: "Our relationship – don't take this in a funny way – is like a boy and girl . . . we don't get upset about things that boys would normally get upset about. We can swear at each other. If it's serious, I might sulk for a while, thinking they're not my friends anymore and things like that and feel very down. Then, a few minutes later, it's all blown over."

Robert, for his part, insisted: "Obviously we have to sell records to survive . . . at the same time, we've retained enough ideals – well, I have – despite what we've been through. The way that we do things is more important than the actual outcome of things . . . We're not mainstream and we never will be unless the mainstream changes to us . . . We can convert people along with other groups I admire like PiL and Siouxsie & The Banshees, groups like that. If people could realise there's as much in what groups like that are trying to do, instead of just buying ABBA and stuff, then there'd be a new mainstream."

The band began to tour the album immediately.

Robert:

"I didn't realise what effect it would have on the group. I thought we could just merge the songs in live, and the other songs would balance but it affected everyone. Those songs had a downward spiral effect on us – the more we played them, the more despondent and desolate we became."

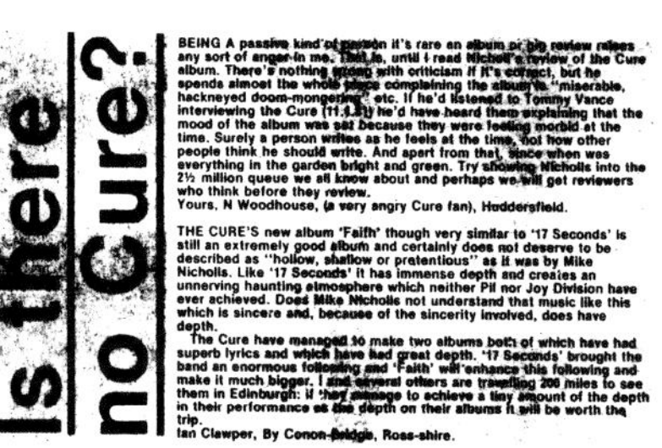

Is there no Cure?

BEING A passive kind of person it's rare an album or gig review raises any sort of anger in me. That is, until I read Nicholl's review of the Cure album. There's nothing wrong with criticism if it's correct, but he spends almost the whole piece complaining the album is "miserable, hackneyed doom-mongering" etc. If he'd listened to Tommy Vance interviewing the Cure (11.1.81) he'd have heard them explaining that the mood of the album was set because they were feeling morbid at the time. Surely a person writes as he feels at the time, not how other people think he should write. And apart from that, since when was everything in the garden bright and green. Try showing Nicholls into the 2½ million queue we all know about and perhaps we will get reviewers who think before they review.
Yours, N Woodhouse, (a very angry Cure fan), Huddersfield.

THE CURE'S new album 'Faith' though very similar to '17 Seconds' is still an extremely good album and certainly does not deserve to be described as "hollow, shallow or pretentious" as it was by Mike Nicholls. Like '17 Seconds' it has immense depth and creates an unnerving haunting atmosphere which neither Pil nor Joy Division have ever achieved. Does Mike Nicholls not understand that music like this which is sincere and, because of the sincerity involved, does have depth.

The Cure have managed to make two albums both of which have had superb lyrics and which have had great depth. '17 Seconds' brought the band an enormous following and 'Faith' will enhance this following and make it much bigger. I and several others are travelling 200 miles to see them in Edinburgh: if they manage to achieve a tiny amount of the depth in their performance as the depth on their albums it will be worth the trip.
Ian Clawper, By Conon-Bridge, Ross-shire.

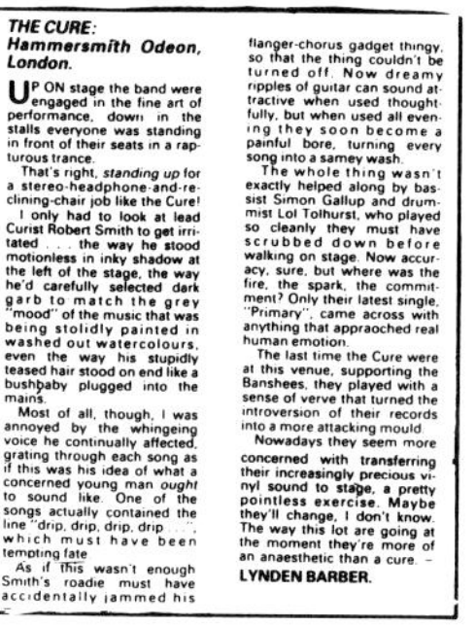

THE CURE:
Hammersmith Odeon, London.

UP ON stage the band were engaged in the fine art of performance, down in the stalls everyone was standing in front of their seats in a rapturous trance.

That's right, *standing up* for a stereo-headphone-and-reclining-chair job like the Cure!

I only had to look at lead Curist Robert Smith to get irritated . . . the way he stood motionless in inky shadow at the left of the stage, the way he'd carefully selected dark garb to match the grey "mood" of the music that was being stolidly painted in washed out watercolours, even the way his stupidly teased hair stood on end like a bushbaby plugged into the mains.

Most of all, though, I was annoyed by the whingeing voice he continually affected, grating through each song as if this was his idea of what a concerned young man *ought* to sound like. One of the songs actually contained the line "drip, drip, drip, drip . . .", which must have been tempting fate.

As if this wasn't enough Smith's roadie must have accidentally jammed his flanger-chorus gadget thingy, so that the thing couldn't be turned off. Now dreamy ripples of guitar can sound attractive when used thoughtfully, but when used all evening they soon become a painful bore, turning every song into a samey wash.

The whole thing wasn't exactly helped along by bassist Simon Gallup and drummist Lol Tolhurst, who played so cleanly they must have scrubbed down before walking on stage. Now accuracy, sure, but where was the fire, the spark, the commitment? Only their latest single, "Primary", came across with anything that appraoched real human emotion.

The last time the Cure were at this venue, supporting the Banshees, they played with a sense of verve that turned the introversion of their records into a more attacking mould.

Nowadays they seem more concerned with transferring their increasingly precious vinyl sound to stage, a pretty pointless exercise. Maybe they'll change, I don't know. The way this lot are going at the moment they're more of an anaesthetic than a cure. – **LYNDEN BARBER.**

Robert:

"For the public, there was no way out. The critics said the gigs were religious ceremonies, and it was true. Most of the time, I left the stage crying. It was horrible but, at the same time, a good experience, bizarre and intense. We only played the 'Faith' album and one or two numbers from '17 Seconds' and because we felt so much what we were doing, if someone shouted something, Simon and I would go mad, we'd often even jump into the crowd and sort things out."

Simon:

"'Carnage Visors' worked for us in a way because we'd find out what an audience was like by their reaction to it. If there were lots of cat-calls and throwing things at the stage, it would wind us up a lot and we'd go out and be really aggressive."

On 22 May, The Cure played the Dublin College May Ball.

Robert:

"A most ridiculous night and about the only time on the tour we felt happy. We were supposed to be playing mainly for the students, but it was good because the gig was invaded by the local Dublin punks who broke through security en masse to see us.

"We went on stage at 2am and I was so drunk I couldn't see. We were really getting into playing and a group of punks down the front were calling out for 'Grinding Halt' and stuff but the rest of the audience became really agressive and started jeering and throwing cans at us. We suffered about 20 minutes of this and then we stormed off, went straight to the beer tent, erected a table as a barrier, and drank ourselves into a coma.

"On the way out the next morning, there were lots of people gesticulating at us, going 'Ha! Ha!' so we drove over a couple – it was the least we could do!"

On 8 June, The Cure played the Stadthalle, Freiburg in Germany.

Robert:

"It was very hot and only 32 people turned up – with the roadies, there was almost more of us than them! I remember singing, sitting on the edge of the stage with my legs hanging down – I really liked that moment. After the gig we just jumped down and had a beer with the crowd!"

The Cure next embarked upon a tour of Holland in a circus tent – a bid, on their part, to avoid playing the usual venues.
Robert:

"It started off well but, at Sittard on 24th of June, just before we went on stage for an encore, someone came up to Lol and told him to phone England urgently. They told him 'Your mother's dead' – simply, just like that. We went back on stage and played 'Faith'. Lol started, played for about a minute, and then stopped and just sat there without moving. We all returned to England the following day and we played the cassette of that concert at his mother's funeral. It was very strange.

"After the ceremony, we went to get drunk and Lol decided we absolutely *must* restart the tour or he'd go mad. It was very hard . . . horrible, even if the music *was* perfect for the circumstances . . ."

On 5 July, they played a festival in Werchter, by the sea, in Belgium.
Robert:

"We'd only been on for about half an hour and everything was running late so Robert Palmer's road crew started motioning to us to stop. This bloke ran on and said 'If you don't stop playing, we're gonna pull the plug'. Simon immediately walked to the mike and shouted 'Fuck Robert Palmer! Fuck rock 'n' roll!' and we started playing a really slow version of 'A Forest' which lasted about 15 minutes.

"It was fucking brilliant. Unfortunately, when we finished, they threw all our stuff off the back of the stage . . ."

On 16 July, the band started recording the next single, 'Charlotte Sometimes'/'Splintered In Her Head' at Playground Studios, named by Robert and newly opened by Hedges. It took two days to complete.
Parry:

"I was really disappointed with it, I thought it sluggish and lacking in vitality. I wasn't around, I stayed away deliberately so Hedges had to come to me. He said 'If this isn't a hit, then you don't have to use me again' and I thought 'Well pal, that's it then.'"

The single was accompanied by a sadly inappropriate and tacky video by Mike Mansfield who, at the time, was having a lot of success with his mini-pantos for Adam Ant.
Lol:

"It was Parry's idea and what a mistake! Embarrassing! We wanted a video which told a story so we went off to film it in an old, abandoned psychiatric hospital, a huge, strange place where there were still a lot of padded rooms."
Robert:

"We gave Mike Mansfield the book, Charlotte Sometimes, to read, and said 'This should be a period setting where the girl time-slips'. We wanted it to be really mysterious. When we saw it, we didn't know whether to laugh or cry."

On 23 July, the band began their second American tour with the first of two nights at New York's Ritz.
Simon:

"Robert and I nearly died that night. After the gig, someone gave us two quaaludes each with the recommendation that we shouldn't take more than half at a time. Well, we took the lot, went out to a club and started to feel really ill, y'know, we'd passed out but we were still walking around. I remember Lol took us into the toilets and tried to bring us back to life and, in the taxi back to the hotel, he was so seriously worried we were gonna die that he picked a fight with us just so we'd react."
Robert:

"I don't remember very much about any of that period of time. I think San Francisco was the night of the Royal Wedding and . . . we couldn't acclimatise to those American dates at all – two nights in New York and then straight across to the West Coast . . . ludicrous really.

"We were completely out of it on that first night and the second night . . . well, Bill maintains it was our worst ever concert. He says he doesn't know to this

day how I didn't fall over. I really don't remember it at all.

"I think we then went straight to Pasadena and then to the Whiskey A Go Go in LA. I remember running to the hotel in tears after that gig so I must have been in a bad way. There were so many people backstage and they were all coming up to me and all I could see were faces . . . faces . . . faces. I think I was hallucinating . . .

"I kept imagining people were threatening me and I was still feeling weird when we arrived in Auckland, New Zealand! It was from the hotel in Auckland that I phoned up The Banshees. I called Severin – they were on tour in Scotland at the time – and I played him 'Charlotte Sometimes' down the phone. I was really proud of it. But, during the phone call, I fell asleep: the phone bill was 480 dollars.The next morning I was exhausted –
and I couldn't understand how or why I was there."

Before the "Picture Tour" reached Australia, the Auckland Press wrote: "Smith wore a Marilyn Monroe T shirt which was the only personality he gave away . . . "

Robert:

"We had a lot of problems, especially in Australia where they'd got used to listening to '17 Seconds' and songs like 'Fire In Cairo'. They were expecting a lighter, poppier show and when we started with 'The Holy Hour' and 'All Cats Are Grey', seven minutes of atmosphere, there was always someone who wanted to break the mood which annoyed us a lot. What we were doing was very different from other bands at the time and it was people like The Specials who were going down a storm over there."

From down under, the tour moved on to Canada where, if anything, if got worse. The shows were in bars and cowboy clubs and 27th of August in the Riviera Rock Room, Edmonton was typical.

Robert:

"Every time we finished a number, someone would ask if we didn't know something faster or they'd ask for Chuck Berry songs. We never thought we'd get out alive."

The band returned home in September where Robert borrowed Lol's drum kit and experimented, writing rhythms, recording them on cassettes. The basic structures of 'Figurehead' and 'Cold' were devised this way and it set the pattern for the relentlessly driving percussion of the next album.

Between 30 September and 17 October, The Cure were off again, touring France where, since the release of 'Three Imaginary Boys', the band had been gaining in popularity. The crowds, however, reacted as badly as the Aussies to the sombre assault of 'Faith'.

Simon:

"The audiences were exasperated and so we'd get angry and jump in. It would have been ridiculous if only one of us had done it so we never went unless we *all* went. When I saw Robert putting his guitar down, I knew the moment had come and, by the end, it was like a dance – we'd jump in to settle accounts, then get back on stage. We didn't give a fuck about being out of tune afterwards!"

Robert:

"I don't really remember many of those shows. I was getting to the manic stage that was going to lead to 'Pornography'. I was due for a break – too much of everything, no respite. I had no control whatsoever over what I was doing. We were committed to taking around quite a big show. Pink Floyd's PA, film equipment, a lot of lights and not getting paid very much money so we had to play virtually every night. This was another of Bill's strategies . . .'"

Gary Biddles, a friend of Simon's who'd previously met Robert and Lol in a record shop in Horley, started to travel with the band on the 'Faith' tour sleeping on the floor in Simon or Lol's room, just along for the laugh. By the time the tour reached France, he was doing the backline.

Gary:

"They were all very young and innocent – short haircuts and a bit of eye-liner, Robert in a blazer. He always had something interesting to say in interviews, he always had an arty answer."

In mid October, 'Charlotte Sometimes'/'Splintered In Her Head' was released.

THE CURE
NEW SINGLE
CHARLOTTE SOMETIMES b/w
SPLINTERED IN HER HEAD
12" version includes extra track
FAITH (recorded live)
on fiction records

Robert:

"Once again, everyone at Polydor said it would be Top 10 and again they were wrong. I was glad because, by then, I wanted to get into something harder."

In America, 'Happily Ever After' was released on A&M, a double album package of '17 Seconds' and 'Faith'. The Virginian Pilot said "Sometimes they sound like Gang Of Four meets Pink Floyd, acid rock for the industrial age, but they never get boring" and LA Weekly called it "Disciplined minimalist post punk from one of the bands that helped forge the gloom movement."

From 25 November to 3 December, the band played Britain, climaxing at Hammersmith Palais.

Derek Block presents
THE CURE
plus GUESTS
26th NOV.
EDINBURGH ODEON
27th NOV.
GLASGOW PAVILION
28th NOV.
BRADFORD ST. GEORGES HALL
29th NOV.
STOKE KINGS HALL
30th NOV.
COVENTRY APOLLO
3rd DEC.
HAMMERSMITH PALAIS
All tickets £3.50 & £3.00
except
Hammersmith Palais, all £3.50

Robert:

"The support acts on that tour were And Also The Trees and 1313 who were Lydia Lunch and Steve Severin. They used to come to our hotels to avoid their bed and breakfasts and Severin used to sleep on my floor. We used to talk a lot – getting to know each other better and better. I didn't like what he was doing with Lydia though – it was atrocious."

At this time, the NME published an article entitled "A Cure For Fun" in which Paul Morley took it upon himself to *become* Robert Smith and to write down his thoughts. Marauding through a tangle of notions about hedonism, total sensory input or overload, exploring and pleasing every sense as a path to enlightenment. Smith/Morley concluded: "We've never attacked, there's been no offense. We've been there for people to like or dislike but always on a very abstract level. We should have played beyond that. That's what we're going to do with the next phase."

Robert:

"I'd been writing a few ideas for new songs and, after 3 December, I went down to this studio called The Windmill somewhere in Surrey. Then Lol came down and did some drum parts, then Simon came. I think Simon and I had had a few flare-ups too many – he was angry because he thought I was going to go off with Severin – that's why he wasn't at the studio all the time. I remember it was snowing, it was really cold and I decided we should have another Christmas party.

"We finished doing most of the demos in about six days and they were really excellent, much more vicious than before, and then I took a break and went to Severin's and spent a few days just wandering around London, hallucinating. Severin couldn't believe what I was doing so he kept an eye on me. I wrote most of the lyrics for 'Pornography' during that period and then went back to finish off doing a few things in the studio.

Simon:

"There was a communication breakdown. Robert was out clubbing a lot and we had a big row because I was getting the hump a bit about him going off with Severin. I'd always prided myself on being his confidant and I wanted it to stay that way.

"I wasn't sure what I'd done wrong to, like, lose his friendship but now, looking back, I see I wasn't willing to listen."

Robert:

"Matty came down on the last day in the studio and the four of us went to the party together. It was a good night, and a good time to get back together. I don't know why I did all that stuff, I just felt I had to. I didn't want to be normal anymore, I just didn't want to feel secure.

"In January 1982, we had a bit of a break for a couple of weeks and then Bill took me round to meet various different producers. I didn't think we should work with Hedges again because the nature of the music was entirely different and I wanted to make a break from how we'd been working before."

Hedges:

"The reasons were also partly financial. I'd just made an album and a single with The Associates, which had gone well and I had several offers where there was a lot of money on the table. The end of our collaboration came naturally enough. The Banshees asked me to produce 'A Kiss In The Dreamhouse' so the parting of the ways came at an ideal time."

Parry:

"I came in with a lot of names, people I liked, like Colin Thurston, people I'd seen and thought were going to be good but Robert wasn't into that. Again, it was all about personalities. He wanted someone young – he had this fixation with youth as if someone old couldn't possibly have a handle on it. I understand, now, Robert's preoccupation with the right face.

"Anyway, we picked Phil Thornalley – he was young and they liked the look of him and, I must say, it went really well."

Thornalley:

"The only thing I knew by them was 'Killing An Arab' – a good song but too tricksy for my taste. I was very naive, I didn't even know they'd had hits so I treated them like normal people which produced a sane sort of atmosphere."

Robert:

"We were booked into RAK between January and April and the first two days, I thought we were heading for disaster. Phil was so nice to me and I was so horrible. He was wrong to be so polite when I was anything but. I wanted to make a horrible record and I remember he told me he didn't like the guitar sound I was making."

Thornalley:

"His guitar style was his pride and joy and perhaps I shocked him, I don't know . . . When you're used to being flattered, it's always a good idea to have someone tell you what they really think."

Robert:

"What annoyed me was, right then, I *didn't have* a guitar sound. '100 Years' and 'Figurehead' didn't sound like me at all. Nor could Phil tolerate me being late. So I told him, if it didn't suit him, we would find someone else who'd enjoy making the record more. But we talked it out and everything ended up fine."

Simon:

"It was such an intense album to do that things blew up again. I think Robert really wanted to get out of The Cure – I can't to this day put my finger on exactly what it was but I could understand it. A lot of people were calling us a long raincoat band and I wanted to go out and prove them wrong, prove we were more than that. I think Robert did too but it took so much out of us . . . sometimes we'd work right through the night, have a couple of hours sleep, and then go and do it again." The NME notes at the time: "It seems not much recording gets done but plenty of Babycham gets done with brandy. Fair enough: The Cure were only grim for one day back in 1979."

Robert:

"It was the first time we were in control of everything. For the first three albums, Hedges was the buffer between me and the others but this time I knew exactly what I wanted and I told them. Once Simon had finished the bass and Lol the drums, it went very quickly, though I don't think they could understand me – it was very bizarre.

"I had a sound in my head but I couldn't manage to explain it so they all thought I was trying to exclude them, especially Simon. Biddles and Lol would just set up camp at the end of the studio, tell each other stupid jokes and get drunk most of the time and it started to get out of hand because we were in a completely unreal environment.

"We were all living at the Fiction office and, for three years, we'd been almost constantly together. I'd spent more time with Simon and Lol in that period than I had with my girlfriend Mary so I was beginning to feel I'd had enough of being in a band all the time and the cycle just got worse and worse. We'd leave the flat at 10 at night, get drunk, go and record, finish at 10 in the morning, go to the pub, get drunk and then go to bed.

"I slept on the floor behind the setee with a blanket drawing-pinned to the wall so it was like a tent. I had all these little bits, things I'd found in the street and taken back to my nest. It really got out of hand. Simon, Biddles and Lol were in another room and I wanted to kill them . . . We should have met in the middle but it had all gone too far and I knew this album would be the end. It was too violent. I wanted 'Pornography' to be the best but I thought they didn't give a fuck."

Simon:

"Sometimes I'd forget that, besides Robert the friend and Robert the musician, there was Robert the producer and he couldn't allow himself to crack or come and get drunk with the rest of us all the time. He had to concentrate 20 hours of the day and we only had to do it for 12. We had fights – I didn't understand and it was completely my fault. I was distracting him."

Lol:

"It was a bit crazy. In one corner of the studio we'd piled up all the cans and bottles we'd drunk, and there were so many by the end, you could completely hide among them."

Thornalley:

"It was one of the recording sessions I've enjoyed most. We understood each other, we all had the same background. There was only one time when I didn't understand a single thing and that was when Robert had taken something and we did nothing at all for two days."

Robert:

"We took over Fiction and refused to let anyone in the door. The record company closed for that period. We couldn't bear it – y'know, people would *smell* different, they were coming into our cave. I became obsessed and all the inspiration – the time at the Windmill, the time with Severin, the latter stages of the last tour, being in the studio, they were all disconnected. I couldn't remember what I'd done or where I'd been. I really lost touch with what was real for a couple of months."

Biddles:

"Simon and I would dance around the studio and Robert would go 'Why are you doing this? I'm trying to make an album!' He was very serious and he didn't want anyone else encroaching. I was going out and buying two boxes of drink a day so how anything ever got recorded I don't know. One day The Associates would come in, the next day The Banshees – it was like party time and Robert was consuming vast quantities of everything yet fighting against it."

Parry:

"I used to go to RAK at 10 o'clock at night and leave at one, bored. I've got to be honest, the only track that didn't bore me was 'A Strange Day'."

Robert:

"I was on the rampage really – trying to co-ordinate it and I couldn't even co-ordinate myself! Sometimes I'd flip back into reality and join in – things like the can mountain were really good – but then I'd go back into this manic state."

Biddles:

"I think it's the best thing they've ever done, energywise. Because of the pressure, things were so heartfelt, you can feel it, y'know . . . something is about to happen in that record, it's a real stormer."

Parry:

"The first album was done in naivety, the second with clear cut vision, the third under difficulty and 'Pornography' was all those three rolled into one. It was a mess.

"Anyway, I had to try and put bums on concert seats because, if I'd said to Robert 'Well, that's a pretty fucking average album', he'd have hit the roof. He'd just sit on the island of creative exclusivity and fend things off, y'know, 'Bill, you don't understand, just book the tour'.

"That's not to say 'Pornography' is a bad album, it's just heavy, a difficult one to take so, ergo, films, technology, screens, all those sorts of things came in to try and make it a *show*."

'Pornography' was reviewed by the music press in mid April. Rip It Up wrote "Ian Curtis, by comparison, was a bundle of laughs."

Filth hounds

THE CURE
'Pornography'
(Fiction FIXD 7)***

THE TITLE is appalling, the music inside is terribly icy the whole way through, and as an entity in time in space and rock criticism the Cure are in themselves a dreadfully easy target. Are they part of the New Progressives? The production is so horrible and obvious, it makes you wonder, is R Smith all that clever really? In short, the mistakes the Cure make are as clear as the fractured daylight the Imaginary Boys themselves like so to chat about.

If they'd called the thing 'Dirty Books' or 'Filth' or something slightly more poetic it would make the whole lp better. As it is that initial, fatal misnomer sums up the Cure as a symptom. If Simple Minds are the SDP of rock then poor Cure are the equivalent of Mary Whitehouse. The title! Sheer Whitehousian! The problem is, R Smith has a grasp of the truth all right, but he transmits it in a manner that is doomed from the outside.

On 'Porn' (that's better!) the Cure sound like a chunky New Order. Like the middle class boys they are, they are prone to the most overt plagiarism, which naturally leads to that one single main motive of the Cure/Smithian oeuvre. Guilt.

Smith sings about "never being clean again" and "will somebody give me the (wait for it Curefans) Cure". We know what he means! He means well, he has talent, at the bottom of this heavy handed, sub NO and (still) sub Banshees stodge, there is a genuine pop talent still at work.

But the Cure have a knack of sounding like artifice of the worst, the most blatant kind. I'd have to be very kind to like 'Porn', as liberal as a Cure fan. But the heavy handedness, the unfortunate turn of phrase, never mind the generally too obviously angst-sounding backing (a monotone of would-be despair), push the Cure to that periphery from whence they really ought to be trying to crawl.

'Porn', has too much music, too cluttered a backing for Smith's well-intended observance. There are too many 'nice hi fi effects', there is a constant baulking away from the savage in the music, to project what Mr Smith has to say.

The last, title track, for instance, tries to copy Cab Voltaire, all shuddering tape noise. And they do it in an antiseptic, full-blown, blown-dry production! One is tempted to believe at such juncture that Mr Smith is doomed in his own unseeing woolly bourgeouis comforts.

'Porn' carries too much of an inward knowledge of the effect the music it's making will produce in its all too captured audience. It is already loaded with appreciative sighs of awe and wonder from its grammar school, studenty crowd of Cure fans. This is indeed a bad way to be in, again especially as Robert dear has talent (still). He ought to quit Surbiton and start dossing real soon.

'A Strange Day' is good though, mainly because it stops the sickly compulsiveness of the sound with a gap (Magic!). But even here the title is copied from New Order! In 'One Hundred Years' (these titles!) Smith is the m-c kid wanting to write 'War And Peace', and in 'Short Term Effect' he is the m-c kid copying the words of Maggie Thatcher.

While Cure fans are insidiously locked in the Cure (otherwise this musical crap wouldn't exist), Robert Smith seems locked in himself, a spiralling nightmare that leaves the Cure like (their once opponent) the Fall, a possible 'new progressive', making a pompous sounding music that is, when all's said and done, dryly meaningless.

DAVE McCULLOUGH

COLD TURKEYS

However, I feel that 'Pornography' was not designed to be objectified or probed, but taken *en bloc* as a very dense wash of emotional colour, portraying one soul on a leash, fighting back the panic in the dark. And, as such, it really works. The confessional returns, fragile, frightened, horribly forlorn, and very finely drawn. A killer of its kind.

Don't have too much fun, now.

Dave Hill

Blue movies

This time around, I'm hard pressed to find any redeeming features. It was possible to view "Faith" as The Cure working single-mindedly to stake out some territory of their own, refusing to be hurried by New Romantics or cult vendors of any stripe. And at least they threw in "Doubt" and "Primary" as breaks in the clouds.

But "Pornography" refuses to move on, replaces self-sufficiency with a refusal to peek through the curtains into the street once in a while, and finally plummets like a leaking submarine into depths unfathomable by man.

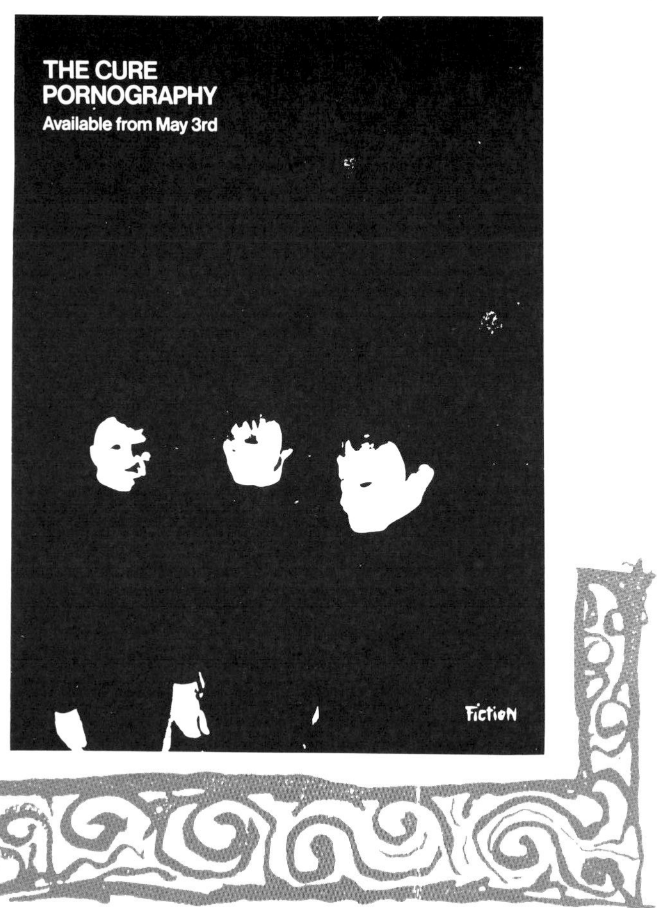

THE CURE
PORNOGRAPHY
Available from May 3rd
Fiction

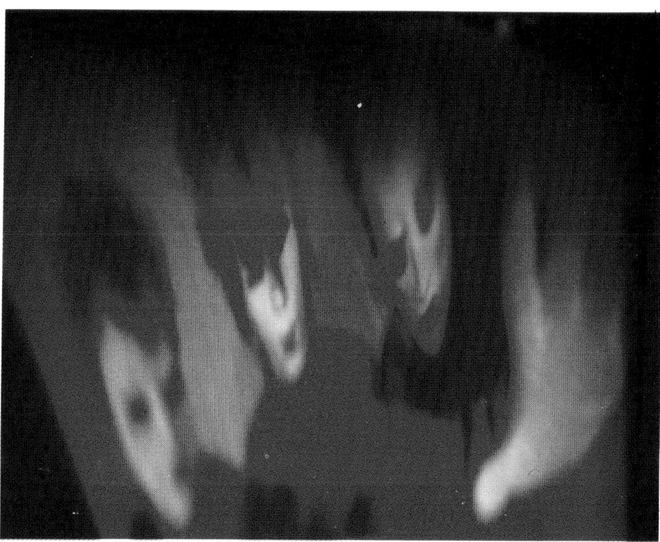

Later, Richard Cook of the NME put it in perspective – "At a time when The Song was ascendent again, The Cure made 'Pornography' and split its mother atom into fragments. The collected shrapnel, an icy, tuneless roar, was laid out on a record that literally destroyed a group" – but, at the time, David Quantick could only find "Phil Spector in hell."

Robert:

"'Pornography' is well put together. It's made up of little bits of experience scattered throughout the songs. To understand the album, you'd have to have it explained line by line. On the 'Faith' tour, I'd started to read books on clinical insanity, psychiatry, asylums, y'know, mental health in general. I thought about what sort of existence one must have in care, about the way you get treated and I thought, if I'd been alone, that could have happened to me. Instead of singing to an audience, I could've found myself singing to a wall."

The line "A charcoal face bites my hand" from 'A Short Term Effect' was culled from a book in which a patient drew people, in charcoal and then had nightmares in which they came alive. Shooting the 'Charlotte Sometimes' video in the old asylum had also had a profound effect. Robert had found some old paintings and sculptures in a cupboard there and had taken some home.

'Hanging Garden' came about "when I was at home, listening to the noises of cats outside . . . It made me go strange . . . I wanted to go out in the garden . . . so I did . . . stark naked . . . stupid . . . "

while 'Siamese Twins' was written about the ugliness of love:" It's despairing, as if I was getting rid of a whole piece of me. I thought I wouldn't be able to keep the two parts of my personality, that the balance was impossible. Once 'Siamese Twins' was written, I realised I didn't want the other side of it anyway – that it was seductive and exciting but in a deranged sort of way, that there was no substance to it. I had to detach myself from a lifestyle.

"To call the album 'Pornography' was my idea and Lol and Simon laughed and joked about how it was gonna be about sex. We had a big discussion about what exactly pornography was and I was surprised because everyone had a different idea. Bill thought of it in terms of the hit parade but I thought of it as in the way people are treated who don't conform to certain ideas or standards. To some people, someone obese in a newspaper with no clothes on is pornographic but, for me, it's the way people open the paper and laugh. It's not the subject which is pornographic but the interpretation of it.

"Seeing someone fucking a monkey doesn't particularly shock me. I get much more shocked by someone attacking someone else for doing it. For a lot of people pornography is tied to old morals and tired values. But, after all this discussion, Simon still wanted to call it 'Sex'!"

Lol:

"We thought most things were self-justifying – there's always a hypocritical side to polite people, and 'Pornography' is a protest against that. For the first time, in a way, we were being political. Political and humanitarian and very intense."

Robert later told the NME: "It wasn't really violent, it was the inability to be violent."

With the album finished and out, The Cure went straight onto the "Fourteen Explicit Moments" tour. Supported by Zerra 1, they played around Britain from 18 April to 1 May and then spent a month touring Europe. From the start there were problems. Robert objected to Parry choosing one of his mates to drive the band round and Record Mirror noted that "Robert Smith seems to be paying the price for his heavy boozing these days – he's getting quite chubby. Better stick to your favourite Peruvian snuff Rob – at least there's no calories in it."

'Be 2'

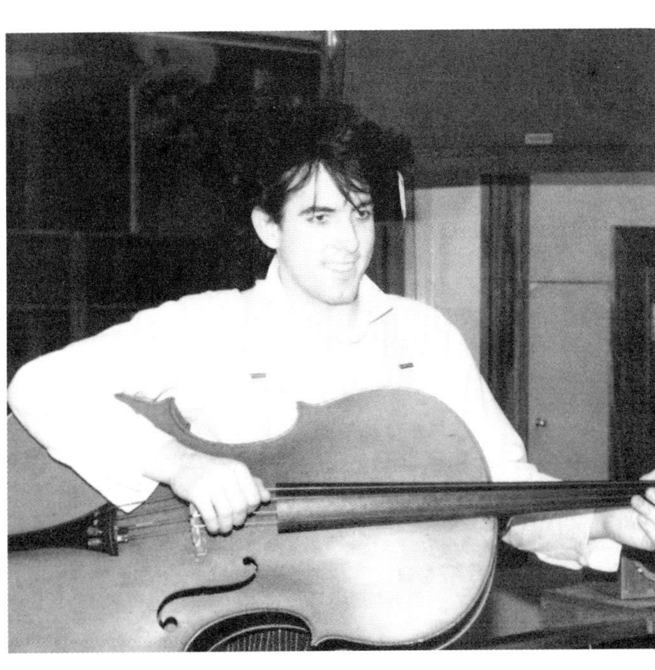

Still no cure for the Cure

THE CURE
Hammersmith Odeon, London

THE closest the Cure ever come to touching a core of humanity beneath their fraught facade is, unwittingly, through the inherent, though probably accidental, humour that mocks their very name. Seldom have a modern showband saddled themselves with such a self-consciously stark and inappropriate misnomer, seldom have three young people in pursuit of a clutch of aimless atmospheres, achieved so little with such panache.

The Cure – that's a joke. More like a symptom. Where contemporaries like the Clash play-act toy soldiers, point fingers, stick their necks out and look stupid advocating simplistic slogans, where Killing Joke share and shoulder despondency, offer no glib solutions but rally round nonetheless in blind, bitter anger, the Cure are content to whimper slightly and wallow, mirroring the meaningless mess of our lives – are, to be over-generously positive, perfectly pedestrian.

Here, in the Hammersmith Odeon, they'd dearly like to make an art-rock cross-over and abdicate into stylish Gothic performers a la big buddies the Banshees. But the place is too vast, the sound too thin and spineless, the light show too spartan and the songs themselves too intimately miserable to communicate anything other than boredom.

The audience, strangely, gets off on this image of three up-dated Al Stewart bed-sitter boy students squeezing their pimples and translating Camus prose into Shelleyian stanzas. Titles like "The Drowning Man" evoke "O" level angst, melancholy musings like "Siamese Twins" and "The Funeral Party" beg mothering instincts from doe-eyed girl fans. The Cure need a good clip round the ear.

Not extreme enough to stretch to exorcism nor even to elicit widespread sympathy, they only ever urge participation when they wrap their moaning in Bunnymen melodrama and a half decent tune and churn out their biggest hit "Primary".

As I sneaked out without so much as the slightest twinge of guilt or regret, Robert Smith was still demanding of no-one in particular: "Is It Always Like This?" I wish some wag had shouted back: "It Needn't Be!"

What the Cure ignore in their stifling, senselessly cyclical self-examination is that rock music may never provide effective sociological answers but, through joy, release and a rare sense of community, it may act as preventive medicine.

And, as any doctor of words, tunes or potions will eagerly testify, prevention almost always pre-empts the Cure. – **STEVE SUTHERLAND.**

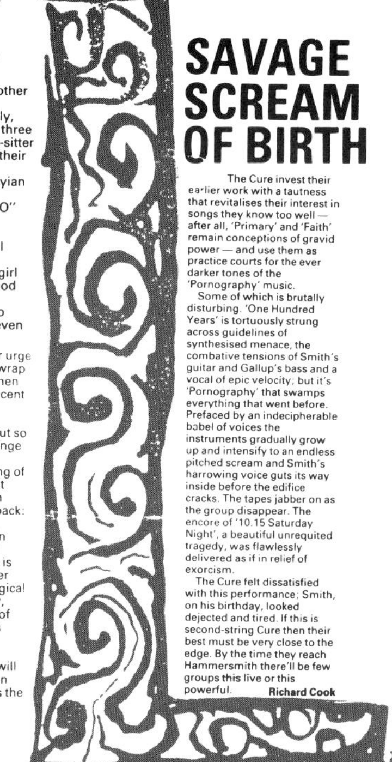

SAVAGE SCREAM OF BIRTH

The Cure invest their earlier work with a tautness that revitalises their interest in songs they know too well — after all, 'Primary' and 'Faith' remain conceptions of gravid power — and use them as practice courts for the ever darker tones of the 'Pornography' music.

Some of which is brutally disturbing. 'One Hundred Years' is tortuously strung across guidelines of synthesised menace, the combative tensions of Smith's guitar and Gallup's bass and a vocal of epic velocity; but it's 'Pornography' that swamps everything that went before. Prefaced by an indecipherable babel of voices the instruments gradually grow up and intensify to an endless pitched scream and Smith's harrowing voice guts its way inside before the edifice cracks. The tapes jabber on as the group disappear. The encore of '10.15 Saturday Night', a beautiful unrequited tragedy, was flawlessly delivered as if in relief of exorcism.

The Cure felt dissatisfied with this performance; Smith, on his birthday, looked dejected and tired. If this is second-string Cure then their best must be very close to the edge. By the time they reach Hammersmith there'll be few groups this live or this powerful. **Richard Cook**

Robert:

"Things got worse the longer we played. At this stage we were really confronting people and the collectiving personality of the group completely changed. What had really been a jovial experience became an aggressive one, and there was real viciousness, real vindictiveness in some of the practical jokes that were being played."

Simon:

"It was very hot in Europe and we weren't in the best frame of mind. We had to play near enough every night and it was hard to play the songs with the intensity they demanded without taking some sort of tension out on somebody. Unfortunately, Robert and I took it out on each other."

Robert:

"It was like Matthieu all over again – Simon started picking on Lol because he couldn't get to me. It just built up and up and Simon would come off stage, go off with the road crew and travel with the truck drivers. I don't suppose I was very good company anyway, I was in a world of my own. We couldn't bear each other anymore but it made us good on stage.

"I didn't go out much. I tended to spend my time alone, at the hotel bar or in my room. I'd get drunk and end up sleeping in the bathroom and I wasn't myself, I hadn't really recovered. People couldn't speak to me because I wanted everyone to be as I was. You had to actually *want* to be part of it and people hated us hated those concerts, even most Cure fans.

"The fighting extended to everything around us – in hotels, at the concerts, backstage, security people, the whole thing. It was mental."

Biddles:

"Simon was as popular as Robert – a big crowd puller – and it built up from there. They'd be in a mood with each other at the end of the show and it just got worse and worse, not just for them, but for everybody. I think I'm the only person on that tour who didn't have a row with someone – all the roadies were fighting, the lighting man going spare with the sound guy, just a huge mess."

Parry:

"Pornography was a bad tour, bad feeling, the worst. Simon was a lost soul. He was left believing in this Cure thing only to find that he believed in it for all the wrong reasons. He believed in it for cameraderie when it was patently obvious that Robert was going through a very cold period in his life and, when Robert is searching himself, when he's looking within, he doesn't care about other people.

"Robert can be very cold you see and one has to be wary of it. Simon wasn't."

The tensions came to a head on 27 May in a club after the gig in Strasbourg.

Simon:

"I was about to leave when some guy came up and told me I hadn't paid for my drinks. He thought I was Robert. I was knackered but the bloke took me up to the bar and Robert appeared to see what was going on. I hit him, he responded and we had a fight."

Robert:

"I was on the first floor of this club when they came up and told me there was a problem downstairs. Simon was so wound up that no-one could talk to him – he was screaming at the barman, this young kid who was nearly in tears. By himself, Simon would never have behaved like that but he was surrounded by the road crew so he was behaving the way he thought a rock 'n' roller ought to behave.

"He didn't want to pay for his drinks because he thought I wasn't paying for mine. I told him to shut up and he punched me. It was the first time he really laid into me, we had an enormous ruck and I said 'That's it', walked out, got a cab back to the hotel, got my suitcase, my passport from the tour manager's room and got on the first flight to London. That was at 6.30am and I was home by half past 10.

"I left a note saying I wasn't coming back. Simon returned the same afternoon. I'd left so I suppose he thought he could do the same. Good idea . . . we had three days off!"

Lol:

"The pressures of having to keep up the intensity and aggressive sentiments of 'Pornography' turned Simon into someone different though, at the time, I don't think he noticed. Or didn't want to . . . "

The last gig was in the Ancienne Belgique, Brussels on 11 June.

Robert:

"Before the concert, Lol and I sat in the dressing room, miserable because we knew it was the end. The show was quite flat and, during the encore, Biddles came on and started singing 'Smith's a wanker, Tolhurst's a wanker, only Simon's worth anything in this band'. I was drumming, so I stopped, threw the drumsticks at the back of his head and told him to fuck off. Everyone looked at each other . . . and that was it."

Simon:

"Zerra 1 were on stage too. Lol was playing bass, I was playing guitar and, to start with, it was great: but then it got stupid so I stopped and, gradually so did the others."

Robert:

"I slept right through the journey back the next day and then I said goodbye to Simon. I didn't see him again for 18 months."

SIX

Back in Britain, 'Hanging Garden'/'Killing An Arab (Live)' was released in July.

Reviewed by Adrian Thrills

THE CURE: Hanging Garden (Fiction)
Don't be fooled by the Banshee-esque title, "Hanging Garden' is a dismal exercise in rolling, tumbling rhythmic textures. The Cure have drifted disappointingly and indulgently from the idyllic pop invention of their younger days, a decline in standards reinforced by the inclusion of the original versions of 'Killing An Arab' and 'A Forest' on one portion of this doublepack.

It's just as well that The Cure have now jettisoned what was their finest moment 'Boys Don't Cry', a song now being respectfully refurbished in a Glasgow home by The Bluebells, who seem to be the sort of people that appreciate it more.

Believe it or not, I was actually the first person to write about The Cure, although it is not something I tell anyone but my closest acquaintances.

THE CURE
A SINGLE
RECORD ONE
THE HANGING GARDEN
ONE HUNDRED YEARS
FROM THE ALBUM PORNOGRAPHY
RECORD TWO
A FOREST
KILLING AN ARAB
RECORDED LIVE IN MANCHESTER
AVAILABLE IN A LIMITED EDITION GATEFOLD SLEEVE AT A SPECIAL LOW PRICE
ALSO AVAILABLE AS A STANDARD 7"
THE HANGING GARDEN B/W KILLING AN ARAB
Fiction

Robert:

"After we got home and had a few days away from each other, Simon probably thought it had all been born out of the same madness as the record but I knew it was far more than that. I didn't really feel the need to phone him up and say 'You're not in the group' – it would have been a pointless call because I had no intention of playing again at all. I was just fed up and, effectively, at that point, The Cure had stopped.

"I was uncontactable – Bill didn't know what was happening, or where we were, and the group effectively dissolved."

Lol went off to France and Spain for a month on holiday while Robert went camping in Wales.

Robert:

"First I went to see The Banshees recording 'A Kiss In The Dreamhouse': then I went off with Mary – just put a tent in the car and drove off. I stayed in two or three places and I didn't make any phone calls or tell anyone where I was. I just wanted to disappear.

"I would just sit outside the tent and stare at the sky . . . around this time Flexipop magazine wanted The Cure to do a record to go on their cover, so I wrote 'Lament' on my old Top 20 guitar . . . and I was surprised I was writing again, but pleased.

"When I got back to London, I recorded it in two days in The Garden Studios – Mary was there for the first day and, on the second, Severin. It was a really good atmosphere and the session was delirious! Great fun!"

Lol, meanwhile, had returned home and decided to give up drumming. He started taking piano lessons in Clapham.

Lol:

"It didn't matter at the beginning of The Cure who played what and, when I started, I couldn't play, I just found my own style. That's all very well – you can play if you're creative – but there comes a point where barriers loom up because you don't have the technique. We wanted to do more complicated things and I was neither ready nor prepared to practice for years to get there."

Parry:

"I wanted to get them going again so I told Robert I wanted a fun single, something unlike The Cure to break the mould and destroy the Cure myth. It appealed to Robert because he wanted to destroy The Cure anyway, he was up for it and I just voiced the idea – y'know, 'Let's kick this thing into the ground'. We had a meeting and Lol was up for it too because he was as anxious as I was to get Robert back into the fold. I moaned a lot at Lol at that point, we were good buddies. He'd come in regularly and I'd tell him all the things that were wrong with The Cure in my view, all the things that had gone wrong and why they'd gone wrong.

"I'd pick around at a bit of this and a bit of that but I couldn't really find my place anymore – my marriage was breaking up so I wasn't prepared to see *this* thing

die. That's when we went into what I called the 'Art Under The Hammer' Sessions which were basically demo sessions to find a pop song. It was a ploy to confuse the fuck out of everybody who'd hitherto known and liked The Cure. And why not? I thought it was ridiculous of Robert to drop everything after five years without getting any fun out of it. I mean, that's what had killed Robert and Simon – it had all got too serious, too important."

With sessioneer Steve Goulding on drums, Robert and Lol eventually came up with 'Let's Go To Bed' and 'Just One Kiss'.

Robert:

"It's a foolish title and the lyrics don't mean a thing. Musically, I mixed in everything bad I'd heard for years but even when we'd recorded it, I still didn't think it was horrible enough. So Bill remixed it and there it was!"

Simon:

"I was living at Fiction because I'd split up with Carol and one day I answered the phone and it was a fan wanting to know which studio Robert and Lol were in. That was when I knew I was out."

Robert:

"I would've liked Simon to tell us he was leaving the band. I didn't wanna behave like a dictator and throw him out. But, on the outside, people were saying 'that horrible Robert Smith has chucked out Matthieu after Michael and now the bastard has thrown out his best friend.'

"It wasn't really like that though. We were more like a couple who didn't get along anymore. If I hadn't liked Simon, I'd have had no trouble in telling him to leave. I just hoped he'd phone and leave out of pride but he didn't. What a stupid ending – there was too much pride between Simon and me and we were too young to react differently."

Simon:

"I wanted to talk it over but, after the fan's call I knew it was too late. For the next six months I was bitter and sour and, even after that, when I saw them on Top Of The Pops, I kept thinking 'That should be me."

Parry:

"We used the in-house Island studio because they'd made a lot of hits there and I thought 'We need a fucking hit'. We ran the 'Let's Got To Bed' session over four days and on the fourth, Robert decided he didn't like it but I thought it was great, a ball, totally sacriligeous, a great form of musical vandalism.

"I've always backed Robert – if he doesn't want something out, he doesn't have it out, even if all logic down to my last molecule screams 'This is a fucking suicidal move commercially' – but I went against him with 'Let's Go To Bed'. He came back and said 'I don't want it out under The Cure's name. I want it out under the name 'Recur' or something.' I said 'You made it, you sang it, what are you trying to do *pretend* it's not The Cure? It's done and it's coming out as The Cure'. He said 'If you're so sure it's gonna be a hit Bill, put it out under another name' and I said 'But that's not the point Robert – the whole point is that we want to come out with an irreligious record and it has to be put out under The Cure or it's a waste of time."

Robert:

"Bill reckoned it was gonna be a big hit and I didn't believe him so we had this bet – it if didn't make the top 20, he'd release me from my contract so I could do a solo project. That's why I let him do it, because I hoped it would let me work later without having to use the name The Cure, I'd be able to do what I wanted. Later, though, he typically claimed never to have agreed!"

Parry:

"He wanted a double A-side but I refused because that would just have confused the radio programmers. But he bad-mouthed it enough to kill it. He bad-mouthed the ass off it and people were wondering why the fuck they were interviewing Robert Smith at this point. I arranged them all, all the interviews because I thought I'd be fair – he didn't want it out so he can talk about it and explain why. I wasn't gonna try and muzzle him.

"But I still think it's a great record."

Having decided the record was coming out, it was logical to shoot a video, despite the band's previous bad experiences. For 'Hanging Garden', they'd used the crew that had made such a wacky success of Madness, but the desired humour didn't come across.

Parry:

"The night before we mixed 'Let's Go To Bed', Robert, Lol and myself sat down and really had fun visualising it, so we were looking for someone who was a bit different. I'd seen Tim Pope's showreel and I liked it, liked the 'Bedsitter' one for Soft Cell, so I investigated and found he was fairly new to the game and a bit freaky. It was worth the risk though because, for the only time ever, we'd strictly choreographed it – we asked him what he thought and he said 'great'. Robert was after something quirky, something that took the piss out of the other pop acts that the song was supposed to be in competition with."

Pope:

"I knew a little bit about them and I thought they'd be well devoid of humour, y'know, well doomed out. I liked 'A Forest', I liked the drum sound and I remember when I first met Robert at Fiction, I thought 'This can't be the geezer who makes all these doomed out records' because he was such a funny little chappy with hair that all stood up.

"I liked him immediately and we had a good relationship because I think he sort of *feels* film, understands it. They'd had a lot of bad experiences on video so they'd come up with this script but I was given a lot of freedom with it. I remember taking it away, looking at it and thinking 'Fucking hell, this is completely incoherent' so I had to structure it into some kind of feeling. I wasn't entirely successful. Robert was such an odd character, he was really quiet and I remember, as we were filming it in this studio in St John's Wood, I began to push him more and more because he'd never *performed* in a video before. That's where we started to breed and develop that eccentric little character which we now all know and love! On the first take, he was very calm but on the second, I don't know why, I saw him as a clown – funny but also tragic.

"He's a good character, he's got a good face and he's crafty. His lyrics are neat, they always give me ideas. All The Cure videos follow strange little logics.

For 'Let's Go To Bed' it's a huge V. We did 13 takes and, for each one, Robert and Lol changed places until the finale when Lol had to fall out of the top bunk with Robert in the one below. He had to move just at the right moment and they were terrified of mistiming it!"

Robert:

"Pap, as he is known in Cure circles, gave things a highly coloured and stupid side. He made something for the song that really wasn't there. I told him I wanted to look like an idiot so it'd be impossible for anyone to imagine it was us being serious. When I actually saw it though, I wondered if I *really* wanted to look like that. There are a lot of people who *still* haven't grasped the irony."

While he was recording 'Let's Go To Bed', The Banshees came to the studio and asked Robert to rejoin them for their British tour.

Robert:

"I'd slipped back in as part of the set-up during the recording of 'Dreamhouse' and Severin said 'I don't think McGeoch's very well, I don't think he's quite there'. So he asked me to join and I knew I'd be there for as long as I wanted because there were some European dates lined up as well."

'Let's Go To Bed' was released in November and Robert told Record Mirror: 'I don't think it's a Cure song. I wanted it released under a different name like we did with Cult Hero a couple of years ago. It's not that Cure songs are a formula but they do share a central core. This single has been released to get major daytime radio play and it's disappointing to me because it's the first time we've been seen to be involved in current trends or fashions . . . There are probably only a few thousand people who've held us up as an example to themselves but, if I were one of them, I'd feel let down. For us to be seen to be bothering in an arena I don't respect upsets me. When you spend time in a band trying to achieve certain goals, you don't want to betray them . . . For the first time I'm conscious of being seen as someone who could make money. I resent it. At first they respected me for not wanting to write hits, then they saw me as some kind of halfwit and now they're trying to goad me by saying I can't do it anyway. I suppose I've let them get to me with 'Let's Go To Bed' but, as you can see from the video, I don't take the song seriously and that's its saving grace."

***THE CURE 'Let's Go To Bed' (Fiction)** Let's not. Let's drone over a sub-funk backing and talk about the implications of it, eh Rob? Buuuuuut, the insidious timing and uncanny production could well stick this little stocking filler a fair way up the charts.*

Robert later pointed out the flaw in Parry's masterplan to Alternative Tentacles fanzine: "It was an experiment to see if we could write a chart single but, under The Cure banner, it failed two-fold – prejudice against The Cure wouldn't let it sell and fans who bought it would feel betrayed.

As to the state of the band at this time, Robert told Record Mirror he'd "completely lost track of the central core of The Cure . . . There's a lot of things I'd rather do than trek around countries being drunk and playing to drunk people. The last tour was like a re-run of the worst movie you've ever seen. It's as if you're leaning against a wall, eyes closed, and when you come to, you're in the same place you were a year ago. You see your own graffitti up in the dressing rooms and the next band's posters replacing yours as you leave town. We were cracking up so the people offstage began to fall apart as well. Twenty three people reverting to primitives is not a pretty sight; we were more like a rugby tour than a Cure tour . . . ' . . . I began to feel like some doddery old rock 'n' roller who needed a few beers so he could go onstage and turn it on."

Robert saw joining The Banshees as a means of escape – from 'Let's Go To Bed', from The Cure, from responsibility . . .

Robert:

"I don't remember much about the English tour but the atmosphere was good and they were glad to have me back. Bill was pissed off though so I reminded him of his promise – 'Let's Go To Bed' hadn't been a hit and, therefore, I should have been released from my contract. He said it had been a joke and I really started to hate him. He simply didn't want me to stay with The Banshees.

"But I wanted to be with them because I was pissed off with being the vocalist and the leader of the band for so many years. I just wanted to be a guitarist, to see if it was different being in another band, I wanted to see if my experiences were different from theirs.

"Bill didn't understand though and he tried to get me to leave through legal recourse. I got a letter threatening to sue so I rang him back and said if he tried to stop me I'd come round and break his legs.

"He was worried that people would think The Cure no longer existed but I didn't give a fuck – we could always reform. I hated being looked upon as a source of money and being with The Banshees was a reaction against that. I remember Bill said he'd spent five years building up The Cure but what about *me?*

"We hated each other. He thought The Banshees were using me because of my name and that I wanted to be with them to form a supergroup. But a month later, Bill approached me again. And this time he apologised, which surprised me no end."

Parry:

"To start with, Robert was only supposed to do

締 切
CLOSED
日本航空

締 切
CLOSED
日本航空

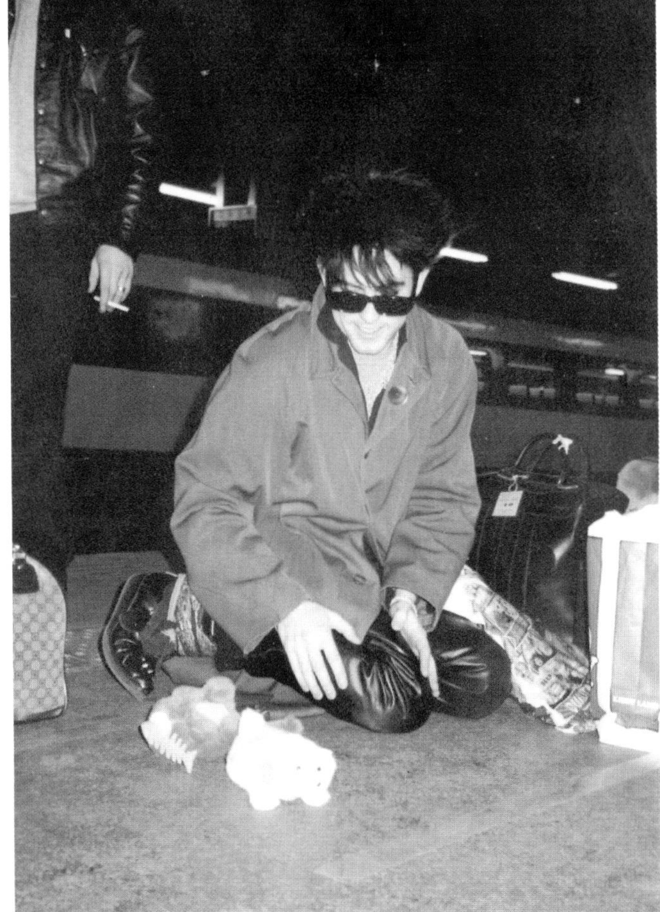

the English tour with The Banshees and then he became a full time member which was stupid – as far as I was concerned, he was going from one dead end to another. I soon stopped blocking Robert but I was determined to make it register."

Lol:

"I knew Robert would go off with The Banshees to get rid of his responsibilities for a time. I also knew that the day would come when he would no longer be able to stand not singing and playing his own songs."

While Robert was on tour, Lol produced And Also The Trees and, on his return, Robert revitalised the Dance Fools Dance label and released a single by Animation.

Robert:

"It was a bit of a disaster. They'd been playing for two years in Crawley and they couldn't get any other gigs. I thought, if they had a record out, people might take them more seriously but it was terrible and they broke up, so I decided my forte wasn't in that side of the record business after all!"

At this stage the press, not surprisingly, were in some confusion over the future of The Cure, especially as Robert told Record Mirror: "Talking about it now is like going back to an old toy or a game whose rules you've forgotten . . . I don't despair about losing touch with The Cure. It's more despairing to realise I'll never reach the heights of a Bach or a Prokofiev."

And he told Melody Maker: "People keep saying 'You mustn't break up because it's become an institution'. That almost gives me the incentive to pack it in anyway. I think it's really awful, just seeing bands disintegrate slowly in a stupid way, don't you?". but, he admitted: "I know it's strange but people are interested in us the way I'm interested in the confusion of other people. I mean, someone can stand up and say 'I believe in God', someone else can say 'I don't believe in God' and someone else can say 'I don't really know' and all three statements are the same. Some people are attracted to belief, some people are attracted to the opposite and some are attracted to the centre, the middle ground which is, I suppose, where we stood – not in relation to religion but in general. I don't know whether we were ever successful in conveying that . . . I never really considered that I've had anything of importance to say to people on record and yet I sometimes underestimate The Cure's achievements . . . We get hundreds of letters from people very concerned about what we've done, it's almost been like a soundtrack to their crises."

During January and February of 1983, Robert toured Australia, New Zealand and Japan with The Banshees and he outlined to Shake magazine his relationship with Siouxsie: "I get on very well with her, which is quite strange because I'm one of the few people who does. I think it's because I don't take her very seriously and it's very novel for her to have someone to tell her to shut up because most people are too scared.". Later, he told NME: "My attitude towards playing with The Banshees is . . . I beat them at pool, they get ratty."

On his return to London, he was approached by Nicholas Dixon, a young choreographer with the Royal Bellet, and asked to write the music for 'Les Enfants Terible'. Robert was intrigued but hesitant so, as a test, he suggested they try out a choreographed Cure song. A spot was offered on BBC 2's Riverside and, with Lol on drums, Severin disguised under a hat on bass and the Venomettes on strings, Robert played 'Siamese Twins' live in the studio while two dancers danced. It was an interesting if not entirely successful experiment, and the ballet project was indefinitely shelved.

That Spring, he told the fanzine Alternatives To Valium: "The Cure as an idea, or as an instinct, has probably finished its useful life . . . It would be a real freak if The Cure had ever had a hit single or ever did hit. 'A Forest' was about the closest – if we'd released it two years later we could have been Tears For Fears!"

Between March and May, Robert and Severin finally brought to fruition a long-nurtured project, The Glove, named after the murder mitten in The Beatles' 'Yellow Submarine' and intended to be an ironic psychedelic pastiche. Ever since the 'Faith' sessions, the two had been trying to find time to work together and now, with Siouxsie and Budgie off pursuing their Creatures project, they went into Britannia Row to demo.

Parry:

"I didn't want Robert to sing on the album because it would have been too like a Cure record and it would have damaged Fiction – someone else would have got the royalties while he was still under contract to me."

After searching and searching for a suitable vocalist, The Glove finally settled on Budgie's girlfriend, Jeanette Landray, a dancer with Zoo who'd appeared as a nurse in a Pink Floyd video. The scene shifted from Britannia Row to Morgan to Trident to The Garden as the pair experimented and pissed about.

Robert:

"We chose Britannia Row out of irony. It was Pink Floyd's studio and the album was psychedelic. It was terrible actually, I was out of my head the whole time – I didn't know where I was or what I was doing. To start with, I lived in an hotel but I couldn't stand the stares from the staff when I came in at 10 o'clock every morning so I went off to stay at Severin's flat where we'd endlessly watch videos like 'Bad Timing' 'Videodrome', 'The Brood', 'Evil Dead', 'Helicopter Spies' and 'Inferno'.

"For four weeks we lived a cultivated madness because we wanted to disorientate ourselves in order to make a good record."

Later, he told Melody Maker: "It was really an attack on the senses . . . We were virtually coming out of the studio at six in the morning . . . and watching all these really mental films and then going to sleep and having these really demented dreams and then, as soon as we woke up at four in the afternoon, we'd go straight back into the studio so it was a bit like a mental assault course by the end . . . We must have watched about 600 videos at the time! There'd be like all these after-images of the films we'd watched cropping up in the songs . . . it sounded like 15 different groups, like a K-Tel compilation album . . .

"The other thing that influenced it was the amount of junk we were reading, the amount we spent on idiot magazines . . . we were making big murals of all these cuttings and pictures and stuff, big Day-Glo posters."

In the same article, Severin said: "The idea that The Glove could get away with anything vanished very quickly because it became a real responsibility to get it to sound not indulgent". Robert told International Musician: "We didn't want it to sound like a self-indulgent album made by two ageing hippies . . . it's light in texture, up-sounding" and he revealed to Shake magazine that they'd watched the videos in slow motion and that one track, 'Sex Eye Make-Up', was typical - inspired by "Bad Timing" and a letter Robert had read from a madman to the queen.

At the time of recording, Robert told Flexipop: "I need a holiday. I keep making plans to go every week but every week I'm in another group!"

Suddenly, in April, The Cure were offered a spot on The Oxford Road Show. The programme's director wanted two songs – 'Let's Go To Bed' and 'Just One Kiss' but, out of sheer perversity and because he wanted people to realise The Cure *did* still exist, Robert elected to play '100 Years' and 'Figurehead'. All he needed was a band.

Parry had a tape of Brilliant and was impressed with the drummer, Andy Anderson, who'd played with Hawkwind among others; he was drafted in along with Derek Thompson of SPK.

Robert:

"It was a real pleasure. I was singing live again for the first time since Simon had left and I realised, then, how much I was missing it."

Parry:

"Whilst watching the replay of the Oxford Road Show with the group, Peter Powell and the BBC Staff, I was filled with an immense joy as at that moment I knew my struggle with Fiction, The Cure, was not to end so lamely."

In May, Robert decided The Cure should record again:

Robert:

"After 'Let's Go To Bed', I wanted to do another dance number but a harder one, more like '100 Years' but, as I knew nothing at all about recording electronic music, I thought we would need a specialist. We chose Steve Nye because I really liked his work on Japan's 'Tin Drum'. We hadn't had a producer as such since Bill on 'Three Imaginary Boys' and, as The Glove had been quite haphazard, I thought it would be good to do something structured, and gorgeous to go in and have someone say to me 'That vocal isn't any good, you'll have to keep doing it'.

"I didn't care if it worked or not – no-one was expecting us to do anything anyway. It was a really funny way of working because we'd never done it before – sitting there, programming things, hearing them back straight away, putting down drum patterns and listening back to them without having to shout at a drummer! It was done quite fast – in under five days – and the actual recording itself was quite boring. But Jam Studios had a good pool table and a pretty garden with tables and chairs where I could write, and I learned a lot of technical things just from watching Steve Nye work."

Lol:

"Our collaboration with Steve Nye worked well apart from the fact that he smoked 60 filterless Gitanes a day."

Parry:

"I didn't want to get involved. I'd done my little bit with 'Let's Go To Bed' so it was passed over completely to Steve Nye and they decided to do a four track, 12 inch which I thought was a good idea. Value for money – very important."

The year before, Robert had told Flexipop: "I've taught myself to remember my dreams and write them all down because they help me write songs" and, sure enough, the EP was heavily dream-inspired. The cover was designed by Porl and Undy from an idea of Robert's – a return after they had refused to do the cover for 'Let's Go To Bed' because they didn't like the song – and the video was directed by Tim Pope.

Pope:

"It was the best thing I'd done by a long way. Something happened where I developed and they developed and we started getting close to Robert's true personality. He suggests ideas – he's pretentious but in a funny way, and he knows it. We improvised a lot and Lol insisted on wearing a dress though I've never quite worked out why to this day. They were standing in this paddling pool and no-one seemed to understand it but I didn't think there was much to understand – it was just a big fucking laugh.

"I like Robert's lyrics because they're like a spider's web, they're made up of clues, they never present things in an obvious way. It's perfect for film-making because every phrase has a corresponding emphasis.

"I remember we filmed against a black background which was pretty rare at the time and, for every take, Robert and Lol would change their make-up – which they did themselves – and their clothes.

Robert:

"I was the only person who thought 'The Walk' would be a hit but, just after we'd finished it, New Order released 'Blue Monday' which had exactly the same overdub set-up and it was so similar in sound, we actually debated whether or not to release it. But we decided it was different enough although, of course, people accused us of plagiarism!"

He told Sounds at the time: "It's nice that it's got in the charts for the sole reason that it'll be heard on the radio. I'm not being big-headed but I think it's better than 90% of what you hear on the radio now" and he informed International Musician: "I didn't expect it to get so high but I'd suspected something was up when my mum liked it. She normally hates any Cure stuff I play her . . . It occurs to me that a lot of idiots must be buying 'The Walk'."

Parry:

"I had the sailing bug and I got the message that it had banged in the charts at number whatever in the Top 20 – 17 or 18 or something – and I felt over the moon. I sailed round to Jersey, ordered the biggest seafood platter I've ever had in my life and ate and drank myself into a stupor. I was really happy - happy for myself and happy for them because I felt we'd actually got over it all, that this was a turning point."

Pope:

"We had this big toy box for Robert to take shirts out of and, as with all my videos, I tried to do it so that the images didn't correspond literally to the lyrics. I always try to make the film and the song work in parallel. In my head, I throw the song in the air and let it rest for a moment in my subconscious.

"Robert's lyrics are pretty esoteric – he follows his own logic and no-one can understand them as well as he does. The ideas of the old woman comes from there, she's around to interpret Robert's lyrics. My cameraman and assistants looked at me as if I was mad when we were shooting 'The Walk' so I knew the video was gonna be good. Oh, and the green stuff that droops around, sticky stuff . . . was all to do with rude things going on in the background . . . I think."

Lol:

"The BBC didn't want to show it because we had make-up on and they thought we were gay!"

'The Walk' was released in July and, astonishingly, went straight into the charts.

THE CURE: 'The Walk' (Fiction)
The poster sleeve folds out to reveal The Cure looking a little green around the gills.
Mind you I'd feel pretty sick if I'd spent all my royalty cheque earnings in an expensive recording studio only to come out with a load of fly blown rubbish like this.

THE CURE 'The Walk' (Fiction)
Robert Smith actually sounds in a fairly good mood here, but I'm sure it's just a silly phase he's going through. In fact the whole song smiles more than usual, bucked up by some beaty electronics.

the cure the walk 7" available in a limited edition
poster bag plus 4 track 12"
Fiction

Robert told the NME: "All the singles we've done are just odd things we've thought of, dumb singles . . . I've had people writing to me that we've sold out for doing that but I don't see it at all. It's still a side of me." and to Sounds he confessed: "I've been having really good mental dreams . . . I can't wait to get back at night. I write them down in the morning. Maybe I could do a dream album or something . . . "

While 'The Walk' was doing its business, Robert was also recording with The Banshees, appearing on Riverside with The Glove playing 'Punish Me With Kisses' and twice undergoing the ritual of Top Of The Pops.

For their first appearance, Andy Anderson drummed and Porl, who'd been around the studio, mimed bass in shades but he couldn't make the second show so, as Lol had bumped into Phil Thornalley again while The Cure were making 'The Walk' video, he was asked to stand in.

Robert had also been offered the headline spot at Elephant Fayre, an outdoor festival in St Germains, Cornwall and, after consulting The Banshees who'd played there the year before, he accepted because he was beginning to realise the convenience of having a working band on stand by. Both Phil and Andy stayed put and The Cure played the gig as a fourpiece.

Phil:

"I was happy to get out of the studio and, to be honest, I thought after 'Pornography' that they'd call on my services again. But they did the two singles

without me so, when Lol asked, I said 'I'm your man'.

"We played two warm up dates – one in Bournemouth and one in Bath and we'd only been rehearsing for a week so they were horrible. I was playing the wrong basslines, Andy was playing the wrong drums but, strangely enough, it didn't seem to annoy Robert at all."

Robert:

"I remember this tiny little club with the audience only a yard away. Our equipment wouldn't fit in the room and I sang louder than the PA . . . it was so small, I didn't even need a microphone."

A week after Elephant Fayre, the NME quoted Robert as saying: "People came up after we played and said 'Oh, it was really enjoyable' but I didn't want it to be. It was so nostalgic, all those songs we played. Somehow I feel I've compromised it, this big leap between 'Pornography' and what we do next, by allowing us to play live. I've recognised the history of The Cure again. And then by the end of the set, I felt I wanted to do them over but properly. God knows what it'll be like in America, probably awful."

Four months later, though, he told Zig Zag: "It was something of an obligation to play all the old songs but that was the whole reason for doing it. I just wanted to play those songs just once more; it's probably the last time we'll play most of them. We knew that was the case when we played the Elephant Fayre so it gave an added poignancy to the performance – like the end of an era for us I suppose."

SCREAMING UNDER THE STARS

THE CURE

Elephant Fayre, St Germans, Cornwall

A FEW months back, if anyone had been laying odds on a Summer artistic renaissance, The Cure surely wouldn't even have figured in the reckoning. What with Robert Smith off doing his bit as a part-time Banshee and collaborating with Severin under the banner of The Glove, Lol Tolhurst denouncing his drum kit and starting on keyboards from scratch, Simon Gallup quitting altogether, no live action for nearly 14 months and the last single, "Let's Go To Bed", proving a half-hearted and unsuccessful disappointment, The Cure were, to all intents and purposes, widely considered a lost cause.

Strange, then, that when or if July '83 is at all remembered popwise, two peaks will belong to The Cure. The first, a fragile, hallucinating shock hit single called "The Walk", acts as a timely reminder that, even off-beam, Smith still figures among our acutest sensory autobiographers, vividly imparting his brooding introversion with all the organised passion of Ian McCulloch and some of the clipped authority of Siouxsie.

The second, last weekend's retrospective at the Elephant Fayre, was testament that not only does the spirit of The Cure still exist despite (or because of?) its creators' extra-curricular activities, but that, in the risky corporate decision to ration its action, The Cure positively *thrives*.

The Elephant Fayre, no matter what anybody feared beforehand, was not some Philistine promotional cash-in by a hastily concocted line-up. Far from it. After two warm-up (sweat out!) club dates, this temporary Cure functioned inspirationally, often on adrenalin alone, and achieved what few gigs on the last Cure tour managed – to convince the crowd that Smith's obsessions are worth investigation.

Still scarred, but recovered from the sapping monotony of that last tour (which, incidentally, very nearly *did* scupper The Cure), Smith responded energetically to the challenge of coaxing and cajoling a novice band through a set of songs obviously sacred to the thousands of spellbound Cure fans who'd made the trek south west. More animated and eagerly expressive than most of us can ever remember, Smith flirted with disaster and came through smiling.

Without trotting out the usual platitudes about performing on the edge evincing more stimulation than strict rehearsal, it's true that this experimental Cure was the most eloquent ever. Andy Anderson is a magnificently muscular and sensitive drummer, producer Phil Thornally is a nervy bassist revelling in the opportunity to indulge in a little exhibitionism, and Lol is still a basic keyboard operator, stripping "The Drowning Man" and "At Night" down to their bare, painful essentials.

Screaming there, in a field under the stars, The Cure treated the Elephant Fayre to a set that evolved from tension through realisation to exasperated ecstacy – "In Your House", near the start, was furtive and taut with caution completely complementary to the song's frozen fright; "Primary" and "Three Imaginary Boys" were looser excuses to stretch out and test their new rhythmic possibilities and, when they hit "100 Years", they were beginning to believe that the telepathic mayhem that finally overcame the encores was well within their grasp.

From something old sprang something new, and although there was no attempt to introduce new numbers or premier clues as to where The Cure might go from here, it was a show of strength with the power of trance; a dominant blue fused from a doubtful grey.

For one marvellous, all-too-brief midnight, The Cure were back and, thanks to the Fayre (easily Britain's best true "event"), we need no longer worry; they've assured us there's a Cure present and all the signs are that The Cure future will be well worth the wait.

● STEVE SUTHERLAND

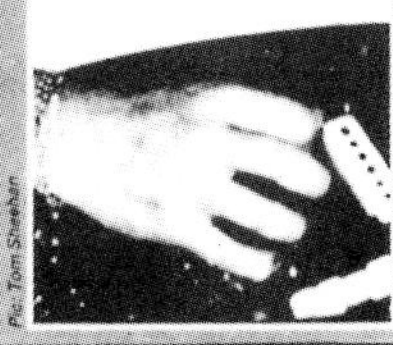

Pic: Tom Sheehan

In August the band played a short tour of America and then flew to France where they recorded the next single in the Studio Des Dames, Paris.
Parry:

"It was probably the best recording session anyone ever had in the whole world. The studio was in the most dodgy area of Paris, but the restaurant next door did great food which they arranged to come in on a platter. The studio was owned by Polydor and run by the son of the head man and he had every possible video that was ever made. It was perfect. It was champagne time, it was girlfriend time, fun time, party time.

"I remember it was so good that I took the multi-track back to London with me. I cuddled it all the way home."
Robert:

"The idea for 'Lovecats' came from The Aristocats. I knew all the words by heart, I even bought the film, and I was completely obsessed . . ."
Parry:

"We mixed it at RAK and Robert wasn't happy with the horn sound so I went to Genetic and got this brass player who, even to this day, Smith maintains doesn't exist because, y'know, at Martin Rushent's studio they can synthesise anything. But it was true, he played and it was really good, multi-tracked, mixed down and I sent it to Robert who was busy with The Banshees or whatever he was doing."

Robert loved the track but loathed the electronic double-tracking on his vocal so Parry drove him back out to Genetic where the engineer, Dave 'Dirk' Allen, removed it. Allen was young and fresh and Robert liked him immediately.
Robert:

"He took sides with me against Bill – always a good sign!"
Allen:

"Before I met Robert, I thought The Cure were y'know, really boring and depressed, like their music, but they turned out to be quite the opposite."

Tim Pope, again, shot the video.
Pope:

"As usual I had two days notice – not like everyone else who gives you a month – so I met up with Robert and he had his say and I went away and came back again and had my say and he sat there with a meaningful look on his face, nodding, the dimple in his chin tightening, looking like he knew what I was talking about. Then he had his say again and I nodded and looked like I knew what he was talking about and everything just came together on the day."
Robert:

"Good night that. We told this estate agent we were thinking of buying this house in Hampstead, got the keys took the whole film crew in, shot the video and took the keys back first thing next morning."
Pope:

"The Estate Agent? Such a sweet little story, I wouldn't want to argue with it."
Robert:

"We invited lots of people and had a party. I did all the close-ups first and, by the time we came round to doing the group sequences at about four in the morning, everyone was totally out of their heads."
Lol:

"We had about 30 cats altogether and they wouldn't do anything we wanted them to. There was loads of cat food in strategic places to encourage them into the shot but they hated the stuffed cats so they all ran away."
Pope:

"It's not my favourite video because I think it's a bit *too* easy to like. Maybe I went a bit far but the song's kinda playful anyway. Robert's image – sort of delirious – worried him a bit but I like the way his personality develops from 'Let's Go To Bed', through 'The Walk' to 'Lovecats' . . . he was coming more and more out of himself. My way of working is very close to the way Robert works in the studio – y'know, he knows the feeling of a song, he knows its structure but he doesn't know all the details in advance."
Lol:

"I terrified an old Rastafarian at about six in the morning. He was walking along the road and I came out of nowhere in a cat suit. He must have thought he'd had too much 'erb!"
Pope:

"That's true about Lol in the catsuit and the ganga-ed out Rasta, Lol always gets those roles. Robert told me, in the 'Hanging Garden' video, it was about seven in the morning, really cold, and the director came on and said 'Right, who's gonna wear the animal suit?' and everyone said 'Lol!' There's such a theme of persecution in their videos it's untrue!"

In mid August, The Glove's single, 'Like An Animal', was released. Written around a story in an American newspaper, it focussed on the claustrophobic madness of a woman who lived in a tower block and started dropping small things on peoples' heads below until she finally snapped and lobbed out her washing machine.

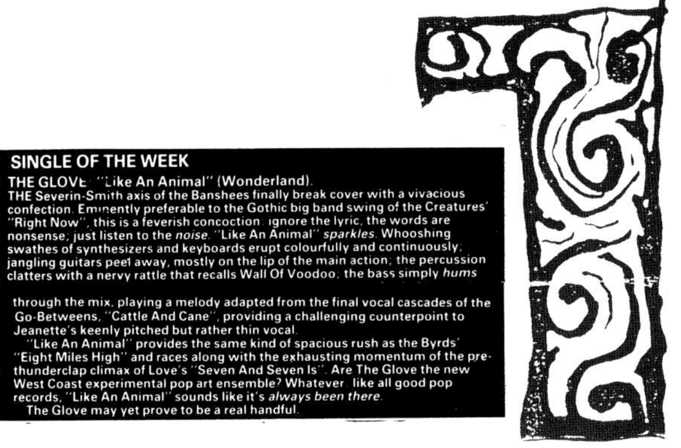

SINGLE OF THE WEEK

THE GLOVE: "Like An Animal" (Wonderland).

THE Severin-Smith axis of the Banshees finally break cover with a vivacious confection. Eminently preferable to the Gothic big band swing of the Creatures' "Right Now", this is a feverish concoction: ignore the lyric, the words are nonsense; just listen to the *noise*. "Like An Animal" *sparkles*. Whooshing swathes of synthesizers and keyboards erupt colourfully and continuously; jangling guitars peel away, mostly on the lip of the main action; the percussion clatters with a nervy rattle that recalls Wall Of Voodoo; the bass simply *hums* through the mix, playing a melody adapted from the final vocal cascades of the Go-Betweens, "Cattle And Cane", providing a challenging counterpoint to Jeanette's keenly pitched but rather thin vocal.

"Like An Animal" provides the same kind of spacious rush as the Byrds' "Eight Miles High" and races along with the exhausting momentum of the pre-thunderclap climax of Love's "Seven And Seven Is". Are The Glove the new West Coast experimental pop art ensemble? Whatever: like all good pop records, "Like An Animal" sounds like it's *always been there*.

The Glove may yet prove to be a real handful.

In September, Robert played in Rome with The Banshees before the entourage moved on to Venice where Tim Pope joined them to shoot the video for 'Dear Prudence', a Mansonised version of the old Beatles' song and Robert's first recording as a Banshee.

Pope:

"For some reason I never gelled with The Banshees like I did with The Cure – I don't know why. It was really weird when Smithy turned up with them because it was like working with a bit of The Cure and a bit of The Creatures, who I'd also worked well with so it was interesting but somehow unsuccessful.

"I remember we went out to this disco owned by the richest gondolier in Venice or something, Sioux and Budgie were having an argument, Smithy was up on the dancefloor singing along to ABBA songs and everyone got really pissed. I left with Robert and Severin, just walking the streets, and they wanted to set fire to some flag. Then, I remember, they wanted to set fire to me! They chased me through Saint Mark's Square and, y'know, I'd always thought of Robert as quite a quiet little chappy and suddenly he let out this scream like I'll never forget and, right out of the blue, he threw this bottle of beer at this huge plate glass window.

"The noise was terrifying and we fled. That's when I realised there was something odd lurking within the Smith persona, something completely mad. It was understandable, I think, because one week he'd be with The Banshees and the next he'd be with The Cure, one week introverted, one week in charge . . ."

The Banshees moved on to play in Israel.

Robert:

"It was very peculiar there – I sort of liked it and I hated it. I remember hiring a big old American car and driving The Banshees to the Dead Sea. I lost my shoes there – I think I was drunk . . . all I remember is this shoal of flying fish . . ."

On this tour Robert started writing for the next Cure album and cracks began to appear in his relationship with The Banshees. They'd been trying to record on and off now, for months, Robert attending when his Cure commitments would allow. In Italy, the posters read 'Siouxsie & The Banshees With Robert Smith' and it was irritatingly obvious to all involved that Robert's loyalties were becoming strained.

In September, The Glove's 'Blue Sunshine' album was released – named after a B Movie neither Robert nor Severin had seen about a particular batch of acid that causes homicidal madness in those who've taken it exactly a decade after their trip.

INCURABLE

I refer to Richard Cook's interview with Robert Smith. In it he describes The Cure's 'Pornography' as "Devoid of any rhythmic impetus, chained to drumbeats and guitar lines of spiritless presence, it was The Cure smashing into the buffers of a dead stop, almost terrifying in its emptiness, impenetrable and virtually unlistenable". Couldn't he have just said he thought it was crap?

John Brown, Edinburgh.

Richard, being freelance, gets paid by the word. Pithiness

Robert:

"The Glove was always aimed at Japan actually. We'd really liked it there when we went with The Banshees so we decided we'd be this mysterious Western group and do this short disco tour of Japan with Lol as the support act but it didn't come to anything. I don't think Polydor even released the album in Japan!"

Two weeks later, 'Dear Prudence' was released and quickly became The Banshees' biggest ever hit, peaking at number three in the British singles charts.

SHOULDERS

SIOUXSIE & THE BANSHEES: Dear Prudence *(Wonderland/ Polydor)* A beautiful sleeve and a less than astonishing cover. As Siouxsie's pop standing dissolves from light to dark and back again the records of her group are getting fogged and indecisive. Whirlybird guitars and even some nostalgic phasing scarcely paper over a cracking and underfed treatment of a dried-out chestnut. And it goes on, and on. What will they do next – "The Continuing Story Of Bungalow Bill"?

On 30 September and 1st October, The Banshees played The Royal Albert Hall. Both shows were videoed and recorded.

Talking to International Musician, Robert revealed: "Over the four years The Cure have worked with Fiction and Polydor, they've realised that, the more they pressure us to do something, the less likely it is that it'll get done. They've learned to tolerate me like an awkward but inexpensive halfwit in the corner. The fact that we've never been in debt to a record company has allowed us a great deal more freedom than most bands . . .

"I've never seen The Cure as a career. It can't progress consciously – it could just as easily stop as keep going for years. It doesn't worry me, I don't plan . . . at the moment I'm involved in so many things because I get sick of being tied down to one area, to one set-up. The only disadvantage of doing so much is that it's not allowing me as much free time as I used to have to do things away from music. It's difficult to disappear – I haven't had a day off for about three months now and it's really getting to me."

On his relationship with The Banshees, he said: "A lot of the time I'm still trying to play John McGeoch's guitar parts and failing . . . If I went on like this for another few months . . . um . . . I'd be the next one to have a breakdown. No, it's fine at the moment. It's a balancing act, and as long as I don't fall over, it'll be alright . . . "

In late October, 'Lovecats'/'Speak My Language' was released in another Porl sleeve and Robert claimed in No1, it would be the last of the fantasy trilogy: "'Pornography', took you to the edge of the cliff, the next one will plunge you over it."

THE CURE: "Love Cats" (Fiction)

AS if some macabre folly cast Vincent Price instead of Jeremy Irons in "Brideshead Revisited", or some sinister senility chose Tobe Hooper to direct a series of Jeeves, "Love Cats" is a post-modernist's dream of a nightmare, a purrrfectly corny example of the past purrrceived impurrrfectly, the flaw maliciously irritated and then put to use. In this purposeful madness, the last of The Cure's "fun"-single trilogy, Robert Smith's imagination is squirming proof that, though TV, radio and most especially video, the past now plays as active a part in the present as the present itself, revitalised through easily available images, ravaged out of its rituals and roles and reinterpreted as a malleable source of fractured associations.

"Love Cats" is Smith's masterpiece of disorientation, a mental collage of history unhinged. Herman Munster takes spiked tea with Jean Cocteau while a taxidermist twitches the net curtains in anticipation of a cannibal feast. But how to praise something so zany? How to approach its kaleidoscopic approaches? Well, at a pinch its psychedelic cocktail jazz, a strychnined nursery rhyme where every allusion (illusion!) triggers off a tunnel of flashbacks, but it's so much sillier than that.

Sing the slap-dash chorus, swoon to that devil-may-care decadent swing. Single of the week? Single of the year(s)!

During the next month, Robert forgot the words to 'Lovecats' on Top Of The Pops, the band started wearing crumpled grey suits, the single entered the top ten and Smash Hits were informed "Being alive is quite nice at the moment."

The Glove's second single, 'Punish Me With Kisses' was also released, closely followed by 'Nocturne', a double album and video of The Banshees' Albert Hall concerts boasting "No overdubs" on the LP's gatefold cover.

Robert:

"I didn't think 'Nocturne' was as bad as everyone thought at the time. I didn't so much go for the video but the live album would have made a good single LP. I don't think The Banshees really knew what they were doing at the time and I don't think I had any clear idea of what they wanted me to do."

Just before Christmas, 'Japanese Whispers' was released, a compilation of all the fantasy singles and B-sides. Initially it was only intended for the Japanese and German markets but, as Lol puts it, "the record company got greedy."

PURR-GATORY

THE CURE

Japanese Whispers: The Cure Singles Nov 82: Nov 83 *(Fiction)*

Hamm; "*Can there be misery–(he yawns)–loftier than mine? No doubt. Formerly. But now?*" (From *Endgame*, a play by Samuel Beckett.)

LET'S FACE it: some folks can make a profession out of misery. Robert Smith is one such. Mean-voiced, sombre-mooded, and balanced on the knife edge of both post-punkish (fashionable) nihilism and mass popularity, I like The Cure for the contradictioins they embody, but loathe them for the vision of the world they depict.

Pop meets gloom in The Cure, and I'm on pop's side, 'cos this collection of singles shows them seemingly to wallow in being underground when any old fool could tell them that there isn't any underground, or subculture or whathaveyou, worth being in anymore. (Or, at least, not one that spans the whole gamut of human experience from Neasden Comp to Eton and back again, like punk did.)

They are reaching out for bigger gestures than they can make on their own, but not realising how hollow they sound. Smith's hazy mixture of lyrics claim the world (apocalyptic imagery and the lot) but haven't got anywhere to put their frustration, anger and the sense of futile desire; so they turn in on themselves and burn all their anguish out in visions of failed relationships, duff forms of communication ('Speak My Language') and sombre nightmare versions of power used against loved ones.

This is what I hate about The Cure, because they don't seem able to see that all they are mourning is the wrong placing of a set of ideals into a sphere that cannot possibly fulfill them. They are the hollow men, but they don't seem to know it. And they depict women as if they are to blame for what is wrong with their worlds.

But I like The Cure for the gaudy terseness of their tunes. Those parts of their music hold all the emotionality, wistfulness and drive that all the post-punk underground-homelessness denies. I like them when they aren't trying to make big claims, but settle for the nuances of mood and subtleties of attraction that lurk in any one particular relationship.

The Cure are the *angst*-ridden *doppelgangers* of the pretty boys of pop. They seem to be able to externalise everything and feel very little of it. They need a cause. Perhaps '84 will give them one.

Amanda Root

The sleeve, replete with Christmas angels, was Robert's own design. Sounds' Bill Black informed the public "Beware! All the signs are that Smith intends to return to the plodding ground of past work the next album so get happy while you can" and Robert told Smash Hits: "I think it'll be really odd if we do something serious. People will think it's really morbid and they'll go 'Oh, this is a bit of a change for The Cure. I thought they were a pop group.'"

Asked how some of the older Cure fans had reacted to the singles, Smith replied: "Some feel cheated, I really detest them. It's like we're their pet band and how dare I tamper with our mysterious image . . . I never asked for blind devotion . . . I resent it because they're trying to shrink me into a one-facetted person who's only allowed to produce one style of music. That's another reason why I wanted to do something totally stupid and off the wall."

He also told Zig Zag: "It's more exciting to be in The Cure now than it's ever been. There's less pressure because we can now use it when we want to. There's less risk of becoming complacent than ever. The Cure don't *have* to make records ever again."

On the special Christmas edition of Top Of The Pops, Robert appeared with both The Cure and The Banshees. The Evening Standard reported he was "Of no fixed abode", desperate for a place of his own but with no time to look and he told them "I wouldn't like to have children. I would hate to impose life on somebody else" while Zig Zag had him claiming "I don't think I'll feel young again maybe that's what the songs are about."

During the Spring of 1984, Robert continued his schizophrenic existence, working simultaneously on The Banshees' album, 'Hyaena', The Cure album 'The Top', and Tim Pope's single 'I Want To Be A Tree'.

Robert:

"We'd started 'Hyaena' about 10 or 11 months before and, in that time, The Cure had done 'The Walk', 'Lovecats', released 'Japanese Whispers', made three or four videos, played the Elephant Fayre, gone to America and recorded most of 'The Top'. The Banshees just seemed to be getting slower and slower and, although they often blamed me for not being there, I knew it wasn't all my fault.

"It was so frustrating. I'd turn up and they'd all go out for an Indian and leave me alone in the studio with Hedges saying 'Right, you've got three hours. When we come back, we want to hear a guitar part' and I thought 'This isn't what I wanted to join The Banshees for – it's really stupid'. So they'd come back and I'd be sitting there, drunk, refusing to work. It was a hopeless situation because they said 'Well, you should be here all the time then' and they did have a point.

"It dragged on and on, being recorded in spare moments. At the beginning, everyone had three or four ideas for songs but they were exhausted pretty quickly so I found myself doing guitar for a song where I didn't know the title or the lyrics and Siouxsie didn't like it anyway, saying that it wouldn't go with the words she couldn't give me because they weren't finished yet!

"I suddenly wondered what the fuck I was doing there. No-one knew what was going on."

Severin:

"Robert was torn between 'Hyaena' and the hits he was having. He was always late arriving at the studio and he kept having to go off with The Cure. We tried to carry on but it was very frustrating."

Robert:

"I had to finish 'Hyaena' because I wanted to stay friends with Severin. Of the 10 songs finally chosen, four are good and six are boring. I thought the album would be a hybrid of 'The Scream' and 'A Kiss In The Dreamhouse', I wanted it to be really hard but, obviously, the others didn't see it the same way. I didn't mind – I'd lost interest in it really, it had become a really grinding process and it was beginning to wear me down. The funny thing is, I was only in The Banshees to get away from all that – I thought it was going to be really vibrant. I could understand their irritation with me not being there all the time but I got a bit fed up with their dismissive attitude towards what I was doing with The Cure.

'The Top' was being recorded at Garden Studios, Trident and Genetic with Dirk engineering vocals and guitars and mixing and Howard Grey doing drums, bass and additional guitars. Robert played and composed all the basslines himself because Thornalley was off in Australia engineering Duran Duran's long-winded 'Seven And The Ragged Tiger' LP. The session soon assumed a familiar pattern.

Lol:

"Pub, studio, bye-byes. We never stopped drinking."

Allen:

"I think I convinced them I knew what I was doing. I was pissed off with working with electronic music so it was a good experience, recording without restraint."

Robert:

"We were living in a village pub near Genetic which meant we'd work all night and arrive at the pub at 10.30 in the morning, sit there, have lunch, sleep in the afternoon, get up about 7.30, have a bar meal, drink sixty pints of beer, take some drugs and then work all night again. That took its toll on everyone and a strange lethargy came across in some of the songs.

"I'd written most of the words while I was with The Banshees because I had nothing to do while Siouxsie and Severin were doing interviews. I just spent a lot of time on my own, writing and walking about. I didn't have access to any instruments and that was probably good because it meant it was all saved up inside of me.

"But as soon as 'The Top' was finished, I wanted bits of it to be different; but it was too late to re-record it because I was working to such absurd deadlines to keep The Banshees thing going as well. I'd never really had that before – an album always took as long as it took to make it good but this time it had to be finished by a certain date and I was going back, stealing odd days out to overdub things thinking 'God, this ought to be faster' or 'that drum shouldn't sound like this'. It's not that I was unhappy with it all, it's just that I could see the flaws."

Pope:

"Dave Allen told me 'The Top' was terrifying. Robert got really obsessive and it sounds like that on the record."

Although hamstrung by writing and playing most of the material himself without the benefit of a real band set-up to bounce ideas off, Robert liberated himself lyrically and vocally on 'The Top'. 'Shake Dog Shake' was aggressive and brooding, "about me during The Banshees tour", 'Bird Mad Girl' was about "a mentally ill girl" and 'Wailing Wall' was obviously influenced by his visit to Israel: "I went to Jerusalem and I lost my shoes. The roads were dirty . . . it was revolting . . . but the wailing wall itself was brilliant . . . the most beautiful noise I've ever heard . . . total religious insanity."

'Give Me It' was written for The Glove and based, partly, on Nicholas Roeg's film 'Bad Timing'.

Porl:

"I was going into the studio, showing them how the cover was coming along and one evening Robert asked me to play sax on 'Give Me It'. Then he asked me to stay for the tour. No-one ever said to me 'Come back' but, little by little, our relationship became more open and I stayed."

Robert:

"I realised there'd need to be five of us on stage in order to play the songs. I couldn't play all the guitars, Lol couldn't do all the synths and Porl could do both."

'Dressing Up' dealt with Robert's feelings before he went on stage while 'Piggy In The Mirror' was a throwback to 'Pornography'. 'The Empty World' was, Robert says, about 'Charlotte Sometimes' and Simon, "how proud they both were", 'Bananafishbones' came from a Salinger short story and 'The Top' itself was a mosaic of seemingly unrelated influences.

Between recording commitments, Robert found time for an exhausting and increasingly strained tour of Australia with The Banshees.

Robert:

"I'd never really got on with Dave Woods, their manager. We didn't appreciate one another. He thought I should have left The Cure for The Banshees because, for him, they were the most important band in the world. This attitude annoyed me and it wasn't a very happy tour."

In March, The Banshees released 'Swimming Horses' and The Cure released 'Caterpillar'/'Happy The Man'/'Throw Your Foot' (the latter track on 12 inch only).

Robert:

"I thought 'Swimming Horses' was the wrong choice for a single. I thought 'Caterpillar' was much better and I used to say so – very contentious as you can imagine."

In a Banshees interview in Record Mirror at the time, Siouxsaid "Fat Boy Smith is nothing to do with the new album except that he actually plays on it" and Severin added "He's off making another space opera with The Cure". Both, the writer noted, were laughing.

Tim Pope was responsible for the 'Swimming Horses' video.

Severin:

"The basic idea was to use the three males as a screen onto which a swimming horse could be projected but it didn't work very well. As with everything at this time, it was done in too much of a rush."

Pope:

"It's a failure as a video. The only funny thing in it is Robert in his wide white shirt."

'Caterpillar', a track to appear later on 'The Top' was to prove the more successful of the two singles with a better, brighter video.

THE CURE 'The Caterpillar' (Fiction)

Smith? . . . impossible. After the pastiche of 'Love Cats', a record so gorked on the cream of its own smugness it made motorists accelerate at any passing feline whenever it came on the car radio, the Cure scrape some new-found claws all over the vacant face of pop and out flows a truly distinctive alternative. A highly viable one as well.

This song does everything wrong commercially and because of it sounds completely right. Acoustic guitars, violins, and a superpretentious lyric bursting with the kind of colour references which only spring from the use of illegals, all on a voyage into the human zoo.

Brilliant.

THE CURE: "The Caterpiller" (Fiction).

AFTER the surprise and much deserved success of "Love Cats", Tolhurst and Smith relax their grip on commerciality. "The Caterpillar" sees The Cure re-treading their steps into quirky pop territory, and despite the joyful sing-along riff after the squeaky violin intro, the song simply isn't strong enough or catchy enough to convince in chart terms.

Beautifully constructed, it's still a smashing record with folky guitars, prodding bass and delicately presented vocals to tempt you.

THE CURE: Cool for caterpillars

Pope:

"Another video where they gave me a days' notice. We wanted butterflies but, at that time of year, they haven't hatched yet so we had to settle for caterpillars – a typical cock-up. It's not the best video I've done, not that much fun but I remember they did a massive wind-up on one of the crew that day, something about a big pile of vim . . . "

In March, Robert toured Europe with The Banshees, returning just in time for The Cure to play The Oxford Roadshow with a mate of Howard Grey, Norman Fisher Jones of The Umbrella, on bass. While Robert was away, Lol produced And Also The Trees 'The Secret Sea' and Baroque Bordello's 'Today'.

Between 24 April and 10 May, The Cure toured Britain with Andy Anderson on drums, Lol on keyboards, Phil Thornalley back on bass and Porl playing sax, guitar and additional keyboards. Robert admitted to No1 at the time that, prior to the tour, he'd cracked up and spent several days in bed and that "Sometimes I feel like I'm in a computer adventure game with all these people moving me around on a giant chessboard . . . I prefer commitments that are left unsaid. That's why I'm glad that The Cure aren't a proper group anymore. You see, I feel responsible for everything that happens to The Cure and, at the moment, that's just me. If it was a group then I'd feel very responsible and, at the moment, I can feel very irresponsible."

Early in May, The Banshees released 'Dazzle' off 'Hyaena' as a single and Smash Hits' Ian Cranna called it "An absolutely titanic meeting of the Onedin Line and Sixties wall of sound". Meanwhile 'The Top' was also released, Robert informing Melody Maker that "Writing it was like starting again, like writing 'Three Imaginary Boys'. I did loads of stuff, *loads*, lots of nonsense and worked from that. There was so much it might have gone anywhere."

TOPSY-TURVY

THE CURE

THE TOP

Fiction FIXS 9

TRYING to get to the bottom of "The Top" is a bit like trying to decide whether a happy lunatic would be better off sane. It's silly and sinister, like Syd Barrett. It's selfish, irresponsible, perfectly amoral and completely incompatible with anything else happening now or, indeed, anything that's probably ever happened. It's playing practical jokes where the victim dies. It's Vincent Price in "Theatre Of Blood" – plotting, delighting to saw the head off another nice song.

In a way it's as carefree and cocky as the Beatles' "White Album" album but it never sounds wilfully disorganised. Its logic is strict, just unhinged that's all. We shudder but sympathise, giggling.

"The Top" is psychedelia that can't be dated, the sounds and shapes of somebody revelling in an identity crisis. It's a pose on purpose, as preposterous as it wants to be. There's no way I could criticise it even if I wanted to because it didn't set out to do or prove anything so it couldn't fall short, now could it? It recognises no values but its own existence; no rules, no precedents, no preconceptions, nothing. "The Top" is perfect freedom.

I've yet to meet anyone who can tell me why The Cure are having hits just now of all times – it's one of those brilliant things that confounds all those theories about only clones of clones surviving. Have we discovered something in Smith's busy lethargy (two bands and still dreaming all day!), and if so, in heaven's name what? Or has Smith uncovered some twitching nerve near our funny bone that reacts instinctively to his whimsical tortures? Whatever's going on, Smith's kept his sulk to himself and done what all the Wellers have been bleating on about; he's escaped his past and wriggled out of the cul-de-sac that we knew and loved to death as The Cure. He's stomached the violent monotony of the wretched "Pornography" and thrown it all up. He doesn't care what we think anymore – he's not the guitar hero in black with a head stuffed with Camus but he could be next Wednesday if he felt like it. He just doesn't give two hoots, he howls when he wants to.

There's not a straightjacket designed by the critical canon that could restrain "The Top". It could be a joke or anything. Smith's voice is all over the place, play-acting mock passionate, whining, daft as Steve Harley, devious as Devoto. Where his head's at's something else. Most of the lyrics on "The Top" – "Dust my lemon lies" . . . "Oh I should feel like a polar bear" . . . "Shapes in the drink like Christ" – sound like video cues to egg on Tim Pope to weirder excesses. They circle their subjects like vultures, swooping to peck at some sense, squabbling over morsels, then fluttering away again, glutted with their own being. Every line on "The Top" is a song in itself.

Could it be drugs? "The Wailing Wall" could be an acid trip in Israel. Could it be The Banshees? "The Top" itself worms around similar tunnels. Could Smith be a hippy? "Dressing Up" is a gorgeous acoustic ditty yawning and stretching like vintage String Band. Could it be cunning? Oh, very. Just as "Love Cats" teased cocktail jazz like a cat with a moth, so there are clues in "The Top" of Smith's inspiration. The flutey feedback of "Wailing Wall" is Hendrix's "If Six Were Nine", the "Give Me It" vocals echo Nick Cave's "Mutiny In Heaven". Smith's a great taxidermist.

Still, attempting to account for "The Top" is like trying to account for someone's dreams; you add up all the reactions and reasons and there's still something missing. The more I think about it, the more I reckon either Smith's gone mad or we have. Maybe both? Who knows? Who cares? Love it!

● STEVE SUTHERLAND

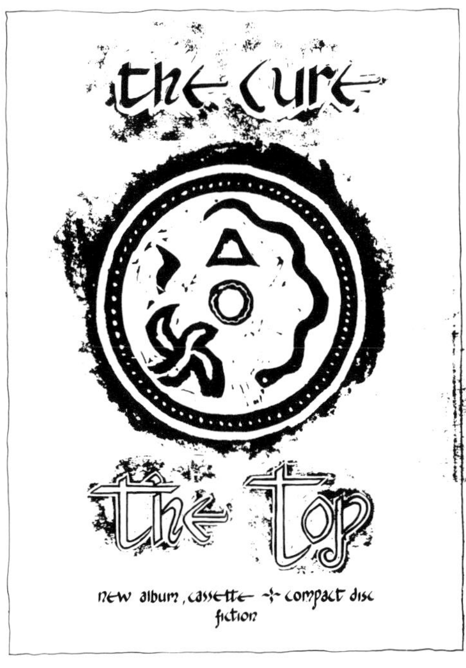

TOPSPIN FALLS FLAT

'The Top' will test the patience of all but the most resilient Curist. If it has any value it's only as a vivid illustration of the ease with which even the flagship bands of the cleansing turmoil of the late '70s can slide into the same miasma of self indulgence that nurtured the sickness we thought had been purged forever. In this case, the Cure is as painful as the disease.

Danny Kelly.

The tour culminated with a gig in Oxford followed by three nights at Hammersmith Odeon, all recorded on the Manor mobile. To co-incide, the NME ran a piece entitled "Top Cat – He's An Intellectual" in which Mat Snow described Robert as "Only a mite overweight . . . stuffed into his suit (black, natch), leaving a fully buttoned-up white shirt billowing down untucked. He seems ill at ease with his body, jamming hands into pockets for want of a more graceful move. A smile of exquisite inscrutability plays on his placid features – more, one feels, out of shyness than smugness. That great pale face is framed by an excruciatingly teased and back-combed mass of big hair, lending him not so much the aspect of Nick Cave as of an old and comfortable Persian cat. Yet his is no feline lope – more a sort of pigeon-toed, floating shuffle; trailing perhaps just a hint of scent in his wake. And, like a moggy replete with Whiskas, Robert's long pink tongue is in the habit of licking his empurpled lips.

"I was determined to take the puss and so asked him if being a cat appealed. ' It does, yeah, but just because they seem to do very little except make little funny noises, and fuck, and eat, and sleep . . . "

Robert described his state of mind as "Happy but very muddled. I don't think it'll last – I just think I'm going through a mid-life crisis . . . The point where I stop working in contemporary music at all, I think, becomes increasingly close. In fact, it's very close . . . I just don't want to have bits of me falling off in public. I don't want to do it in front of cameras."

But, theoretically, he argued The Cure could go on forever: "I never adhered to the philosophy of the dinosaur, I never accepted the fact that a group or a person could only have a limited timespan . . . You can't run out of things to say unless you can put yourself up as saying anything in the first place, and I've never claimed to be saying anything".

Snow considered Robert a *fan* of post punk music too impressionable to grow beyond *wearing* influences to *assimilating* them. And Robert considered the interview with Snow "The most boring hour of my life."

HAMMERSMITH

Mick Brown

The Cure

THE CHART success recently enjoyed by the Cure, under the guidance of Robert Smith, flatters to deceive. Love Cats and particularly The Caterpillar illuminated a group that has always seemed predominantly sombre with flashes of quirky, individualistic humour. Both records toy with unusual musical idioms — hep-jazz and a sort of inebriated folk music. The Caterpillar put one in mind of a pixillated Incredible String Band; both are wildly atypical of what the Cure are actually about.

The Cure's audience — more knowing — come dressed in black. And so does the group: Smith's white mascara, gallows smile, dark shrouds, and crucifix suggest the possibility of unholy inquisition followed by a perfunctory reading of the last rites. And certainly you leave the concert feeling closer to death than when you went in

This is a performance built on fastidious perfectionism; the lighting is starkly effective; the use of film on a screen behind the stage hauntingly appropriate; the playing pristine and flawless. Seldom can an atmosphere of bleakness and futility have been conjured with quite such thorough professionalism.

The Cure's music hints at the tumult and mystery of psychedelia, but with the emphasis on darkness rather than light. The songs cluster around a martial drum beat and Smith's clanging sepulchral guitar gathering intensity to become a throbbing onslaught of black noise. Occasionally, a glimpe of chilling beauty may be discerned in a particular chord sequence, or the rub between guitar and synthesiser; more often it is like being kicked repeatedly about the head by a metal toe-cap.

The epigrammatic titles of the songs themselves are shot with ambiguous menace — Cold, The Empty World, The Top — but Robert Smith's high, reedy wail never clearly conveys the exact meanings behind them. But the audience was a message in itelf. Nobody smiled, nobody danced; all filed out looking dazed and comatose. The Cure achieved the difficult task of making New Order seem radiantly, effervescently optimistic.

Between 13 and 31 May, The Cure toured Europe.

Robert:

"I was going to the same places as I'd just been with The Banshees and it was unreal. Going out on stage, I found I couldn't concentrate – I was thinking I was with The Banshees and about to start a Banshees' song!"

Adding to the strain of exhaustion, there were troubles with Andy Anderson.

Robert:

"He kept flipping out. The weirdest time was in Nice on 18 May. He was walking around this plush hotel in army fatigues and a security guard thought he was an intruder and, without asking, sprayed him with mace. Andy, understandably, went on the rampage and hammered a door in. Well, unfortunately, the mayor's daughter just happened to be having an illicit affair with some bloke behind that very door so we had to smuggle Andy out of France in a truck."

While the British music press were getting to grips with Robert's claim that he took a *live* lamb on tour (He told Smash Hits he found the staff at one hotel feeding it while he told Sounds it had been a present from a fan and was now living on his brother's farm in Wales – "I went to see it recently. It didn't remember me at all."), he was becoming severely run down and, on 26 May, he called Severin from Hamburg to say he couldn't fulfil his commitment to The Banshees.

Robert:

"I couldn't sleep. I was so bad that each night in the hotel, I'd be sitting there in bed, really wild-eyed and shaking and sweating and I thought 'It's finished – I mustn't seriously damage my health just for the sake of not letting The Banshees down'. So I phoned Severin and got his answer machine. I left a very long message explaining myself – I called about 10 times. The next morning, Severin rang me and I said I'd do the British tour but not the American one and, even then, I couldn't guarantee I'd be able to finish the British one. "When he'd got my message, he'd been really pissed off and couldn't believe I was serious but, listening to my voice, he could tell I was in a really bad way and he was really concerned. He asked me to come back to England to see them and I agreed. So The Cure cancelled two gigs and I flew over – but I was really cursing them because it was the worst flight I'd ever had; the plane got hit by lightning, all the lights went out and I was thinking 'The bastards! It's all their fault! I'm gonna plummet from the sky!' That was the last straw.

"When I got back, instead of going to see The Banshees, I went to see my doctor who I hadn't seen in about seven years and he was quite horrified at the state I was in and insisted I check into a health farm immediately or he wouldn't be answerable for the consequences.

"I refused – I had to finish The Cure tour – so he wrote me a certificate explaining I needed a complete rest and I sent that to The Banshees. Sioux was furious and kept going 'How come you can do The Cure tour but not The Banshees tour?' but I think Severin understood and anyway, by then my mind was made up. After all, I'd given them two weeks' notice which was longer than any guitarist had given them before!"

Robert returned to finish The Cure tour, Tim Pope's 'I Want To Be A Tree' was released and widely ignored and, after over a year in the making, The Banshees finally released 'Hyaena'.

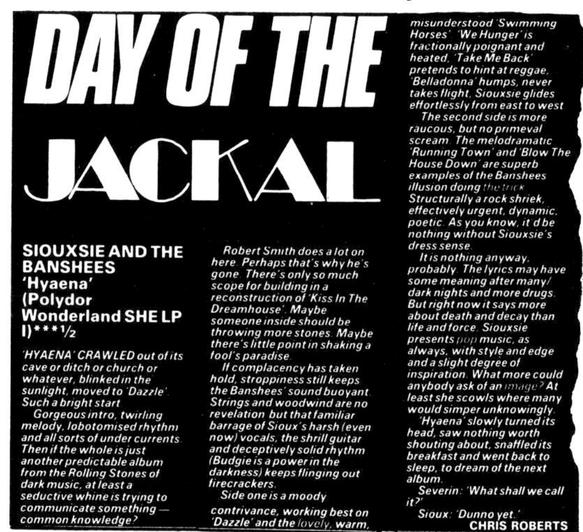

DAY OF THE JACKAL

SIOUXSIE AND THE BANSHEES 'Hyaena' (Polydor Wonderland SHE LP I)*½**

'HYAENA' CRAWLED out of its cave or ditch or church or whatever, blinked in the sunlight, moved to 'Dazzle'. Such a bright start.

Gorgeous intro, twirling melody, lobotomised rhythm and all sorts of under currents. Then if the whole is just another predictable album from the Rolling Stones of dark music, at least a seductive whine is trying to communicate something — common knowledge?

Robert Smith does a lot on here. Perhaps that's why he's gone. There's only so much scope for building in a reconstruction of 'Kiss In The Dreamhouse'. Maybe someone inside should be throwing more stones. Maybe there's little point in shaking a fool's paradise.

If complacency has taken hold, stroppiness still keeps the Banshees' sound buoyant. Strings and woodwind are no revelation but that familiar barrage of Sioux's harsh (even now) vocals, the shrill guitar and deceptively solid rhythm (Budgie is a power in the darkness) keeps flinging out firecrackers.

Side one is a moody contrivance, working best on 'Dazzle' and the lovely, warm, misunderstood 'Swimming Horses'. 'We Hunger' is fractionally poignant and heated, 'Take Me Back' pretends to hint at reggae, 'Belladonna' humps, never takes flight, Siouxsie glides effortlessly from east to west.

The second side is more raucous, but no primeval scream. The melodramatic 'Running Town' and 'Blow The House Down' are superb examples of the Banshees illusion doing the trick. Structurally a rock shriek, effectively urgent, dynamic, poetic. As you know, it'd be nothing without Siouxsie's dress sense.

It is nothing anyway, probably. The lyrics may have some meaning after many/dark nights and more drugs. But right now it says more about death and decay than life and force. Siouxsie presents pop music, as always, with style and edge and a slight degree of inspiration. What more could anybody ask of an image? At least she scowls where many would simper unknowingly.

'Hyaena' slowly turned its head, saw nothing worth shouting about, snaffled its breakfast and went back to sleep, to dream of the next album.

Severin: 'What shall we call it?'

Sioux: 'Dunno yet.'

CHRIS ROBERTS

Robert:

"After the tour, I went to Wales again with Mary. I played football on the beach, went for walks and listened to cassettes of old Cure concerts. I remember realising how close I'd come to being a total idiot, that I'd done it all without thinking why I was doing it. I was stupefied, unhappy and sick but I came out of it eventually and, when I came back from my holiday, The Cure did the Rock Around The Clock TV show from Barrowlands in Glasgow and I felt fresh and enthusiastic again.

In August, Robert at last bought a flat in London and took another break in the Lake District where, on the banks of Lake Windemere, he listened to the remainder of the 160 or so old Cure tapes.

Robert:

"It was fun, I listened to everything in chronological order and it made me realise how much we'd changed and I wanted to do something with the tracks that no-one would expect from a band in our position. The live Banshees album had been such a luxury item, I wanted the opposite."

Mixing 'Concert' with Dirk, the live album taped on the last British tour, Robert decided to put out a selection of the old tracks he'd been listening to on the cassette version so it became a double package with 'Curiosity – Cure Anomalies 1977 – 1984' on the B-side, featuring, among others, 'Heroin Face' from the Rocket days and the first demo version of 'Boys Don't Cry' all "made listenable" by Phil.

On 30 September, The Cure set off on a tour of New Zealand, Australia, Japan, Canada and America. The gigs went well at first but, again, there was trouble with Andy.

Robert:

"He was drinking too much. In Sydney, on 12th October, I had a big stand up row with him in a club which turned into a real ruck. It was just one of those arguments that takes place in clubs at two in the morning – y'know, 'You don't give me enough space man' nonsense. I never really understood it, but I was constantly having to reassure him which I eventually got really fed up with.

"We left Australia the next day, arrived in Japan, and drove to Tokyo, to play a couple of concerts. After the shows I went out to this club with Andy and, again, he went completely beserk. We went back to the hotel and he just went on the rampage. It was about 4.30 in the morning and I was feeling a bit saki'd up so I said goodnight and went to bed.

"I didn't hear anything more, I was in a sort of a coma, just collapsed on the bed, but I found out everything the next day. I got the story second-hand so I still don't know exactly what happened – I don't suppose anyone does because everyone'd been out – but the police were there and every one of our doors had a security guard outside. Apparently, Andy had attacked Phil, Bill, Mac, security guards, anyone . . . he'd just been running through the hotel beating people over the head. He'd just taken the place apart.

"He was locked in his room with a policeman outside the door who kept saying 'Look out! Wild man in there!' Eventually I had to go in and tell him he was on the plane home. Obviously he wasn't very happy about it but he said 'I respect you, you're the only one who's dared come to see me' so I just left him in his room and arranged for him to get to the airport and get a plane home and that was that. Andy's the only person to whom I've ever said 'You're out of the band'."

After a few weeks rest, Andy went on to play with ex-Orange Juice drummer Zeke Manyika's band.
Robert:

"So we arrived on the West Coast of America with a three week tour ahead of us, without a drummer and in a bit of a panic. We were in this bar deciding whether to cancel the tour or whether Lol should drum and we should carry on as a four piece when Phil phoned up a mate of his, Vince Ely, who used to drum with The Psychedelic Furs but who was now living in this beach house with someone from The Go Gos, mellowing out as a West Coast producer. Vince hadn't drummed in a band for about two years but he was up for it so he did a day and a half's rehearsal with us and played 11 concerts, 40 minute sets, learning the songs in soundcheck. Unfortunately, he was doing advertising work, producing jingles or something, so we knew he'd have to leave the tour somewhere around Texas. Again we thought of playing as a four piece but again Phil put out a call, this time to Boris Williams who he'd met drumming with The Thompson Twins and Kim Wilde."

The Toronto Globe And Mail said of The Cure at the time: "While much drone music remains barely listenable, Smith has adapted a stylistic compromise – a sort of bitter pill wrapped in sugar coating. His clashing, jangling guitar hits the ears as if it were held in a shifting envelope of sweet overtones. The remaining members of The Cure support Smith's sound with harmonically complimentary keyboards, propulsive, almost funky basslines and the thunderous tom-tom style of the band's new drummer, Vince Ely, formerly with The Psychedelic Furs.

"Coincidentally, The Cure often brought The Furs to mind on Monday night, not so much in sound as in the direction it has taken in demonstrating how a cultish English group can make selling-out look good. Both bands have exchanged inventive but limited exploratory styles for greater popularity and, in the process, have pushed mass taste in an interesting new direction."
Robert:

"Boris had actually already come to see us play at the Palladium in Hollywood, just to see the band and say hello to Phil so we called him up and, when Vince left, he joined up at the First Avenue Entry in Minneapolis on 7th November and he knew all the songs! He'd learned them off a tape in the interim – it was brilliant."
Boris:

"I'd just finished a tour with The Thompson Twins and I was on holiday in LA with Cynde, my girlfriend, when Phil, who I'd met when he worked as an engineer for the Twins, asked me to drum for The Cure for a few weeks. I had to learn their songs as fast as possible so I ran all over LA looking for their records and, from then on, it was in at the deep end. We started doing really short sets and added one or two songs a day until, at the Beacon Theatre in New York, we played for an hour and 50 minutes.

"Actually, it wasn't too hard to learn their songs once I knew how they started and how they finished! Ha ha! It was a big change for me – really refreshing. At last I was *really* playing the drums. With the Twins it was all electronic and precise whereas The Cure gave me more freedom and they were creative and fun."
Robert:

"We had to smuggle him in and out of Canada because he didn't have a permit but, by the time we played the last concert in New York, it was really good, just like when Andy was playing. Boris learned the rest of the songs in soundchecks and we did a complete set and there was a really good reaction, so we asked him if, when he got back to England, he'd get in touch with us instead of going back to the Thompson Twins.

"Meeting him was just a happy accident really. He liked what we did because, with The Thompson Twins, he had to repeat the same thing exactly every night whereas, with us, it's slow one night and fast the next. We got on well too – he had a Cure sense of humour. The only thing he was dubious about was the money because he was obviously getting paid an extraordinary amount with The Thompson Twins. But we kept saying 'Boris, Boris, think of your *art*' and he eventually agreed. He made the right decision!"

While in America, Robert told Shake magazine: "I lie a lot . . . To lie to gain someone's confidence or to get close to someone is a bit stupid . . . I make things up but just through boredom a lot of the time. I mean, a lot of what goes on in The Cure is just completely made up anyway. We spend a lot of time just talking rubbish at each other . . . I feel immensely younger than most people my age because I've never worked so I'm bound to feel young."

Back in Britain, 'Concert' was released in late October and Robert told Record Mirror: "It's all been done very plainly. We only spent four days mixing it and it's not a very big budget number. It's a very trashy record. It doesn't glisten . . . it actually sounds like a concert."

CURIOUSER AND CURIOUSER

THE CURE

CONCERT & CURIOSITY

Fiction FIXHC 10

THE great thing about this double-play cassette is that it confirms everything I've ever claimed about The Cure – that they started off preposterously talented but too easily led, that they hit a kind of bloated, droning nadir in the early Eighties when they attracted the so-called long-raincoat brigade, and that they went gloriously mad early this year, starting to do all sorts of weird, uncool stuff that was so off the beam they found themselves teen idols and the whipping boys of the startled press.

Strange. The Cure '84 are the finest incarnation ever, grey gone DayGlo, frigidity fractured. There was a warmth and adventure and sensual humour about "The Top" which exasperated those who had Robert Smith asphixiated as some precious bard's tongue in aspic. Smith, simply, stopped peering in the mirror and putting on weight, grew his hair and started having fun.

So what? So when the dust finally settles on 1984 and the theses have all been written and the made-up minds unmade by the changing tricks of retrospection, The Cure discovering a unique identity might well prove more rewarding and inspirational than any number of Frankie effects and shades of eyeshadow.

"Concert" supports this notion simply because it's exactly what a band in The Cure's position shouldn't do. I mean, all live albums are naff aren't they, fillers to cover for constipated creativity, easy ways to fleece the fans? "Concert", oddly, is none of these things; it's perfectly part of the couldn't-care-less Cure that's reaping shimmering rewards.

The actual "Concert" stuff, recorded live during May on the last British tour, is something of a greatest hits given a fair going over by the latest band. It was a delightful shock, Smith deciding to go out and give it some after the claustrophobically soporific "Pornography" tour and it led to a chemical redefinition of The Cure's career. As the tour wound on and what was essentially a makeshift incarnation (Phil Thornally on bass, Lawrence on minimal keyboards, Porl Thompson on additional guitar and sax and Andy Anderson on thundering drums) began to find their stage legs, stuff as signed, sealed and delivered as "Killing An Arab" started sprouting wings and limbs and scampered off in all manner of whimsical directions. Smith was, perhaps unintentionally, proving a point to himself: The Cure were frantically, desperately *alive,* not some statuesque institution.

"Concert" features The Cure seemlessly steaming, submitting past and present ("Hanging Garden", "A Forest", "10. 15") to a single hot black metal dimension. "Shake Dog Shake", a slightly ugly anachronism on the weird and wonderful "Top", rages with a manic intensity, "Primary" rips off its precious shroud and shimmies and "The Walk" is stripped to a surreal disco jaunt. Shame there's no "Caterpillar" though.

The second side of the tape (unavailable on record) is a collection of Cure anomalies from 1977 to 1984. Rescued from Smith's private collection of momento recordings, it tells the whole tale, shows where The Cure were right, went wrong and rediscovered themselves in an ecstacy of freedom. Few bands with an eye on their image would allow skeletons like these out of the closet and it's pleasing that Smith, a man much maligned as some spaced-out aesthete, should see fit to laugh and rejoice at himself.

It travels time from the punky "Heroin Face" recorded in The Rocket, Crawley, through the Jammy "Boys Don't Cry", through the stagnant "Drowning Man" (solemnly majestic on record but drained of impetus and urgency live) to the final frantic "Forever", recorded in Paris in '84 and segueing splendidly back into "Concert" with a howling dervish of improvisation. Fun *and* fascination.

Not solely a souvenir, not a makeweight, not an indulgence, the "Concert" package is a fresh perspective on a band captured at its creative peak and, as such, deserves a place alongside any album, Cure live or otherwise, that you care to cherish.

● STEVE SUTHERLAND

On returning home, Robert had a field day with the English press. He revealed he'd had a cocktail recipe broadcast on ORACLE on TV – "Orange juice, Rum, Apple slices, Calvados, Lemon juice, Everything mixed up" – and told Record Mirror: "I lie a lot, people know I do and sometimes they stand there horrified at me. If we go away or if we're being taken out by people, I just create whole mythical worlds about me . . . never repeating the same anecdote twice.

"I really hate being in the company of people who take themselves seriously. I always have done but it's become pathological now. I can't stand people who sit and talk to me in a very serious way . . . when I go abroad, I'll do three interviews in one country and give three different answers to all three, knowing that many people will read all of them and they won't be able to take you seriously because the whole thing is so absurd."

7

Seven

With the band on hold, Robert reviewed the world tour and began looking to the next album.

Robert:

"The whole tour had been quite easy and enjoyable: I actually stopped drinking in America . . . I used to discuss the Bible with Phil instead. In Japan we were going onstage and doing the first song and suddenly it would be the end of the concert and I'd have no knowledge of what had gone on in the middle: so I decided I had to moderate, Bible meetings instead of binges. I used to sit there with Phil and get quite intense about the Book of Revelations.

"We were getting on well so I asked Phil if he wanted to continue playing bass for The Cure. But he decided that as he'd just done a bit of TV on his own, got his own deal, his own single, he wanted to have his own creative freedom, wanted to get back in the studio so people didn't think he'd given that up."

Lol:

"I asked him and Robert asked him maybe five times if he wanted to carry on with it and be committed for the next year at least and five times he said no. He had his own single out but, when it didn't do as well as he thought it was going to, I think he reversed in his mind what he actually said. The last time I talked to him was for about an hour on the phone and he was feeling a little bitter."

Thornalley:

"I never considered myself a permanent member, they always treated me as the sound engineer on a break from his studio. It was good for me though, I *was* a frustrated musician and I did lots of idiotic things on tour, went round the world, had a good time. I learned a lot about myself and the others, undergoing so much unreal pressure, discovering my weak points and strengths and those of others. I wanted to stay but I was too late."

Robert:

"I was doing some demos and buying furniture for the flat and it was getting near Christmas and one day Biddles phoned me up and asked me if I wanted to go for a drink with him and Simon, and I just thought 'Fuck it, this has gone on too long, Porl's back, it's all too silly'. So I went along."

Simon:

"When I didn't hear from Robert and Lol, I moved into a house with Matthieu and stayed there for about a year but we started to row so I thought it must be me that's the catalyst for all the rows and I changed my whole approach to things, I thought, 'I'm not gonna be nippy all the time. I'm not gonna argue, it's not worth it'.

"I remember 'Lovecats' coming out. I used to go to this really trendy half-pub half-disco in Horley and they used to play the singles and the album and people would come up and say 'Bet you're sick now'. Well, I was but, at the same time, I felt proud that they'd made it, that they'd got there, that there were so many people who wanted to put The Cure down and Robert had the last laugh. I got really protective when people used to slag them off and when 'Let's Go To Bed' came out, I really wanted to call them but I couldn't – too much pride.

"I thought 'After the way they've treated me, I'm not gonna make the first move' and I suspected Robert hated my guts so I didn't want to phone up to say 'Hi, how are you?' and give Robert the chance of saying 'Fuck off!' Subsequently, I found out that Robert felt exactly the same way – he didn't want to ring me up in case I said that to him.

"I saw the band at Hammersmith Odeon on the second night and I thought Robert was really good, so was Andy but the sight of Phil annoyed me – still does if I see him on video. Anyway, I formed a band called Cry with Biddles singing – he'd left The Cure set-up a couple of tours after me – and, for a while, Matthieu, but there was another band with that name so we had to change it and we chose Fools Dance."

Biddles:

"When Simon came back to Horley, it took him a while to get over the split but then he realised it was no good sulking and he decided to start a band and asked me to sing. I'd only sung with The Cure a couple of times, during encores and at Christmas parties and messing around at soundchecks but this was very serious – trying to say to The Cure, '*we* can do something'."

Simon:

"Fools Dance put out a mini LP, 'Priesthole', – good songs but just demos really – and we toured Europe, small dates, that's all. Then Robert was in Europe and he sent me a postcard which I thought was really nice. Biddles had kept in touch with them and said 'You should meet and be friends again' and I agreed. It was actually a really nice summery night and Biddles rang him up and said 'Simon's here and he wants to know if you wanna come out for a drink?' I think it was a couple of weeks after he'd come off tour with The Banshees. Anyway, we went down the pub and started to chat and it was exactly the same as the old days."

Biddles:

"They both met round my house and said hello very quietly and it moved on from there. After a few pints, they were talking again."

Robert:

"I saw quite a bit of him up until Christmas and over Christmas and then I said to him that we were going to do some demos for a new record, probably just a single, towards the end of January and did he want to come along and play bass? I did it slowly – first a single, then the album, then the tour because he had his own band and, if I'd asked him everything at the same time, he might have thought I attached no importance to what he was doing with Fools Dance."

Simon:

"Robert said he wanted me to do the next album but the only thing was, I'd have to tour. Well, I said *'Great!'*"

Robert:

"The whole of Fools Dance hated me. They thought I was stealing Simon from them but it wasn't true. I didn't force him back, he just decided to say 'Yes'. I knew it would be good if he came back though – it wasn't *really* The Cure with Phil and Andy, even if it seemed to be."

Biddles:

"I thought it was a bit cheeky of Robert to think he could drop someone and then just pick them up again and I was a bit annoyed. Simon was really into Fools Dance but I could see his point of view."

Robert:

"I'd actually made a cassette of all the stuff I'd been doing at home and, in February, we went into a studio called F2 in Tottenham Court Road. Simon came up one night and we did a song which later turned into 'The Exploding Boy': he just sat down on the flight case and I taught him the bassline and that's the first time the five of us – Simon, Lol, Boris, Porl and me – played together.

"He wasn't there for a lot of the demos – he'd just pop in and out and I was playing all the basslines. It was only really after we'd finished the demos and I took them round to him at his house, just like with '17 Seconds', and he said how pleased he was to be back in the group that I knew it could work. He never really thought Phil should have been in the group anyway. He always thought I should have asked him back sooner, that when Phil joined was time enough for us to have gotten over everything. But I didn't really think it was."

Recording began in the Spring of 1985 at Angel Studios in London.

Simon:

"I was dead nervous of playing with Boris because I knew he was such a good drummer. I didn't know Porl well either – I'd almost not spoken to him since Easy Cure and I was also worried about how things would turn out with Robert and Lol again. It was fine though, the easiest time I've ever had in a recording studio, so much fun. It was almost as if it had turned full circle but this time we could afford more beer."

Robert:

"We played pool a lot and had fun. The atmosphere was stupid, almost childish and we were in a hurry to get back in the studio every day. With Simon, the excitement came back and the band was more aggressive, more vital. He knew me so well that I didn't really need to explain anything to him. We drank a lot more than at any other recording session but this time we didn't take any drugs."

Later he told East Village Eye magazine: "It makes me laugh that there's this image of me as someone who goes stumbling about. I'd be completely incapable of doing anything if I did half as much as they say I do. I prefer drinking and drugs in the social sense . . . Once we went to see 'Re-animator' completely out of it and sat there screaming, all 13 of us in the front row of the cinema. That was a really good night out. If you did that all the time though, everything would take on quite a dulled aspect, everything would become quite drab."

Attempting a different drum sound for each song meant the recording session lasted longer than anticipated and, after a month at Angel, the band moved to the Town House.

Robert:

"I don't think Lol remembers much about it – he was off planet every single night and had to be sent home in a cab. Every night he'd arrive and say 'That's it, I'm not drinking tonight', hold out until about 10 and then the first bottle of wine would go down. The album was great fun to do but it took an extraordinarily long time to record.

" As well as the pool table, we also had a cocktail cabinet, a fridge, an enormous Scalextric layout, video cameras, splatter movie parties . . . and we still managed to make a record! It was a glorious celebration . . ."

Lol:

"It was the most varied album we'd ever done, a bit like a collection of singles – an extended exploration of what we'd done with 'The Top'."

Robert claimed later that he plagiarised himself on the album, using old phrases and dreams to create 'The Head On The Door'. 'In Between Days' was, he said, "what 'Caterpillar' should have been", 'Kyoto Song' (originally called 'The Koto Song' after an instrument Robert discovered he couldn't play - "As if there weren't enough already!") was a dream song: "Half of it comes from a dream Mary had – death in a swimming pool – and half from one of mine about eating someone."

'The Blood', with a flamenco flavour, came from a Portuguese peasant wine called The Tears Of Christ that Robert discovered on tour. Rough old stuff by all accounts – "If you drink half a bottle, you start having horrible visions. On the label, the Virgin Mary holds the baby Jesus under one arm and a bottle under the other!" 'Six' was the culmination of an old idea: "I'd always wanted to do a waltz. I'd intended to with The Glove but Severin never managed to get the rhythm right! The words are about the way I treat people. The six is not that important – it could've been five."

'Push' was about "how you sometimes irrationally hate other people just because they're there" while 'Baby Screams' is "a dance number, something to clap your hands to. It's about the 'this-drink-isn't-cold-enough-get-me-another' me. The band and people close to me know, when I'm doing that, that I'm not being serious". 'Close To Me' is "Frustrated, humming with your head under the pillow, like the end of a day where you feel nothing has been achieved and you're in a hurry to get the day over with so you can start the next one. You tell yourself tomorrow you're going to do lots of positive things. But the next day is just like the one before. Sometimes it goes on for weeks."

'A Night Like This' dates back to 1976, to when Porl was originally in the band, to the days of 'Plastic Passion' when, Robert says, "We wanted to be like Roxy Music . . . ". 'Screw' was about recognising yourself in other people's eyes while 'Sinking' harked back to 'Faith': "Very old Robert Smith".

'The Head On The Door' was completed and mixed at Genetic with Dirk while Zig Zag ran a prying interview by Antonella Black into Robert's private life, typical of the kind of articles appearing now The Cure were accepted in the singles chart: "The idea of an after-life is simply there to give existence a meaning – to give 60 years of banality a sense of purpose. I mean, the idea of the after-life is just as valid as the idea of a hot dinner – it all depends if you're hungry."

Coaxed into talking about his love life, he said: "My relationship with Mary is what most people would consider to be 'liberal' but not in that horrible contrived sense . . . obviously from what I do and what she does, we spend time apart. If I'm on tour, she doesn't come with me because she doesn't like that side of it. She remembers when nobody wanted to talk to me. She can see the hypocrisy of the whole situation – as I can – but obviously it's far more difficult for someone who's close to me to cope with. People tend to ignore her and think she's just another fan. She doesn't tolerate that and nor do I. We understand each other, which is why we've been together so long . . ."

On video, he revealed: "It comes across as nervous because I am. I'm not a natural performer at the best of times. When I get lost in it, I can be but, in a video, the atmosphere is too contrived. I don't really see *myself* in the videos but I can see why I do it – it's the easy way out."

Elsewhere at this time, the press were making a meal of Robert's newly avowed vegetarianism and his claims that he slept 16 hours a day, while, in June, the five piece played their first gig together in Barcelona.

Robert:

"That was a mega night. It was filmed, it was so glorious, so hilarious. Boris was really unsure of the endings of a lot of the songs because we hadn't rehearsed at all for it, and Simon wasn't sure of some of the basslines. But it was the first time we'd played in Spain and the audience went beserk and set fire to themselves. Brilliant!"

The Cure also played in Italy, supported by The Associates and, on 27 July, they performed at a festival in the Antic Panathinaikos Stadium in Athens on a bill featuring Nina Hagen, Talk Talk and Telephone. The night before, Boy George of Culture Club was stoned by the audience and Mary took over the hotel bar.

Simon:

"It was as if England had won the World Cup we went down so well. We were booked third on the bill so we were like underdogs. It was one of our classic concerts, really great."

Back home, Robert was asked by No1 about his health: "I stopped smoking about seven months ago – I just decided one night in Chicago that I should and I've stuck to it. I hate dependency on physical things and I didn't want to get to the stage where I had to have a cigarette. I can't remember ever wanting to give up drink though – I think I've been drunk every night this year!"

He also revealed he'd attempted to waterski during his sojourn in the Lake District to get himself in shape and to win a bet with a head waiter. As it turned out, all he got was a gashed leg and a nose bleed. Of The Cure's escalating popularity, he said: "I'm lucky because I'm quite short sighted so it doesn't matter if there's 1,000 or 100,000 people in the audience – I can't see further than the first row."

As the British teen press began to take interest, Robert was assailed by a whole new onslaught of irrelevance and nonsense. Just 17, for example, wanted to know his Star sign: "If I was born on one side of midnight, I'm Taurus, and if I was born on the other, I'm Aries but no-one remembers. I don't believe in them anyway."

'In Between Days' was released as a single in July, backed by 'The Exploding Boy' which Robert says is him. "I drink too much, eat too much, think too much . . . ha! I'd like to explode. It would be a beautiful death." On the 12 inch version, the additional track was 'A Few Hours After This' which was "supposed to be a party song but went wrong . . . "

THE CURE: In Between Days (Polydor) They're full of little surprises, The Cure. Every once in a while they turn out a completely and irresistably loveable tune, and this one's the best in a long while – since 'Love Cats' in fact. It bounds away at breakneck speed to the rhythm of strumming guitars and a simple little keyboard melody which goes round and round. Even the morose voice of Robert Smith singing about growing old and losing girlfriends can't stop it sounding bright and lively in a Cure-ishly whimsical way. Just the thing for a hot day. Joint Single Of The Fortnight.

THE CURE: In Between Days (Fiction)

● Three thoughts occur. One: how does he do it? How on earth does Smithy keep that face straight as he unloads these records? 'The Top' was a schoolboyishly cruel – legs torn slowly from helpless insects – companion to the Bunnymen's contemporary and equally silly-sod-psychedelic 'Ocean Rain', while his butter wouldn't melt 'Love Cats' routine was sublime, media-mocking TV. The man is a comic to be rated with Keaton.

Two: if I didn't believe New Order to be as rich as Tsars, I'd advise them to grab this record and their own 'Temptation' and 'Power, Corruption And Lies', and to hotfoot it to the nearest court of law. The monstrous scale, nerve and cynicism of Smith's plagiarism, in a world where most claim unique creative genius (Dahling), has, oddly, to be admired.

Three: either because of, or in spite of one and two, 'In Between Days' – a sneeringly offhand debunking of all that Factory's finest seek so assiduously to mystify, is a good 45, easily the best of the week's *pop* crop.

■ My, this *is* artistic! Blurred psychedelic colour group shot and the kind of spindly, scratchy, hand-drawn type that puts the icing on a stale cake.

The video, again, came from the established partnership of the band and Tim Pope.

Robert:

"It's my favourite. I said I wanted something that looked like an old Sixties Dave Clark Five thing, black, and white, normal looking, very unaware of the camera. Pap listened, grinned inanely and said 'I see it all swooping, really sick-inducing . . . I know what we'll do . . . We'll put the camera in a shopping basket on a big rope and I'll swing it at you!

"It did actually get a bit more sophisticated than that – we used these wires they use in the circus to hold up the camera and there was one bloke in the corner who was supposed to take up the slack and make sure the tension was right. But on the first run through they got it all wrong – they'd judged by the weight of the camera and then taken a piece off so it was actually lighter and it came hurtling towards me. Well, I thought 'This isn't right' so I ducked and it went haring past my head and did a complete circle. The crew were really sick – they wanted to call the whole thing off there and then! But it turned out brilliantly. As for the fluorescent socks – there was no good reason for those. Just Pap! As usual . . . "

In late August, 'The Head On The Door' was released.

Robert:

"It was the most accomplished stuff we'd done, more coherent than 'The Top' and yet really spontaneous. It was played as a *band*. We had the songs worked out beforehand so we could actually *afford* to get horribly drunk. It was organised chaos."

Head case

THE CURE

THE HEAD ON THE DOOR
Fiction

No more Mad Bob?
Maybe. Maybe not.

Robert Smith has wormed himself into an enviable but precarious position over the past 18 months. We don't know what to expect anymore. But, then again, we know to expect nothing. He's slipped the straitjacket of brooding depression that seemed to shape "Faith", cleaved through the claustrophobia that stifled "Pornography", checked himself out of the funny farm where he tampered with his nightmares and turned out "The Top", and now roams among us, a harmless, often hilarious, eccentric.

He's changed, or our attitude towards him has changed – he's accepted now for his idiosyncracies, labelled and loved and, even if he's managed to shed all his previous incarnations, I can't help wondering if the magnificent liberty that fashioned "The Head On The Door" won't cement into another image, comfortably digested and, hence, easily dismissed.

Certainly "The Head" is as certifiable as "The Top" in the (non)sense that it's as wilfully enigmatic as ever. The only difference is it's determinedly langorous, nowhere near as tortured or tense as its predecessor and, for all its deliberate variety and characteristic quirks, it maintains a disturbingly even strain.

Sometimes I think Smith could write songs like these *in* his sleep, not just *about* it. They're *exercises* in the manipulation of misery – Smith apparently stopped soul-searching and hair-tearing some time ago and now contents himself matching and juxtaposing emotions in appropriate and inappropriate atmospheres just to see how perverse a pop song can be and still remain popular. It's not so much a craft as a quest, more Don Quixote than Nik Kershaw could ever imagine.

So "The Head" is a collection of pop songs, it's as simple(?) as that. Bursting with potential hits, it staggers under its influences, rescued from dilettantism solely by Smith's steady presence. Some stuff, like "The Baby Screams" – a classic Cure concoction of mixed metaphors and creeping guitar – will satisfy the Faithful. Others, like "Close To Me" – a squirming, sobbing, pleading disco thing complete with handclaps – will seduce just about any Tom, Dick or Vanessa.

"The Head" makes a mockery not only of the accepted parameters of what the radio will play and the public accept (it's miraculous that "In Between Days" is on "Top Of The Pops") but also of what The Cure are supposed to be about. Absurdly straight, there's nothing obscure or sinister about "A Night Like This" – it ascends a perfectly tangible spiral, deals with love and despair in desperate balance, toys with a joyously incongruous singalong and accommodates a sax break more at home with Hall & Oates.

It's a neat ragbag of the arbitrary – each song a separate piece from a different jigsaw. Some shapes bear the imprint of exotic scenes – "Kyoto Song" sounds Japanese while "The Blood" stamps through its paces to flamenco guitar. Others suggest there are more strident, less fickle things ahead. "Push", for example, is stronger, less whimsical than anything that revolved and grew giddy on "The Top", and "Sinking" is more majestic, more honest perhaps, than anything Smith's done since "All Cats Are Grey".

Dark and poised on a precipitous drumbeat, it glides into shape swathed in keyboards embroidered by hesitant snicks of guitar until Smith's gorgeous whine is echoed into epic, richochetted whispers.

As a compilation of possibilities, "The Head On The Door" is perfection of sorts – a romp more than a rage through the closet, trying things on, not tearing them up. This Cure is boisterous but relaxed and reliably unreliable. I'm used to it now and I use it with pleasure.

So, no more Mad Bob. Next time, something *else*. Again.

STEVE SUTHERLAND

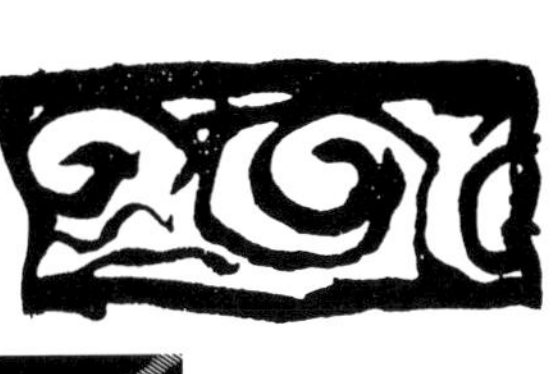

THE CURE
THE TOUR
8TH SEPT · ST. AUSTELL · COLISEUM
9TH SEPT · POOLE · ARTS CENTRE
10TH SEPT · SHEPTON MALLET · SHOWERING PAVILION
12TH SEPT · LONDON · WEMBLEY ARENA
14TH SEPT · BRIGHTON · CENTRE
16TH SEPT · WHITLEY BAY · ICE RINK
17TH SEPT · MANCHESTER · APOLLO
20TH SEPT · BIRMINGHAM · NATIONAL EXHIB. CENTRE
21ST SEPT · LEEDS · QUEEN'S HALL
22ND SEPT · EDINBURGH · PLAYHOUSE
THE HEAD ON THE DOOR
NEW ALBUM
CASSETTE · COMPACT DISC

Robert had fun explaining the title. He told Smash Hits; "It was when I was little. Before I was going to get ill, I always used to see this horrible grinning man who'd appear on top of the bedroom door and laugh. It was like at both ends of a telescope at the same time – really near but when I tried to push it off, it'd be really far away. The last time I had it was when I was 15 and ill with glandular fever. Until, that is, for some reason, a couple of months ago I had a dream about it again and woke up sweating. I thought I was going to be ill but I wasn't."

To Sounds, he said: "One angle I haven't explained is the puppet idea. Did your mum and dad ever do puppet shows, like draw a face on their hands and go 'Waaaargh!' from behind the sofa and really scare you? I've always been fascinated with puppets like Punch & Judy because the tradition is so old. There's something about the way a puppet's head will roll off . . . When they used to decapitate people, they'd put their heads on poles and all your instincts just scream at that. So we were gonna call it 'The Head On The Pole' and then I changed it because of that dream I used to have. It was originally gonna be called 'The Exploding Boy' . . . "

Around the same time, Robert told Smash Hits: "I think I've come through my mid-life crisis. It was the same as anybody's – about growing up. The worst part was getting close to 25 because I'd always convinced myself that I'd be dead by then, by somebody else's hand if not my own. It was a romantic idea but I had it for so long it became truth. I even had the date and everything – February 14 last year. I used to have this recurring dream that I was falling through a window and I could feel all the glass going into me . . . It was only when I got into bed that night that I thought 'Bastards! It didn't come true'. It was quite disappointing in a way!"

While he talked freely of recording an EP of Sinatra songs, he also told Sounds: "I don't expect to be told things in songs or have something illuminated for me. I just want to be amused or inspired or entertained in a huge, umbrella-like sense. I don't expect anyone to impart any knowledge, apart from in a very material way, such as learning words or language . . . All Cure music is a sequence of events or a background to other people doing things . . . "

On the other hand, he admitted, escaping the strait-jacket of image meant "You get to the point where you feel able to go in any direction next, so you lose the ability to shock people. Whatever we did, people wouldn't really be surprised . . . "

And, on longevity: "It's really nice to have been able to go on so long and not compromise anything or regret anything I've done. Some people just want to be rich and famous and have sex but that's a very unreal situation. I enjoy aspects of that from time to time and indulge myself in it, but we've always been on more of a crusade than other bands, which is why we've lasted so long. And there's a strong sense of insanity running through what we do . . . I used to be very morbid but you get to the point where you either accept it and make a career out of it and metaphorically kill yourself or you dismiss it and use it to create an environment in an absurd and slightly deranged way, which is what I chose.

"It's been the catalyst for a lot of the things I've done – not the idea of death so much as the way in which people learn to cope with it, how it all spreads to old age and finding faith. It permeates us without us actually accepting it."

He informed No1: "If we ever have a number one record, I'll disband the group immediately. I'd never let us be seen to be competing to be a number one group. It's all just such nonsense."

And his favourite record?: "'I'm A Moody Guy' by Shane Fenton and The Fentones. It's the first thing Simon bought for me because he thought I was a moody bastard. He posted it through my letter box. In half. So I've never actually heard it, but it's my favourite record!"

In September, The Cure (now dubbed Team Cure and kitted out accordingly in American Football shirts) toured Britain and on the 12th, played Wembley Arena for the first time.

Robert:

"I didn't want to do another long tour ever again but I'd really enjoyed doing festivals so, rather than doing six nights at Hammersmith, I thought 'We'll just play Wembley'. Everyone said we wouldn't fill it on our own but it sold out. Budgie came and thought it was one of the best gigs he'd ever been to. Unfortunately, the rest of the concerts were very disappointing. The venues were too depressing, too impersonal. I think what really went wrong happened early on, in St Austell; it was one of the worst night's drinking in The Cure's history. That didn't really set us up very well and by the time we got to Shepton Mallet, everyone was dead."

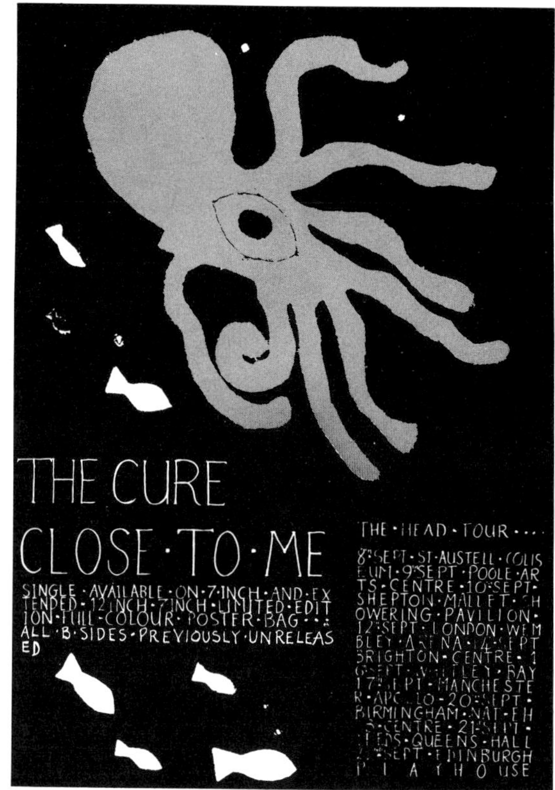

Meanwhile 'Close To Me'/'A Man Inside My Mouth' was released, the first time The Cure had ever allowed two singles to be taken off one album. Robert told the British press that there'd been disagreement over whether 'Close To Me' or 'In Between Days' should have been the single so, as the others were so convinced it was a surefire hit, it was put out in a different version with tipsy Tijuana brass from Rent Party. "It reminds me of 'Jimmy Mack'", he told Record Mirror, "That's the sound I thought it should have."

The B-side of the seven inch recalls Robert's most horrific dream that year, while 'Stop Dead', an additional track on the 12 inch, was another experiment he wasn't totally satisfied with.

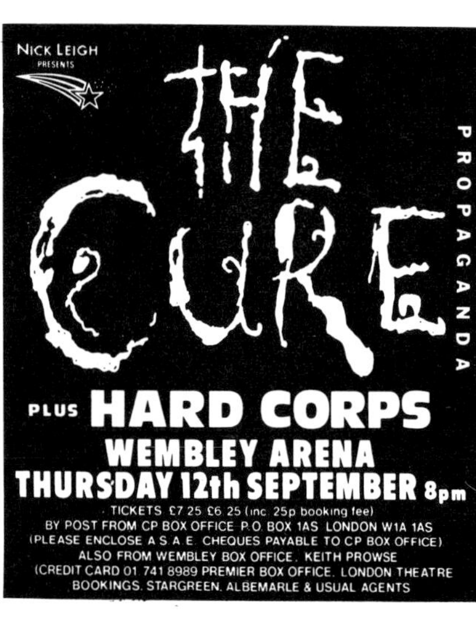

THE CURE 'Close To Me' (Fiction) One thing you *can* rely on The Cure to be, and that is unreliable. Following on from the infectious, if somewhat New Orderesque (not them again) 'In Between Days' 'Close To Me' is Smithy at his eccentric indulgences again. Based around a somewhat mutated New Orleans jazz feel, brass leads you one way as a three blind mice riff on Xylophone goes t'other before joining together again in an eclectic swing.

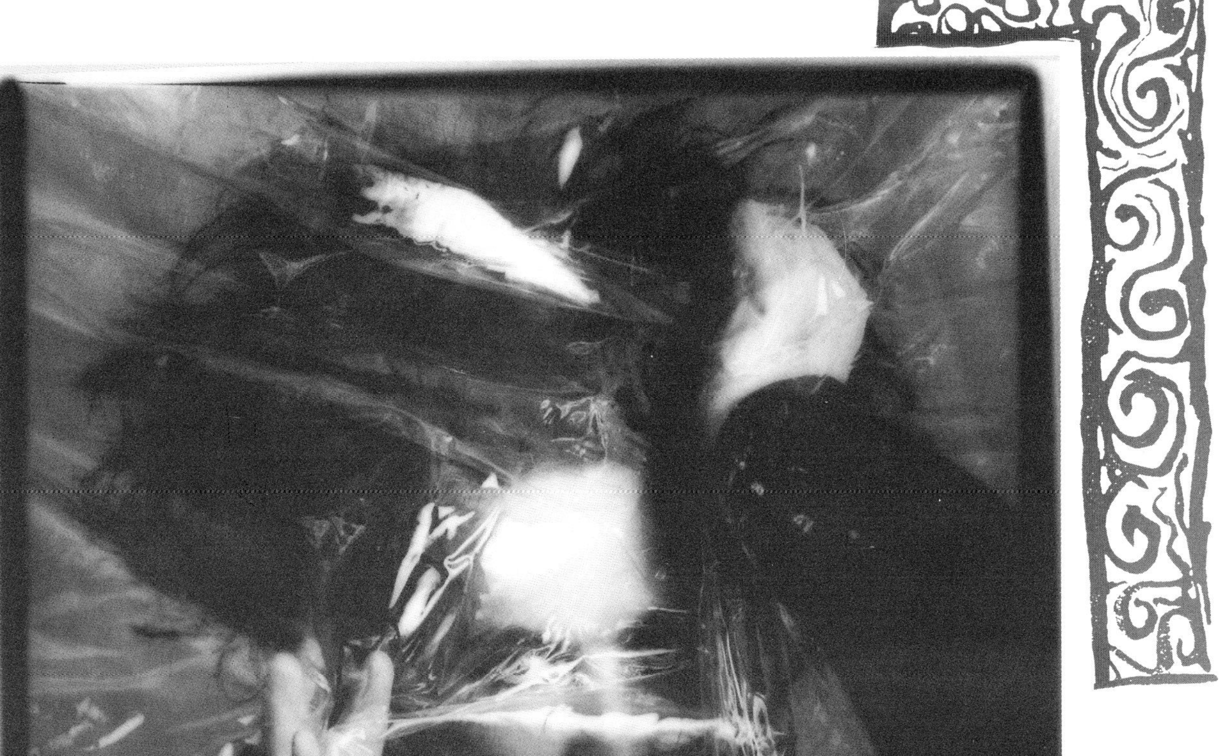

Robert:

"I told Pap the video should somehow capture the sort of claustrophobia you'd get if you were in a wardrobe that you couldn't try to get out of too violently because you were on a cliff edge and, when it came to the day of the video, we found he'd taken it rather literally and we were to be immersed in water inside a wardrobe. It worked out really well but he was unhappy because it hardly got shown at all, least of all on children's shows presumably because they thought it would incite kids to climb into wardrobes and fling themselves off cliffs."

Pope:

"Robert just said 'Make it claustrophobic'. I can't remember where the wardrobe came from but I liked the idea of juxtaposing – there, that's a good film word, juxtaposing – the claustrophobia with the vertigo thing. I just wanted to get the emotion of the song over really, I wanted sweat so we were in this massive studio, the biggest in London, all inside this wardrobe – the Cure, me, the cameraman, the assistant camerman the smallest set in the biggest studio – ha! It was hilarious and it got pretty hectic in there. I don't know if you've ever experienced Laurence's bowels but . . . The crew were really drilled, doing this shot again and again and at about six everybody was really fucked and suddenly I saw the whole crew retract and the band all shot over the other side of the studio but Lol was just standing there with this bestial look on his face, grinning and I had to go outside and throw up. It was so disgusting. One day we'll make a film of the inside of his stomach.

"I think the feeling of persecution finally culminated in 'Close To Me' because, when we all had to go down into this big vat of water, it was fairly sedate until I put Lol in, right in the middle. As soon as the music started, people were holding him under, these fists were coming, clothes over his face, shoes coming in, smashing into his face and feet, kicking him. It's terrible really, a sin . . . when we watched the rushes, we were in tears."

In September, the now defunct Jamming magazine quoted Robert as saying: "Other people have been guilty of taking me too seriously but I never had. I take what I do seriously because I know that, particularly when we started, in the first three or four years, a lot of people looked on us as some kind of inspiration to show that you could do things in a very, very different way and still maintain your integrity. I'm not sure if people worry about that so much with us now. I think that burden's been taken on by other people. I'm not really sure who, people like The Cocteau Twins, who are, I suppose, like the spiritual bearers of that angst sort of thing.

"I enjoyed it at the time but with 'Let's Go To Bed' that was the decision, when I thought 'I don't want this anymore'. I didn't want people to think that I was like that anymore because I wasn't, I'd changed. And I thought that if I want to carry on doing something, we've got to have a very different public image."

Meanwhile, in Record Mirror, Robert claimed: "If I wasn't in a band, I'd start up The Cure now because I still detest the people in the Top 10 as much as I did when we started." And in NME . . . "I *would* be dead if I lived through everything I write about". And in Smash Hits, in an article entitled "I Am Filled With An Overwhelming Desire To Die" . . . "I look less like me than most of the people coming to our concerts."

On 29 September, The Cure embarked on a short but successful American tour, climaxing with a sold out show at Radio City, New York where they were late back onstage for their encores because they got lost in a lift, arrived at the wrong floor and were attacked by an alsation.

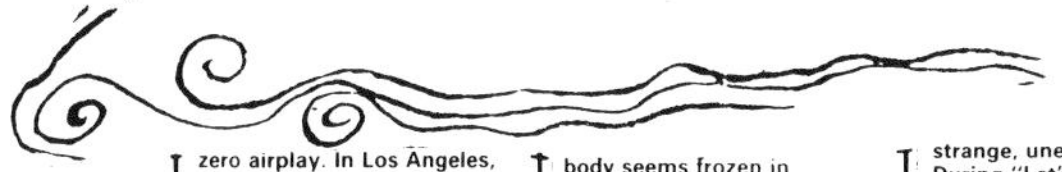

THE CURE
Radio City Music Hall, New York

"WE'VE come a long way, haven't we?" Robert Smith announced to the sold-out Radio City crowd before leading The Cure into "Kyoto Song".

He had every reason to beam. Where The Cure once played to devoted cultists in modest dance halls and glorified bars in this country, this year Smith and company moved over 5,000 tickets in New York alone with almost zero airplay. In Los Angeles, they sold triple that for one show.

The Cure responded to this extraordinary show of support with 75 minutes of bleak, tortured pop performed with demon ferocity against flickering shadow portraits of the band and billowing clouds of pastel dry ice Smith remains a singularly unengaging performer a pudgy doll with a chaotic haystack haircut, wearing a baggy black suit. Yet, while his body seems frozen in position, his voice in spite of its limited range rises and falls in pained extremes, grimly animating funeral marches like "Cold" from "Pornography" then heightening the bullet-punk desperation of "Primary", harkening back to the band's "Faith" days.

Compared to the pouting, humourless Cure that had previously played New York, the Smith Gang on this trip often let its icy cool drop in strange, unexpected ways During "Let's Go To Bed" Smith bounced around in front of the mike in a comic ragamuffin dance. The driving pulse and epic chime of the guitars in "Push" never stampeded over the song's sweet pop outreach and, in the final encore, The Cure went totally teenage with an unexpected brontosaurus stomp through Gary Glitter's "Do You Wanna Touch Me". Smith gone glam? What fun!

DAVID FRICKE

On their return, Robert told Record Mirror he'd recorded a single in 1984 that was such a complete rip-off of Booker T's 'Green Onions' that he thought he'd be bound to be sued so he scrapped it. He also said of his boozing: "It would be awful to have to use a means of escape as a means of being creative. Too many people in recent history have ended up that way, with their creativity destroyed by something that initially helped."

Robert was also featured as the front cover personality in the October issue of The Face. In an hilarious article called "Hair 'Em Scare 'Em" by the cynically erudite Fiona Russell Powell, Robert confessed: "I can imagine one of our songs inspiring people to commit suicide but not to murder." He also told her he'd met the Pope when he was young and that "Drinking's recreational, I think. I used to get drunk on my own a lot but I don't anymore. To use Dylan Thomas as an example, who ended up killing himself through drink; he did it just because it's good fun. I'm not sure it's the same in the latter stages of addiction. I imagine he drank for three reasons. One, because it's good fun, two, because you become almost mythical, it's like you become a legendary drinker which is an idea you can become addicted to, and the third reason is probably because in the latter stages of addiction, you don't have much choice at all! I'm almost an alcoholic now, I haven't had one night this year when I haven't been drunk – a sad admission I suppose . . . "

Having talked himself into this rather flimsy justification for the increasingly infamous Club Smith – vodka and grapefruit – he proceeded to regale Russell Powell with all manner of jocular titbits. He claimed he was writing a book of short stories with no endings called 'The Glass Sandwich', that "I'd rather play football than be an existentialist" and that "I don't put my lipstick on properly because people would think I was doing it for reasons of vanity whereas I do it for reasons of theatricality. I used to wear it when we did 'Pornography', I used to wear red lipstick all round

my eyes and all round my mouth so that, when we were on stage, I'd sweat and it'd run so it would look like someone had punched me in the mouth and my eyes were bleeding. I had to stop it though because my eyesight started to suffer."

In November, Robert told wondrous lies to the Daily Mirror about Mary being a stripper and, on the 19th, The Cure played Camden Palace for MENCAP, the organisation for the mentally handicapped. Part of the show was broadcast live on BBC's 'Whistle Test'. Robert:

"This was quite a difficult one to play actually because we'd become used to playing festivals and big places like Wembley and here we were confronted by an audience in such a small place. I felt really nervous for the first time in years."

Over the Christmas period, The Cure played in France and then took a break. Their contract with Polydor was up and Robert decided on putting out a singles compilation album because "If we didn't release it how we wanted it, they'd just release it anyway."

With that in mind, during the Spring of 1986, Robert re-mixed and re-recorded the vocal on 'Boys Don't Cry' and, together with Tim Pope, put together a collection of all The Cure's videos.
Pope:

"We spent a lot of time on that, going through The Cure's history, and it was a fascinating story – who leaves, who comes back, it's like a game of dominoes. While we were putting it together, whenever Smith went out the room, I'd always manage to have 'Charlotte Sometimes' on the screen when he came back in. And what I admire about him is he didn't care – he decided to put the whole thing out, just taking the piss.

"That's what I like about Smithy, he's a very paradoxical character. Everything he is, he isn't. He's very pretentious but he isn't. He's always black yet he's white and The Cure are one of the stupidest bands you could ever work with yet they're the brightest, the most intelligent. They're the noisiest but they can be the quietest – that's what I love about them. Robert says he's like a child but he isn't, he's too intelligent. Since 'Head On The Door', he's changed. Has he talked about death wishes or anything recently? I find him very perverse and I think he *knows* what is gonna happen. He may build The Cure up and get so happy and then he could destroy it all, just to hurt himself. That wouldn't surprise me – he's one of those people."

The show in Athens had been videoed and shown throughout Europe and suddenly, as Parry told The Face, Robert was big in France. In April, 'Close To Me' was high in the French charts so The Cure returned to Paris for a TV appearance. Porl and Boris were on holiday at the time so Lol mimed the drums and his flatmate, Martin, who worked in the City, mimed keyboards. Robert told Record Mirror, who'd gone along for the ride: "Sometimes it's necessary to be absurd . . . Things generally are absurd and pretty awful most of the time but I'm in a better situation than anyone I know so it seems two-faced of me to walk around moaning. Everyone in any room I'm ever in is going to die the same as I am so there's no point in bleating about it."

He also revealed the band's new found sense of fashion: "My idea of hunkiness is Simon . . . before, when it was just me, Laurence and Simon in the group, no-one ever really bothered about what we looked like, which was fine. Now we have to. With five people you have to, otherwise it looks like the Village People. We just had five suits made each so that, wherever we go, we look similar. It's so we don't lose each other – a bit like wearing a yellow flag above your head. Who's in the band this week? Ah – *he* must be, he's got the suit on."

He concluded: "I'd rather be in this particular Cure than any of the other ones."

On 25 April, they played the Royal Albert Hall, headlining the last night of Soundwaves, a week of

benefits for Greenpeace.

ALBERT HALL

Adam Sweeting

The Cure

THE CURE stepped boldly from the shadows to close the series of Sound Waves For Greenpeace shows with a towering set which lasted nearly two hours. They've been through some curious cycles in their career, from an early dalliance with skeletal pop to bouts of suicidal gloom, more recently developing a knack for idiosyncratic catchiness.

Robert Smith, the fluctuations of whose biorhythms seem to determine The Cure's progress, still looks like a rag doll in a shapeless suit, his hair exploding madly from the top of his head like an experiment with a devastating new type of fertiliser. However, he was able to guide his group easily through a variety of moods, raiding the back catalogue for a number of seldom-heard pieces such as the dolorous Other Voices.

In a more whimsical vein, they played In Between Days and the perfect Close To Me, Smith becoming increasingly skittish as they did so, while A Forest built to a New Orderish climax of stupefying power. The longer they do it, to paraphrase Tina Turner, the better it gets.

THE CURE
BOYS DON'T CRY
7 INCH AND 3 TRACK 12 INCH

Record Mirror's Eleanor Levy wrote: "The Cure managed something only the last night of the proms is rumoured to do. They got the Albert Hall moving . . . Queen Victoria must be turning in her grave." And Robert later told Sounds: "We did 'Faith' for the first time in years and I was crying through it . . . It's like re-reading a page of your diary, like Christmas Eve 1975 and all the hopes you had; it really cuts you up sometimes. When I hear it, I have to stop listening. I wish everything I did had such a strong effect on me."

The remixed 'Boys Don't Cry' was released as a single in April backed wtih two ancient previously unreleased tracks, 'Do The Hansa', a piss-take of their first record company's expectations of them, and 'Pillbox Tales'.

THE CURE
Boys Don't Cry (Fiction)
I WISH Bob would put that bottle down and cheer up a bit. This is the old gem tidied up and ushered along rather unnecessarily by a newly-recorded vocal. Without the cracks and the pauses it's rather like a singalong competition winner and for a song that can make millions cry so easily, that's a shame.

The video, again by Pope, featured the original trio almost invisible behind a screen while three small boys mimed their parts. Michael Dempsey, who'd played as a session musician with Roxy Music and The Lotus Eaters since leaving The Associates, was working on incidental music in Holland with Stephen Emmer.

Michael:

"Robert rang me and it was quite a surprise. I don't know whether he meant it as a nice gesture or whether it just fitted in with the general scheme. It was nice anyway because I'd been to the Albert Hall to see them and . . . well, I don't really enjoy The Albert Hall at the best of times but what I preferred to watch from my vantage point – which I had to pay for – was the audience adulation. I don't know where they can develop from there, stuck with those people who copy their hairstyles, their every movement. I always thought they would carry on for years and years at the level I left them but the way the thing has grown!

"When people from the press talk to me now, they always tend to be more interested in me being an ex-member of The Cure than in anything I happen to be doing at the moment but I suppose that's only natural. Do I regret it now? Yes and no. I regret not being part of what looks to be quite an exciting opportunity to get around and have a look at a lot of things. But to start with a group and still be with them in 10 years time, there'd need to be something there far more intimate than what we had. The circumstances under which we parted were a bit grim and continued to be so for some time so it was nice to see you could still talk to these people."

8

Standing On A Beach', a compilation album of The Cure's 13 singles to date was released in May, its title taken from the first line in 'Killing An Arab' and the cover depicting a gnarled old man.

Lol:

"The picture of that man is a lot more honest than a picture of the band in a lot of ways. When a person sees the cover, he doesn't know what to expect. If we had a picture of us, the person would guess at what type of music might be on it and might not buy it just cos he or she didn't like the way we looked."

WAVING NOT DROWNING

THE CURE
STANDING ON A BEACH: THE SINGLES
Fiction

THERE aren't too many prizes for guessing anymore – most everything you hear makes perfect sense, scared stiff of shaking a leg in another direction or dipping a wick in someone else's pond.

That's why Robert Smith, with his daft disrespect, his scarecrow scatology and his maverick mocking of the fascism of fashion, is more *important* now than he's ever been. It's a role he's assumed reluctantly – like Prince, he's shy of the paraphernalia of celebrity, naturally suspicious of its co-called rewards. And, like Prince, he comes in at all the usual stuff we're saddled with from some damn brutal angles and muddles up melodrama with whimsy, dreaming with waking, because *that's the way it is.*

"Standing On A Beach", a chronological retrospective of all 13 of The Cure's singles, is evidence that time has been kind to Robert Smith because he's always been so acutely aware, in awe and afraid of it. He may have been kidding when he said he'd contemplated suicide at the thought of reaching 25 but many a true word's spoken in jest, many a Freudian slip uttered in flippancy. Robert Smith is always on the run.

The sneering sarcasm of "Jumping Someone Else's Train" was as deliberate a detonation of the pretty pop group that gave us the chirpy "Boys Don't Dry" as "BDC" itself must have seemed a happy-go-lucky way out of the existentialist reputation he'd ludicrously picked up through "Killing An Arab".

Smith simply couldn't, and still can't, understand why people want to pigeonhole him, why pop has to be this or that, and the only external consideration that infiltrates his musical self-sufficiency is to escape categorisation. Hence the rancid eroticism of "The Hanging Garden" purposefully dragging the holy adrenalin of that brilliant romantic trio – "A Forest", "Primary" and "Charlotte Sometimes" – to the very depths of angst, a self-parodic purging that was by no means inevitable if you consider some of his contemporaries still trading off familiar manoeuvres.

The immediate progeny were bitter-sweet revenge on those who took for granted that The Cure were serious young men concerned solely with maintaining their cool. "Let's Go To Bed" and "The Walk" ritually assassinated Smith the guitar hero and, with the exorcism effected, "Love Cats" was like a rebirth, not carefree but uncaring, bursting the sluice gates as the freaked-out "Caterpiller" [illegible] as the [illegible] and "Close To Me".

But, idiot-dancing to "Standing On A Beach", it's evident that, apart from Smith's sheer paranoia of the responsibility of image, of having to live up to anything for anyone but himself, there's as much method in the madness as there is madness in the method. Just as Smith has constantly reviewed and renewed the band's direction to avoid categorisation and its attendant temptations to tread water, so Cure songs squirm around in their sockets, taunting their clichés into new shapes and sharper focus.

"In Between Days" may have jumped New Order's train stylistically but that tune you're singing is laced with a lyric that festers with fear. "Let's Go To Bed", too, is the threat *and* the promise, the suggestion of seduction and an escape from another weary day. And, further still, its lame hilarity and slightly laggard disco grind exposes the hollow heart of the mating game and the forced nightclub glee. Significantly, Smith's voice has always been simultaneously as suggestive of sorrow as celebration, of panic as pleasure.

"Standing On A Beach" is a very great record (the cassette version also includes 12 B-sides unavailable on any LP), a tipsy captain's log of a band wilfully all at sea because, after all, aren't we all?

STEVE SUTHERLAND

'Staring At The Sea', the video compilation also named after a line in 'Killing An Arab', was released simultaneously, with the band's first three singles accompanied visually for the first time. Robert told Smash Hits: "When we decided to put it together, it was apparent that the early stuff was appalling. So we made it more exciting by sticking in some old home movie footage to give the thing a sense of history. It starts off in 1976 at the Bandstand in Crawley, then there's a bit of us at the Reading Festival in 1979 supporting Motorhead.

"The first proper videos we did were hilarious. We thought we were apart from image-building so we stood in front of the camera looking like very bored people, which we were. Now we're well known for videos thanks to Tim Pope. He translates our ideas really well. I'm a lot happier now and it shows."

Vicki MacDonald in the same magazine wrote: "In the space of one hour, Robert Smith changes from a fresh-faced, clean cut youth into the shambling, unkempt figure of today which is a bit of a weird trip (man)."

THE CURE · STARING AT THE SEA · THE IMAGES

Later, Robert told the East Village Eye: "I think it's one of the best things we've ever done because it's really self-deflating. There's no preening or glamour in it. We look completely foolish. If I was at all concerned with the image of The Cure, it would never have been made. In fact, it's so much truer to what being in the group is like. It's just interesting to show people how we've metamorphosed over the years. It's incredible how our faces change, really uncanny. It's not just like I'm fatter – I look a completely different person. My face was so hard and angry around the time of '17 Seconds'. What you really feel inside shows in your face because I have since become far more balanced and my face is much more normal . . . "

In an article in Sounds at the time, Glyn Brown wrote: "Instead of a libidinous, drug-headed weasel I found someone funny, hesitant, shy, charming, guarded, clever and haunting", and Robert told her: "I've never accepted that you have to suffer for your after-life. I think you should make a point of not suffering, of being happy . . . My ambition, at the age of 14, was to sit on top of a mountain and just die . . . "

In early May, Robert travelled to America for a string of interviews to promote the album and a tour planned for July. "I could have brought the whole band with me," he told Aquarian Weekly, "but it would have cost a lot more and they would have just gone out and got pissed and I would still have had to do the interviews on my own . . . The only person to suffer from me being the leader is me. The others are absolved from all responsibility . . . They don't envy me at all."

On 15 May, The Cure played the Pink Pop Festival in Holland followed by a stint of miming on "very dodgy Europop TV shows".

On 22 May, the band and their girlfriends boarded the Orient Express for Venice to play a gig in Verona that was cancelled by firechiefs so the jaunt turned into a holiday. The train journey from Victoria to Dover was filmed by the 'Whistle Test' and widely publicised in the British daily papers.

DAILY EXPRESS Monday May 26 1986

The Perfect Cure!

All dressed up and ready to go . . . the band and their girlfriends Pictures RICHARD YOUNG

She went to . . . Cynde Burnier

When the band goes away—the girlfriends go too

By DAVID WIGG on the Orient Express

IN THE old days rock groups used to travel to their shows in clapped-out secondhand vans. Not any more, it seems.

That outlandish young group, The Cure booked a carriage on the Orient Express over the weekend just to transport them to Venice where they were playing a concert at nearby Verona. Deciding to also treat their girlfriends to the luxury of the sedate golden, brown and cream pre-war train, the trip cost them £15,000 altogether.

Mind you, the five members of The Cure can easily afford such lavish comfort having become one of Britain's most successful cult bands selling more than five million albums. They are currently in the Top 30 with their single Boys Don't Cry.

Opportunity

"We did not always travel around in this kind of style," remarked wild haired singer-songwriter Robert Smith, who was wearing as much mascara as his girlfriend Mary Poole. "When we first started we travelled around in an old Bedford van we bought for £45, held together by tape and chewing gum. I have always wanted to travel on this train and now we have the opportunity to do so."

All the girlfriends have given up their jobs to live with their men.

Robert first met Mary at a school open day 12 years ago when he was just 14. She has worked as a model and been a nurse to mentally handicapped children.

"We work such unsociable hours and if the girls have a day job it means we can never see them—it was becoming ridiculous," explained Robert. "We do not take them on tour though. If we did, we would have to wake up three hours before leaving because they take so long getting ready. They are like a separate group—they drink more and are more disturbing!"

Waitress

Guitarist Paul Thompson goes out with Robert's younger sister, Janet Smith, a classically trained pianist; bass guitarist Simon Gallup's girlfriend, Carol Thompson, is a former secretary; keyboard player Laurence Tolhurst lives with one-time cocktail waitress Lydia Browne and drummer Boris Williams dates the only American, Cynde Burnier, who used to work as a tourist guide in Los Angeles.

While the rest of the passengers turned up for the Orient Express in elegantly formal tailored clothes—the scene resembled Ascot—The Cure and their entourage looked an incongruous party arriving in somewhat startling more casual and individual styles. They conformed to the rules of changing into black tie and evening dress for dinner—but didn't alter their outrageous hairstyles.

Over a champagne lunch on the train's 1928 Zena carriage, Robert explained how he put together The Cure with Laurence while attending a comprehensive in Crawley, Surrey.

"Our first performance was a school joke. We pretended it was going to be a choral society in the school hall and then we turned up," Robert wickedly recalled. "We charged 10p a ticket, 500 people turned up and half of them left after the first song."

Robert left school at 17 with A levels in French and English, and after one week as a gardener settled down to writing songs while picking up £12 a week on the dole.

"The good thing about the dole is that it actually encourages you to do something creative," he said. "I used to spend a lot of time in the library just walking about humming."

Advance

The Cure established themselves during the Punk era, after winning a nationwide new bands contest out of 1,200 entries. A £1,000 record advance—which at the time they thought a fortune enabled them to buy new musical equipment.

The Cure are about to release their tenth album Standing On A Beach—The Singles, which contains 13 of their most popular tracks including Close To Me and Charlotte Sometimes. The group are booked as headliners for next month's Glastonbury Festival on June 21 and BBC 2's Whistle Test filmed their Orient Express trip to be shown on June 17.

Back in London, the band started rehearsing and recording demos of 20 new songs in North London and deciding whether or not to call the next album 'One Million Virgins'. Robert informed Just 17: "I don't worry too much about my appearance or anything. I mean, I haven't washed my hair for three and a half weeks . . . " adding " . . . I'd quite like to swop my internal organs. My liver's going to say 'I can't cope with this any longer and I'm going to give up pretty soon . . . " and " . . . I always use gel, not hairspray. It's called KMS or something and it comes with hexagrams on. It's got the most glue-like consistency of anything I've ever come across. I backcomb it a lot too. I did use mousse for a while but it used to drop onto my nose in big globs when I was on stage, which was disgusting."

While the Cure were in Germany playing festivals (14 June, Nuremberg Ring, 15 June, Munich), 'Whistle Test' screened the Orient Express episode, featuring the boys drunkenly strumming 'Home On The Range' and, on 21 June, they headlined Glastonbury CND Festival. Robert told Smash Hits: "My views are pretty much the same as one of my earliest childhood heroes, Spike Milligan. I still think the idealism involved in nuclear disarmament is laudable but the knowledge to create the bomb is there and there's nothing we can do to take that away – nuclear disarmament is really a very naive dream. Nevertheless, The Cure are still playing Glastonbury because there always has to be a level of public and private awareness otherwise people in power become too complacent. With the threat of civil unrest lying near the surface. I hope that keeps certain political leaders from becoming too extreme, knowing they can only go so far without retaliation from the masses."

GLASTONBURY

The Cure's set is their well-trodden *fait accompli* of recent months. Standing on a beach and sobbing out 'the hits', even if it means 6,427 encores. So many cats and cupboards and fingerclicks. Close indeed, and cute and coy, and if popular bands *must* only perform shows that have all the intimacy of a cashpoint machine, then at least let them do it with *gallons of white light in blackness.*

As here, Smith and his *backing band* (let's face it) nobly attempt. 'One Hundred Years' is the only song in the world that lasts as long as its title without ever falling below the 'admirably magical' level. Later, in a corridor, I see a painting called 'Rustic Courtship'.

The customary opener, "Shake Dog Shake", blistered out across the crowd steaming like cattle, a fog of dry ice stobed and blue from the lights momentarily masking Smith's disappointment at Socrates' folly.

A stately "Primary" pursued "Charlotte Sometimes" into the surprise "Strange Day" and it was apparent that the random ransacking of the back catalogue with which Smith shocked and delighted his disciples at the Albert Hall was no one-off. An immensely jolly "In Between Days", a wigged-out "Walk", a majestic "Night Like This" – This Cure are sublime with such ridiculous ease.

There was something in the Official Programme about them coming full circle but tonight's set was more like a spiral, the nagging "100 Years" flaying the audience into petrified silence only for "Close To Me" to get them swaying and singing and "Give Me It" to stun them again.

Peaks were a chirpy "Boys Don't Cry", a gossamer version of "Faith" and a scintillating "A Forest", Smith allowing the song a loose rein, meandering flurries of chords to the climax then peeling away to allow Simon's bass, clapped along by the crowd, to draw the drama to a moving conclusion.

No new songs, nothing radically out of line but not just another Cure show either because, these days, there's not such thing as just another Cure anything. As the lazers blasted the mirror balls and immersed us in a foliage of lights, Robert wished everyone a happy tomorrow and it ceased to rain.

An American Tour started on 6 July at Great Woods Centre For The Performing Arts at Mansfield and The Boston Globe wrote: "With the possible exception of Pink Floyd, no rock band has ever put across such compelling sadness."

Middlesex News called 'A Forest' "New wave surf music" and The Maiden Evening News headlined their review "Punk Is Dead, Either That Or The Cure's Gone Pop", noting "As the show wore down towards the end of a long, ghostly night of lilting, swaying and rocking, teenie-bopper girls dressed in black and white with punky hair-do's risked their lives trying to get past a group of gruff security monsters to give Smith a kiss. Punk rockers trying to get onstage to kiss a group's lead singer? That's not punk. The Sex Pistols would have opened fire on a crowd like that with flame throwers."

Robert told BAM: "I don't know why people like us more than they did five years ago. Maybe we're making more accessible music. Maybe we're making better music. Maybe it's just because people think we're funny.", and he told Creem: "It's very difficult coming to terms with the popularity we have at the moment, reconciling that to the idea of staying outside the mainstream. Because we're inevitably being drawn more and more towards it", while, to the Waycross Journal Herald, he confessed: "The main motivating reason why The Cure was started and why I wanted to sing in the group and write songs is I thought most everything I was confronted with on the radio and TV was dross, I still do. If I thought we had become redundant, I would write the whole thing off."

"The only time I feel like quitting," he told Only Music, "is when I'm worn out by it but over the past 18 months we've really cut down. Now, everything we do seems like a big event. This entire year, we're only doing about 23 concerts so each one is quite special."

The band's American company, Elektra, was now their fourth, (Sire had released 'Japanese Whispers' but dropped the option on 'The Top') and, with both 'The Head On The Door' and 'Standing On A Beach' doing well, they insisted on re-releasing 'Let's Go To Bed' in preference to 'Boys Don't Cry' as the single. The group were upset. The compromise was 'Boys' on the B-side.

Robert told Only Music: "I've given up fighting with the record company in America. As long as they release the album and don't mess about, I don't really care what they release as the single because we never sell a lot of singles anyway so what difference does it make."

It seemed also, though, that, viewing it in retrospect, he'd warmed to the song, informing Creem: "The most amazing thing for me about what The Cure does is there is nothing in what we've done that I would do differently. I would do it differently if I did it all *now*, but there's nothing I would change from when it was done at the time."

He also told Aquarian Weekly: "I had to change people's perceptions of The Cure with 'Let's Go To Bed' because it's ludicrous to suffer just so people can live vicariously through what you're doing. It's such a tired old cliche, living on the edge and everyone sort of pushing you towards it, saying 'Go on, see how much further you can go'. People revel in that whole sense of the voyeur but it's nonsense because, after they'd finished with us, that same vampiric element in our audience would turn to someone else for the same thing. I didn't want to be a martyr, like Ian Curtis". To Creem he added: "Ian Curtis was my generation's suicide. I didn't really want to follow in his footsteps."

Still, The Boston Globe informed its readers that The Cure formed "inspired by the leading post punk group, Joy Division" and reckoned many of their early fans might be somewhat dismayed by their new pop success. Lol told them he didn't give a hoot, describing their early fans' point of view as "'This is very, very deep so, therefore, you'd have to walk around in a long mac and be perpetually miserable to understand it' . . . I hate that kind of snobbery."

Robert insisted in The Associated Press that "The idea of enjoyment pervades everything we do. It's not easily discerned by people on the outside. Everything we do deals with childish abandon. Nothing is ever worked out. That kind of professionalism is anathema to everything we stand for." And Simon informed Boston Rock: "I think if we see anymore of New York, we're dead . . . "

Musician's Charles M Young noted: "Smith's problem is existential despair, metaphysical distress, ontological ungluedation and cosmic meltdown. You would cry too if it happened to you". Robert replied: "When you ponder anything fundamental to your existence, you inevitably end up depressed if you don't have a sense of belief which I've never had. I've always ended up in this . . . well, it's a bottomless pit, really. From time to time I've slipped into it and dragged the group down with me. But I think what's come out of it is like a soundtrack for a lot of people's lives. Everyone I know has suffered the same sort of doubts and depressions . . . We don't take ourselves so seriously now . . . No-one is in this band because of technical proficiency, they are in it because of something they bring as personalities. Laurence, for example, was an atrocious drummer and he's even more atrocious now on keyboards but I can't imagine him not being in the group. And that dictates the tone of the music, if not the direct content of the words. We have to have that balance between fun and the bottomless pit."

In a major feature in the July edition of Rolling Stone, Robert claimed: "I don't think I'm more depressed than anyone else I know. I'm not really obsessed with death . . . Everything I do has the tinge of the finite, of my own demise. At some point you either accept death or you just keep pushing it back as you get older and older. I've accepted it". But he told LA Weekly: "I change my mind all the time. I never feel bound by what I've said in an interview. It'd be a bit ludicrous – I'd force myself into a corner from which I could never escape. And a lot of the time . . . I find reasons for things that are patently untrue just to make people think 'What is he doing?'"

With Aquarian Weekly calling Robert "The male Kate Bush, the thinking teen's pin-up, the security blanket of the bedsit set". The Chicago Sun Times referring to him as "a dark version of Boy George" and The Evening Gazette And Worcester Telegraph waiting for The Cure to become "the next Thompson

Twins", the band were attracting extraordinary attention, especially as Robert had destroyed all preconceptions by having his hair hacked into a crew cut.

"Can it be that the entire world as we know it is in an uproar over Robert Smith's hair?" asked Only Music. "A haircut is hardly a major news event . . . or is it? MTV, at least, broadcast special bulletins nearly every hour when the former mop-top chopped his locks off."

"If it's that important to someone," Robert told them, "I think they need to reconsider why they like us." And to In Fashion: "It's really bad when people recognise you not for the music you make but because of your haircut. I was tired of seeing so many people who looked like me."

"Some kid out there even asked me if it'd been a wig all this time," he told Boston Rock, and "The Messiah of Angst" informed Only Music "I think the amount of people who feel obsessive about me or about the group has been exaggerated. I suppose people like to have something to hold onto. I'd prefer it to be a group like The Cure rather than a lot of other groups because I think we have a better attitude than most other groups. We're not desperate and we're not really worried about what other people think about us, which is a good attitude for anyone to have."

Horror at Cure show

A LOVELORN fan of top British band The Care was recovering last night after making a bizarre and bloody suicide bid at one of their concerts . . . while other fans cheered him on.

Jonathan Moreland, aged 38, stabbed himself repeatedly in the chest and stomach with a seven-inch hunting knife, splattering blood over the packed audience in Los Angeles.

Then Mr. Moreland, wearing a cowboy hat and boots, stripped off his shirt and leaped on to a chair where he showed off his wounds to the cheering crowd and continued to plunge the blade into his tattooed chest.

Eventually he was hauled off to hospital. Police found a note in his car in which he said he was killing himself because of his hopeless love for a girl called Andrea.

The Cure—whose songs tend to be most depressing—refused to comment on the incident.

Rock fans cheer on death bid at concert

by JONATHAN ASHBY

BRITISH rock band The Cure were in shock last night after a fan tried to stab himself to death at their concert.

Jonathan Morland climbed on to his seat seconds before e group was due to appear ı stage in Los Angeles.

He repeatedly stabbed himself with a seven-inch hunting knife.

The audience, many wearing black with their faces painted white like The Cure's singer Robert Smith, at first thought Morland's death attempt was part of the act.

Bitter end

Police sergeant Norman Brewer said: "Morland thought the crowd were cheering him on and, as the crowd grew louder, he stabbed himself deeper and harder."

Morland was taken to hospital in a "critical condition".

He told police: "I tried to commit suicide because I won't ever be able to have the woman I love."

The group were said last night to be too shocked and distraught to comment.

But in London, a spokesman for the group's record company said: "It was a bitter ending for them because it happened on the last night of what had been a successful US tour.

"They could not believe anyone would do that at one of their gigs."

"Unless something really drastic happens on the American Tour," Robert told Aqaurian Weekly, "like if someone flips out completely, I know that this line-up will make the next record. It isn't really something you can forecast – it might just as easily last for 10 years as 10 days". And Lol informed The Newspaper "I think this will be The Cure that you'll see until it stops being The Cure. I can't see anybody else coming into the band. It's really always been a band made up of friends more than anything else . . . but I don't think we have any friends left who can play anything . . . " and he revealed to The Royal Oak Tribune: "At the moment we have the bare bones of about 20 songs. They're all fairly melodic. But some pieces are a bit longer than the ones off our last album. A few other things are more stripped down . . . I have a feeling that where we actually record tends to influence the way we write and play. Before, we've recorded mostly in and around London. And we've been walking out of the studio at four in the morning and it's pouring with rain. It tends to make us feel a little like that. This time we're going to record in America where it's hot and sunny. So we might end up sounding like The Eagles."

Meanwhile, Robert informed Only Music: "I don't see the point in us being produced when I know exactly what we should sound like anyway. We always get whoever's signed us in America saying 'Get a producer. He'll make your records sound better.' But they wouldn't. They would just make it sound like everyone else's album so it will get played on the radio. I don't think that's making it better."

And, in the Orange City Review he claimed he was co-authoring The Cure's autobiography. The book, he said, was to be called The Glass Sandwich: "It's taking forever. I'll never catch up to today's date. It's quite funny . . . Someone once dared me to eat a glass sandwich. I was in a very sorry state at the time and I tried. I cut my mouth to pieces but I didn't swallow it. I wasn't *that* stupid."

Lol revealed to the University Star: "I've often talked to Robert about things and he'll say 'Oh, do you remember when this happened?' and I'll say 'No', because it never happened. I often think he finds it difficult to draw the line between waking and sleeping hours."

And where, asked the writer, would Lol like to be in 10 years time? "In Heaven." So soon, asked the scribe?: "Why not, if it's as good as its supposed to be?"

During August, The Cure played one show in Spain and four in France, finishing up on the 9th and 10th, in an 8,000 capacity Roman amphitheatre in Orange, Provence. The venue had been especially chosen for Tim Pope to shoot live footage of the band on film – his first attempt at a full length feature. Robert:

"I don't think it was a risk working with Pap just because he wasn't really an experienced film director. We could have got in a 'real' director to make a film of the concert, but he wouldn't have known what the band was about and I wanted it to be a Cure film about The Cure. It's actually very cleverly done and it doesn't look like any other live film I've ever seen.

"Initially we were going to make a film that was

very abstract. We wanted to do something like an hour and half of us playing characters like some old Beatles film, but, as it turned out, mainly through time and money, it ended up being purely live performance. You're probably only going to be interested in it if you're interested in The Cure, but Pap definitely recorded a very special event in his own style and with his own perspecctive on what happened. You'd never get that shakey, hand-held stuff in a normal big budget film because people just wouldn't take the risk. It's like Pap running across the stage, trapping my mike wire – only *he'd* do something like that, anyone else would have been too concerned with camera angles.

"Watching the film is like being on stage, not just like watching the group – you see it from both points of view. Many people who've seen it have felt that they now know what it's like to be onstage and face an audience. It's a shame there was no other kind of off-stage imagery or behind the scenes stuff but, as a record of that one performance, it sums it all up perfectly."

Porl:

"It's aggressive and powerful and you feel like you're in the group when you watch it. When I watch it, it makes me want to play!"

Pope:

"You could actually draw a little map of the roles in The Cure and I shot the film to illustrate that, to *filmically* establish their relationship. It's like the way they sit on the tour bus – Robert has the best seat, Simon sits opposite him, Porl sits behind, Boris sits at the back and Lol sits up front and is persecuted. But, without Lol, The Cure really wouldn't exist, there's obviously a great love between him and Robert and I think it's got something to do with security because they've been together so long. It's a fascinating structure.

"Like, there's a bit in the film where Simon goes over and whispers something to Robert and it looks like he's saying something about the music but he's not at all, he's actually telling him some sort of joke!

"The other thing about the film is that it redresses the balance. I mean, obviously the videos did them a lot of good, redressing the doomed-out sort of thing, but, in a sense, we had to be very careful not to make The Cure too wacky and, at one stage, around 'Love Cats', we did. The Cure aren't about videos. Seeing them live, I realised I'd reduced them, put them into a tiny box which is not necessarily what they're about. I think the film represents more the way they really are.

"What's amazing is the diversity of material. It starts off with 'Shake Dog Shake', really metallic-sounding, then they go into 'A Forest', then 'Sinking', which is really emotional, then Robert's in his 'Close To Me' and 'Let's Go To Bed' clown character, then there's 'Faith' and 'Give Me It' . . . . the changes are brilliant. They're ideal for film because they're just like different scenes.

"There's another film to be made of them too, like a perverse, modern-day Beatles because, to me, they are the perfect pop group and yet they're not – there's something desperately wrong with them. But I don't think I could have made a bad film for The Cure – there's just something about them . . ."

When the filming was over, the band took a holiday in Toulon.

Robert:

"It was a disaster. Word got out that we were there and we couldn't move from the hotel for days. We were on the front page of the local paper every day and we were under siege. It was cack not being able to go out without people coming up and going 'You're Robert Smith'. I became less than human."

The band retreated to Jean Costa's studio in Draguignan where they worked further on demos originally put together in Beethoven studios in London earlier in the Summer.

Robert:

"I wrote 'Head On The Door' on my own at home and the group interpreted it like an orchestra would, but this time I insisted that the others give me cassettes of their own music and I got six or seven songs from each one. Boris even made a tape of some weird vampire drumming! Everyone really wanted to be involved.

"We put on all the tapes and everyone listened to them, commenting on them and giving them scores out of 20, and then we took the ones that were the most interesting and started work. We demo'd at Jean Costa's for two weeks and it was really good fun – he had a football pitch next door and we played the locals almost every day . . . very relaxing . . .

"Then we drove across to Miraval and started recording a song a day, sometimes two. Most of them were first takes, almost jamming the songs to get the right feel. We'd spend a couple of hours playing each song through until we became familiar with it and then we'd record it in one go. And it worked. It was a delight, a joy"

Boris:

"It felt completely different to doing 'Head On The Door' because, although I still think it's a good album, I don't particularly like what I played on it. I'd played parts which were set down for me whereas, with this, I really thought out all the parts. It gave me the chance to express my personality within the group."

Robert:

"I wrote words for 23 songs and they were among the best I'd ever written. I astounded myself because usually I get stuck but, this time, I just sat down every day to write and it was easy. Normally I'm struggling to polish the words in a London studio where there's a lot of pressure but in Miraval I knew we had enough music for a double album and I thought 'If I can't come up with enough words, we'll just make it a single album' so there was no real worry.

"I wrote a lot of the songs the way I wrote 'The Walk'. I had a mood for each one and I sifted back through what I'd already done. A couple of songs even refer to incidents I'd already written songs about but they actually capture their spirit far more. 'Shiver and Shake' is similar in mood to 'Give Me It' but lyrically it's broader, it deals with the same incident but it also encompasses *every* time I feel like that. It sums it up.

'How Beautiful You Are' owes a lot to a Baudelaire short story about how you feel you're really close to somebody, that you think the same way as them and

enjoy the same things, but suddenly an incident will happen that forces you to realise that this person thinks in a different way to you about things that you consider really important. And yet you can still get on with them. So, it's about how no-one really knows anyone else, or really loves anyone else in the purest sense because it's utterly impossible . . .

"Taking specifics and writing songs about them is far more challenging than writing 'I'm not feeling very well today' sorts of songs. It's always good to write about mood but it's also good to look at something really hard and to find and take the essence from it.

"I really wanted to write words for songs that the others had written the music for and they turned out well. Like, Porl wrote the initial music to 'Fight' and I would otherwise never in a million years have written a song like that. Porl's three songs on the album and Simon's two are something that The Cure would never have done before because I couldn't write music like that."

"The other noticably different thing about the songs is my voice. On 'The Top', I started trying to change my voice whereas before that I had thought it sacrilegious to even attempt other ways of expressing myself. Most people change their voice to make it more acceptable, nicer or more American, very few will attempt to make their singing more difficult or *worse*. But, again, I thought 'Why not?' so, 'Hot Hot Hot' for example, I sound like my idea of a gospel singer, and on 'The Snakepit' I sound like a psychopath . . . and it was all done quite spontaneously, quite live."

"In the three months The Cure were at Miraval, a remote studio – cum – vineyard in the South of France, the recordings assumed the overall title 'Kiss Me Kiss Me Kiss Me' and naturally developed into a double album.

Robert:

"The only doubt was the precedent set by other people's double albums. There are so few in the history of pop that have worked – the 'White Album', 'Electric Ladyland', the Prince album . . .
I think 'Ummagumma' was a good record and Porl maintains there's a fab Led Zeppelin album too . . . but we thought 'Kiss Me' would make two great single albums, and as there were no weak songs, we went ahead."

While recording, The Cure took time out to appear on French television, miming to 'Boys Don't Cry' and creating a stir by appearing in frocks and make-up.

Robert:

"I've never tried to capitalise on an image. At the French concerts, an inordinate amount of people arrived dressed in black despite the fact that the group never likes wearing black, it's just a myth that's arisen. It's equally as difficult trying to escape the quirky corner. That's why I cut off my hair when we went to America, because I wanted the group to be far more sullen and aggressive than people were expecting.
I wanted to look stark and it was a crucial calculation because, once I see adjectives like 'cuddly' appearing about me, I think 'This is going to fuck whatever we try to do next'. I mean, if a magazine says 'Wouldn't you like to take him home?', it destroys me when I'm next in the studio wanting to sing something that *means* something."

"In December, The Cure re-signed to Polydor through Fiction with the album virtually complete, and Robert went with co-producer Dave Allen to Compass Point in the Bahamas for mixing.

Robert:

"We had this song, 'Hey You', which was just over two minutes long and sounded a bit like 'The Man From UNCLE Theme' but it needed some brass on it. So we went out to this American bar and there, playing saxophone with a terrible cabaret group, was this enormous bloke who was so out of place, so out of it, he was off planet. But he was so good I thought if The Cure were ever going to get a real sax player, it would be someone like him. So we said 'Come along to the studio and play' and he did – he just wailed away over 'Hey You' and 'Icing Sugar' and it was perfect! Both first takes! We didn't even tell him we were recording! I wouldn't have done that a few years earlier, I'd have thought too much about it. But this time I thought 'If it doesn't work, it doesn't work' – a much better attitude."

In January 1987, Robert and Dirk finished the mixing in Brussels and Robert then flew on to Ireland where the rest of the band joined him for rehearsals in preparation for the band's first South American tour. Tim Pope also flew over to shoot a bizarre, fancy dress, choreographed video for the 'Why Can't I Be You' single at Mary Tyler Moore studios in Bray, and Robert complained to Melody Maker "I always thought I was destined for great things but look at me. I'm in the scruffiest, laziest group in the world dressed up in a fucking animal suit!" While Simon, dressed as a crow, informed Robert he resembled a gay viking more than a polar bear, Pope arranged to fly Lol, dressed as a bumble bee, on wires, ecstatically proclaiming "This is it! The video I've always wanted to make. The Cure *dancing* I can't believe I'm seeing this. They're *finished*!"

Sighed Robert: "Any vestiges of reality that surround the group, any accusations of musicianship that might be levelled at us on the release of the album, will be shattered."

In March, The Cure travelled to Argentina where they played two shows in a 20,000 capacity Buenos Aires football stadium and suffered riots outside when all the people gathered couldn't get in and over 100 were arrested. Tour security was immediately taken over by the Ministry Of Interior Affairs and, again, the band were under siege in their hotels until they flew to Brazil for eight more concerts.

These concerts, too, were wild affairs, and the group returned to London after three weeks triumphant but more than slightly shell-shocked!

'Why I Can't I Be You'/'A Japanese Dream' was released on April 10.

THE CURE: Why Can't I Be You? (Fiction) This sounds like Dexy's Midnight Runners! Yes it does! What – don't you like Dexy's or something? (*No* – S. Patterson.) WHAAAAT!? (*Looks aghast*) Huh! Dexy's wipe away The Cure but I quite like The Cure too. This is just the same as . . . whatsit? "Lovecats". It's not a re-release is it? I like it, yeah, it's white soul with burst – I like that. Do I think this is the worst singing he's ever done? Er . . . I wouldn't be able to judge something that subtle sssssss! He's a good song-writer. Don't like his hair much though. Still, it's *his* hair innit? Sssss!

THE CURE
Why Can't I Be You (Fiction)

This is the third time I've heard this record The first time, I thought, "Oh, f***g hell...Come on, who are you kidding?" But this time I really liked it. He's trying to get the big production in, and it's nothing new, but he sounds like a genuine artiste. He doesn't sound as if he's been in the boardroom too much, basically.**

The Gala Premier of "The Cure In Orange" was held on April 23 at the Odeon, Marble Arch.

THE CURE IN ORANGE (U: 113 mins) Yus! The very wonderful Cure! In a full-length feature film! Made by the mad bloke who makes all their brilliantly bonkers videos! Sounds quite good does it not? Well, it isn't. The "story" is this: The Cure walk on to the stage of a stadium in France (which is a massive old building called "Orange" – hence the name!!), Simon Gallup whips off Robert Smith's "funny" wig to reveal his recent super-snipped hairdo, they play a very large number of songs, wave a bit by a statue and then amble off again. i.e. it's an elongated live video, the swizzlers. . . So now you "know".

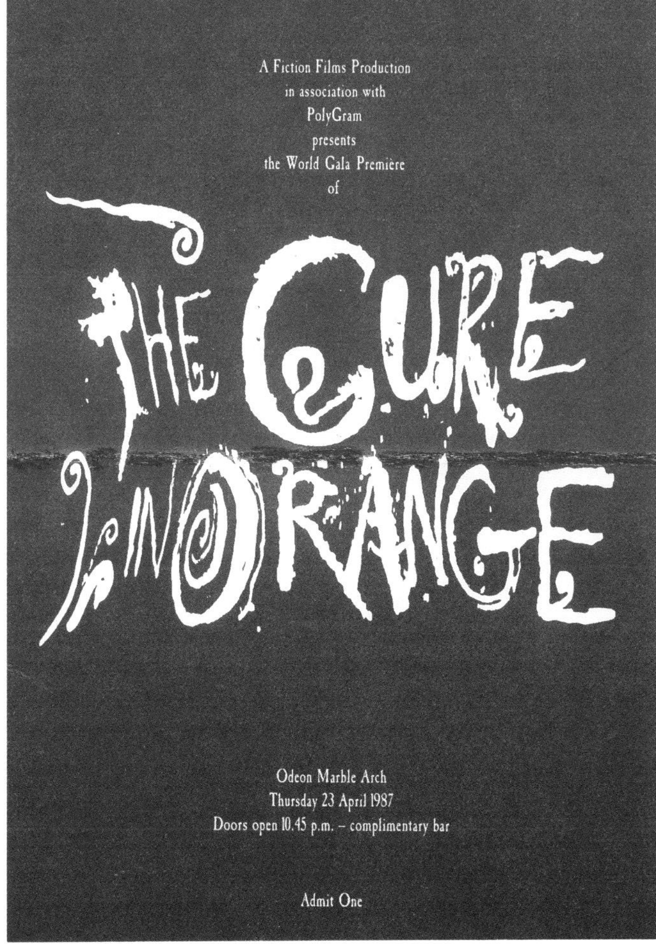

A Fiction Films Production
in association with
PolyGram
presents
the World Gala Première
of
THE CURE IN ORANGE
Odeon Marble Arch
Thursday 23 April 1987
Doors open 10.45 p.m. – complimentary bar
Admit One

Meanwhile The Cure appeared on a round of European TV shows and, on April 24, performed 'Why Can't I Be You?' and 'Catch' on the last ever edition of 'The Tube' (a special elongated version of the programme the following Sunday also featured the band playing 'Hot Hot Hot'). They then 'took part' in the dreadful Montreux Pop Festival and, on May 22, 'Kiss Me Kiss Me Kiss Me' was at last released.

THE CURE: Kiss Me, Kiss Me, Kiss Me (Fiction)
"Kiss Me, Kiss Me, Kiss Me" is a bit like the new Prince LP, really. They're both double albums, they both wander through several squillion musical styles, they're both made by people who almost certainly have "spooks in their brains", they're both chock-a-block with some very weird lyrics and they're both utterly, utterly brilliant. It sounds as if The Cure's whole universe has suddenly gone completely loopy – one moment there's growling, distorted guitars and funeral-paced doominess, the next, jaunty dance tunes and exotic instruments twanging, and the *next*, some beautifully uncluttered pop songs. And one song in particular, "Catch", is quite possibly the dreamiest song ever. It's all quite wonderful.
(9 out of 10)
Chris Heath

THE CURE
Kiss Me Kiss Me Kiss Me (Fiction) ★★★
The Cure carry on in their unique and merry way on this double LP, confounding and delighting us as ever.

They're ten years old now but no one second guesses Mr. Smith. This is a mixture of many styles and moods; from the sombre and dated sound of 'The Kiss' to the jumpy, jazzy 'Hey You'. Some tracks sound as if they were written in ten seconds, cue 'Icing Sugars', others leave you wondering how he could have found time to write them at all ('How Beautiful You Are').

But that's the Cure for you. Brilliant.
PAUL BURSCHE ■

Simon:

"I think every song on the album is a cracker. It's like a mix between 'Pornography' and 'The Head On The Door' – the best elements of both. it works really well because one moment you're flung into despair and the next you're elated. I'm 100 per cent satisfied with the group and, without putting too much emphasis on it, I think this album is perfect."

Porl:

"It feels the same now as it did in the beginning when we were just playing little clubs. It's bigger but the fact that we can still have a laugh is important. I think people understand we mean what we do rather than just playing for effect or because we think it's going to sell a lot."

Robert:

"The Cure has been several groups and it's becoming unique with the reintroduction of Simon and Porl. It's really weird, it's like this particular line up has been inevitable for years. And I can't imagine Boris not being here now – the way he fits in and contributes to the group is immeasurable."

Lol:

"If we didn't bother about it, we could make an album of Cure cliches and there'd be an audience for it. But the reason for The Cure is not purely a musical one, it's more of feeling about *why* you want to do something, *why* you want to make music.

"What distinguishes us from bands who might be our contemporaries is that we realised you can start thinking about things so much you end up just destroying yourself. We're more fatalistic now. 'Why Can't I Be You' may seem flippant but I think anybody who liked us for that other, deeper side will still like us. It's just an age thing. The more you sit there, the more you say to yourself 'Well, I can be angst-ridden and tortured about it or I can get on with it and find some humour in it'. That's what's happened to us.

"We're now a lot of younger people's older brothers in a way, We still don't have any answers 10 years on but at least we can be a bit more lucid about the questions. We've all come through our particular traumas, the things that shaped the songs, and now we've come to reflect on it.

"I see it all as a means to an end, a way to live your life the way you want to because, in the end, that's one of the things music offers and reflects. It offers people a way to live. There are things that tie us but they're probably lesser things than most other people ever have. And that's my goal; to be rid of *all* the fetters."

Pope:

"The Cure are still a small band in some ways and yet they're massive – I don't know how they manage to be both. Everything they deal with on every level is eccentric, soft and hard and human. Everyone seems to like them – they're the band a lot of bands want to be like."

Robert:

"I've always maintained that I'm doing this for selfish reasons and I still do. The main reason is because I enjoy it – I like making records and going on stage and singing. The reason, more and more, that I continue is that it has become more important that I see myself from a third person's point of view as someone to look towards for choices.

"My motivation is to try and make The Cure not more popular but to harden up the whole thing so we are untouchable. Then we reach the point of becoming important and yet still odd. We will never be accepted but we will never go away. *That* is perfect."

Parry:

"Robert started off thinking 'Oh my God, I'm allowed to play and I feel really good about it' but was clever enough not to give too much away, creative enough to move and keep moving, stupid enough to get involved in all the things he got involved in and then lucky and strong enough to get out of them. He can go on and do lots of things or . . . he's a rather gifted bloke and this thing is not going to go on forever; one day he might think 'This Cure thing has become too big a monster, it's got to be slaughtered'. And that's his prerogative."

Pope:

"The Cure's like a big roly poly, it can just turn over and it will be something else. You never know with Robert – But I can just see him giving it up one day."

Robert:

"The more we go on, the more I think we're unique. The longer we go on, the less similarities there are between what we're doing and what anyone else has ever done. The stage we're at at the moment and the public image of the group is so absurd that I honestly don't think there's anything The Cure couldn't do. Anything at all . . . "

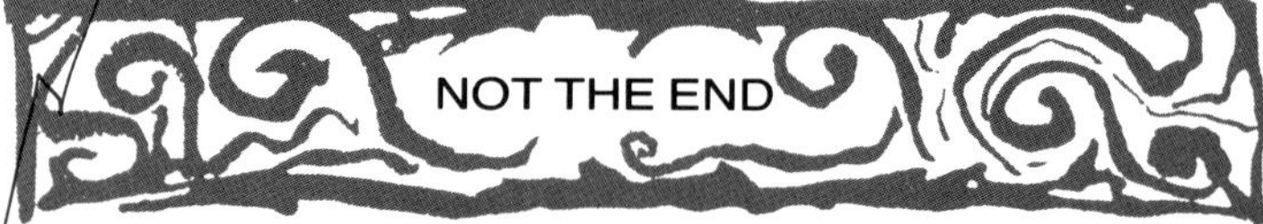

Personal Files

NAME
MICHAEL STEPHEN DEMPSEY
BORN
29/11/58 SALISBURY Southern Rhodesia
(now HARARE Zimbabwe)
FAMILY
Mother NANCY Father WILLIAM
Sisters ANNE (b 4/10/53) THERESA (b 8/4/65)
Brother MARTIN (b 19/1/61)
HISTORY
Moved to SALFORDS Surrey, England in '61
Attended SALFORDS County School '63-'70
Attended NOTRE DAME Middle School '70-'72
Attended ST WILFRIDS Comprehensive School '72-'76
Attended CRAWLEY College '76-'78
Worked for six months as a PORTER at Netherne Hospital.
After leaving THE CURE in '79 joined THE ASSOCIATES
Currently pursuing various hobbies

NAME
MATTHIEU AIDEN HARTLEY
BORN
4/2/60 SMALLFIELD Surrey, England
FAMILY
Sister JULIA (b 29/7/54)
Brother PAUL (b 28/7/56)
HISTORY
Lived in SMALLFIELD until '68
Attended SMALLFIELD Infants School
Attended YATTENDON Junior School
Moved to HORLEY Surrey
Attended BALCOMBE ROAD Comprehensive School '72-'76
Trained and worked as a HAIR DRESSER '76-'79
After leaving THE CURE in '80 worked in a zoo and as a casual labourer for an installation company
Joined and left several local bands
Married '83

NAME
CLIFFORD LEON ANDERSON
BORN
30/1/51 WEST HAM HOSPITAL London
FAMILY
Mother MARIE Father CLIFF
Brothers COLIN (b '44) WINSTON (b '47)
HISTORY
Lived in WEST HAM East London until '60
Moved to RICHMOND West London
Attended WEST GREEN ROAD Infants School
Returned to West Ham and attended HAROLD ROAD Secondary Modern and GEARIES BOYS SCHOOL Secondary Modern
Left school aged 15 and had a few normal jobs before getting involved in music
Since leaving THE CURE he has been doing studio sessions making videos and touring with various bands

NAME
PHILIP CARDEN THORNALLEY
BORN
5/1/60 WARLINGTON, Mildenhall, Suffolk, England
FAMILY
Mother ANN Father JOHN
Brother JONATHAN MAX (b 31/7/58)
HISTORY
Attended MILDENHALL Primary School until '68
Attended CULFORD School, Bury St. Edmunds until '78
Began SOUND ENGINEER Apprenticeship at RAK Studios, London '78
Engineered and produced various records '79-'83
Married JOOLZ FITZPATRICK 15/9/84
Since leaving THE CURE in '84 has been producing his own, and other people's records

NAME
BORIS PETER BRANSBY-WILLIAMS
BORN
24/4/57 VERSAILLES France
FAMILY
Sisters JULIET, CAROLINE, MIRA, SARAH
Brothers MICHAEL, MORGAN

HISTORY
Lived in BELGRADE Yugoslavia until '63
Moved to FARNHAM Surrey, England
Played as Drummer in various groups including TOMATO CITY, FLIRTATIONS, SADISTA SISTERS, KIM WILDE, THOMPSON TWINS '73-'84

NAME
PAUL STEPHEN THOMPSON
BORN
8/11/57 WIMBLEDON London, England
FAMILY
Mother DOT Father TOM
Sister CAROL (b '59)
Brothers ANDREW (b '61) ROBERT (b '63)
HISTORY
Lived in ENGLAND until '62
Moved to MELBOURNE Australia
Moved back to CRAWLEY Sussex '64
Attended SOUTHGATE Crawley Infants and Junior Schools
Attended THOMAS BENNETT Crawley Comprehensive School '71-'74
Played guitar in local groups and worked in various jobs '74-'76
Played guitar in MALICE and EASY CURE '76-'78
Attended WEST SUSSEX College Of Design '79-'81
Played guitar in several other groups including THE EXOTIC PANDAS
Moved to LONDON '82
Formed PARCHED ART with UNDY VELLA
Re-joined THE CURE in '84

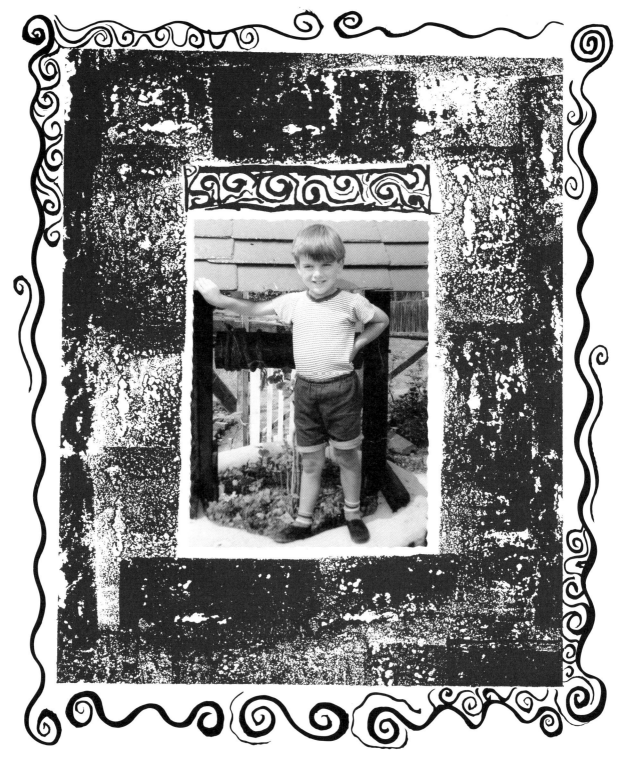

NAME
SIMON JONOTHAN GALLUP
BORN
1/6/60 DUXHURST Surrey, England
FAMILY
Mother PEG Father BOB
Sister MONICA (b 29/12/51)
Brothers STUART (b 15/1/47) DAVID (b 27/7/48) DUNCAN (b 12/5/50) RIC (b 11/10/53)
HISTORY
Moved to HORLEY Surrey '61
Attended HORLEY Infants and Junior Schools '65-'71
Attended HORLEY BALCOMBE ROAD Comprehensive School '71-'76
Worked in PLASTICS FACTORY '76-'79
Played bass in LOCKJAW and THE MAGAZINE SPIES
After leaving THE CURE in '82 formed CRY and FOOLS DANCE and went to the pub a lot
Moved to NUTFIELD Surrey '83
Re-joined THE CURE '84

NAME
ROBERT JAMES SMITH
BORN
21/4/59 BLACKPOOL Lancashire, England
FAMILY
Mother RITA Father ALEX
Sisters MARGARET (b 27/2/50) JANET (b 30/8/60)
Brother RICHARD (b 12/7/46)
HISTORY
Lived in BLACKPOOL until December '62
Moved to HORLEY Surrey
Attended ST. FRANCIS Primary School
Moved to CRAWLEY Sussex in March '66
Attended ST. FRANCIS Junior School
Attended NOTRE DAME Middle School '70-'72
Attended ST. WILFRIDS Comprehensive School '72-'77

NAME
LAURENCE ANDREW TOLHURST
BORN
3/2/59 HORLEY Surrey, England
FAMILY
Mother DAPHNE (d 21/6/81) Father WILLIAM
Sisters JANE (b 27/5/51) BARBARA (b 9/12/60)
Brothers ROGER (b 16/3/42) NIGEL (b 5/8/46. d 21/10/46) JOHN (b 29/11/47)

HISTORY
Attended ST FRANCIS Primary and Junior Schools
Attended NOTRE DAME Middle School '70-'72
Attended ST WILFRIDS Comprehensive School '72-'75
Attended CRAWLEY Technical College and worked at HELLERMAN DEUTSCH and JOHNSON & BLOY '75-'78

NAME
JOHN CHRISTOPHER PARRY
BORN
7/1/49 LOWER HUTT NEW ZEALAND
FAMILY
Mother VIRGINIA Father THOMAS
Sisters VIRGINIA, MARGARET, JOSEPHINE, ANNETTE, HELEN
Brothers DAVID, JAMES, RICHARD, ROBIN, PETER
HISTORY
Lived in UPPER HUTT until '69
Attended ST. JOSEPHS school '54-'61
Attended ST. PATRICKS college '62-'65
Worked as COURT CLERK/SALESMAN/TRUCK DRIVER '66-'68
Drummer with THE FOURMYULA '68-'70
Arrived in LONDON England '70
Married '71
Student '72-'74
Worked as INTERNATIONAL MANAGER PHONOGRAM '74
DAUGHTER born '74
Worked as A&R MANAGER POLYDOR '74-'78

discography

SINGLES

Dec 1978	7 inch	Killing An Arab/10:15 Saturday Night (on Small Wonder label)	Small 11
Feb 1979	7 inch	Killing An Arab/10:15 Saturday Night (re-issue on Fiction label)	Fics 001
Jun 1979	7 inch	Boys Don't Cry/Plastic Passion	Fics 002
Nov 1979	7 inch	Jumping Someone Else's Train/I'm Cold	Fics 005
Dec 1979	7 inch	I'm A Cult Hero/I Dig You (released in the name of Cult Hero)	Fics 006
Apr 1980	7 inch	A Forest/Another Journey By Train	Fics 010
	12 inch	A Forest/Another Journey By Train	Ficx 010
May 1981	7 inch	Primary/Descent	Fics 012
	12 inch	Primary (extended version)/Descent	Ficx 012
Oct 1981	7 inch	Charlotte Sometimes/Splintered In Her Head	Fics 14
	12 inch	Charlotte Sometimes/Splinetered In Her Head/Faith (live)	Ficx 14
Jul 1982	7 inch	The Hanging Garden/Killing An Arab (live)	Fics 15
	7 inch	The Hanging Garden/100 Years/A Forest (live)/Killing An Arab (live) – (gatefold pack of 2 singles)	Ficg 15
Nov 1982	7 inch	Let's Go To Bed/Just One Kiss	Fics 17
	12 inch	Let's Go To Bed/Just One Kiss	Ficsx 17
Jul 1983	7 inch	The Walk/The Upstairs Room	Fics 18
	7 inch	The Walk/The Upstairs Room (picture disc)	Ficsp 18
	12 inch	The Walk/The Upstairs Room/The Dream/Lament	Ficsx 18
Oct 1983	7 inch	The Love Cats/Speak My Language	Fics 19
	7 inch	The Love Cats/Speak My Language (picture disc)	Ficsp 19
	12 inch	The Love Cats (extended version)/Speak My Language/Mr Pink Eyes	Ficsx 19
May 1984	7 inch	The Caterpillar/Happy The Man	Fics 20
	7 inch	The Caterpillar/Happy The Man (picture disc)	Ficsp 20
	12 inch	The Caterpillar/Happy The Man/Throw Your Foot	Ficsx 20
Jul 1985	7 inch	In Between Days/The Exploding Boy	Fics 22
	12 inch	In Between Days/The Exploding Boy/A Few Hours After This	Ficsx 22
Sep 1985	7 inch	Close To Me (remix)/A Man Inside My Mouth	Fics 23
	7 inch	Close To Me (remix)/A Man Inside My Mouth (poster bag)	Ficsg 23
	10 inch	Close To Me (remix)/A Man Inside My Mouth/New Day/Stop Dead (titled Half An Octopus)	Ficst 23
	12 inch	Close To Me (extended remix)/A Man Inside My Mouth/Stop Dead	Ficsx 23
Apr 1986	7 inch	Boys Don't Cry (new voice new mix)/Pillbox Tales	Fics 24
	12 inch	Boys Don't Cry (new voice club mix)/Pillbox Tales/Do The Hansa	Ficsx 24
Apr 1987	7 inch	Why Can't I Be You?/A Japanese Dream	Fice 25
	7 inch	Why Can't I Be You?/A Japanese Dream/Six Different Ways (live)/ Push (live) – (Gatefold pack of 2 singles)	Ficsg 25
	12 inch	Why Can't I Be You? (remix)/A Japanese Dream (remix)	Ficsx 25

ALBUMS

			UK/European	US
May 1979	Album	Three Imaginary Boys	Fix 1	
	Cassette	Three Imaginary Boys	Fixc 1	
Feb 1980	Album	Boys Don't Cry	Spelp 26	*7916
	Cassette	Boys Don't Cry	Spemc 26	*7916
	CD	Boys Don't Cry	815 01112	
Apr 1980	Album	Seventeen Seconds	Fix 4	
	Cassette	Seventeen Seconds	Fixc 4	
	CD	Seventeen Seconds	825 364-2	
Apr 1981	Album	Faith	Fix 6	
	Cassette	Faith and Carnage Visors	Fixc 6	
	CD	Faith	827 687-2	
Sept 1981	Album	Happily Ever After – Seventeen Seconds/Faith – re-packaged		*SP06020
	Cassette	Happily Ever After		*CS06020
May 1982	Album	Pornography	Fixd 7	*SP04902
	Cassette	Pornography	Fixdc 7	*CS04902
	CD	Pornography	827 688-2	
Dec 1983	Album	Japanese Whispers	Fixm 8	125076
	Cassette	Japanese Whispers	Fixmc 8	425076
	CD	Japanese Whispers	817 470-2	
May 1984	Album	The Top	Fixs 9	125086
	Cassette	The Top	Fixsc 9	425080
	CD	The Top	821 136-2	
Oct 1984	Album	Concert – The Cure Live	Fixh 10	
	Cassette	Concert – The Cure Live/Curiosity – Cure Anomalies 1977 – '84	Fixhc 10	
	CD	Concert – The Cure Live	823 682-2	
Aug 1985	Album	The Head On The Door	Fixh 11	160435
	Cassette	The Head On The Door	Fixhc 11	460435
	CD	The Head On The Door	827 231-2	260435
May 1986	Album	Standing On A Beach – The Singles	Fixh 12	160477
	Cassette	Standing On A Beach – All The Hits/Unavailable B-sides	Fixhc 12	460477
	CD	Staring At The Sea – The Singles	829 239-2	260477
May 1987	Album	Kiss Me Kiss Me Kiss Me (double album)	Fixh 13	160737
	Cassette	Kiss Me Kiss Me Kiss Me (single extended play cassette)	Fixhc 13	460737
	CD	Kiss Me Kiss Me Kiss Me	832 130-2	260737

* Deleted

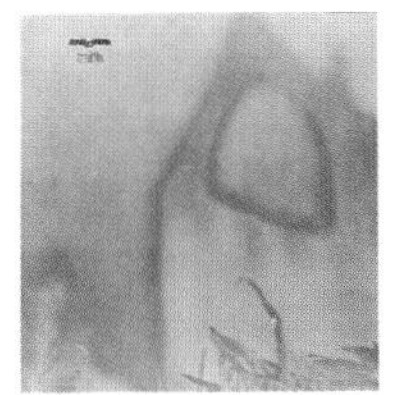
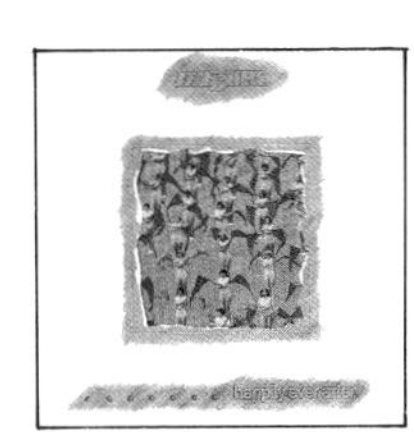
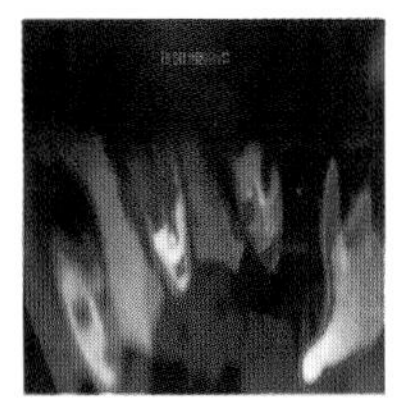

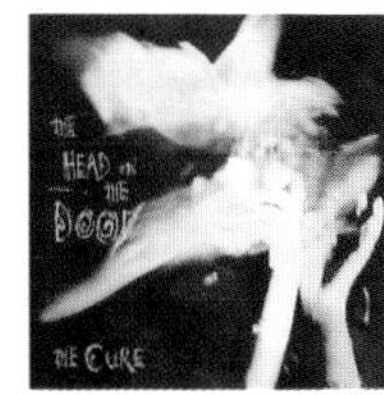

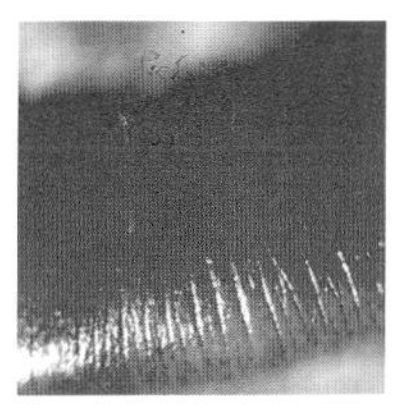

Thanks to the following publications: Crawley Observer, NME, Melody Maker, Sounds, Smash Hits, Record Mirror, Observer, No. 1.

Thanks also to the following photographers: Ebet Roberts, Bob King, Parched Art, P. Musebrink, Peter L. Noble, Paul Cox, Richard Bellia, Steve Rapport, Jim Kutler, Ken Laley, Nick Knight, Marie-France Laval, Frederic De lafosse.

Steve Sutherland is the Assistant Editor of Melody Maker. Among the best things in his life have been that kiss at the Jesus & Mary Chain gig, Southampton winning the FA Cup, shaking Steve Martin's hand, potting a red against Jimmy White, discovering Sashimi, and watching some kittens be born. Among the worst were all the hangovers, getting round to writing this book, and the mysterious loss of his fine head of hair.

Lydie Barbarian has known The Cure since 1980 and started a fanzine for them in France called 'Burning Room'. She has had her own daily radio show 'City 96' in Paris as well as having written books and articles. In 1986 Barbarian came to London as the UK correspondent for the French daily newspaper Liberation.

PRINTED IN BELGIUM BY
proost
INTERNATIONAL BOOK PRODUCTION